THE ASTOUNDING ILLUSTRATED HISTORY OF
SCIENCE FICTION

MOVIES · ART · COMICS · PULP MAGAZINES · FICTION

Publisher's Note: For the chapter timelines, we have omitted direct sequels; but reboots, spin-offs or sequels occurring many years later (therefore acquiring a significance) have been included. Novels which were first serialized in magazines still fall under the 'novels' category; whilst the magazine categories are there to indicate important developments within that industry. The key people whose dates are listed at the back are auteurs of the genre (authors, directors, artists – rather than actors for example). To provide continuity between the historical imagery and a look towards the future, we have also laced contemporary art throughout the book, emphasizing the enduring influence and popularity science fiction still has today.

Publisher and Creative Director: Nick Wells

Senior Project Editor: Laura Bulbeck

Art Director: Mike Spender

Digital Design and Production: Chris Herbert

Copy Editor: Anna Groves

Proofreader: Amanda Crook

Indexer: Helen Snaith

FLAME TREE PUBLISHING

6 Melbray Mews

Fulham, London SW6 3NS

United Kingdom

See our range of gothic, fantasy, horror and science fiction books, journals and calendars at **flametreepublishing.com**

First published 2017

17 19 21 20 18

1 3 5 7 9 10 8 6 4 2

© 2017 Flame Tree Publishing Ltd

A CIP record for this book is available from the British Library upon request.

ISBN: 978-1-78664-527-2

Printed in China

Created and developed in the UK

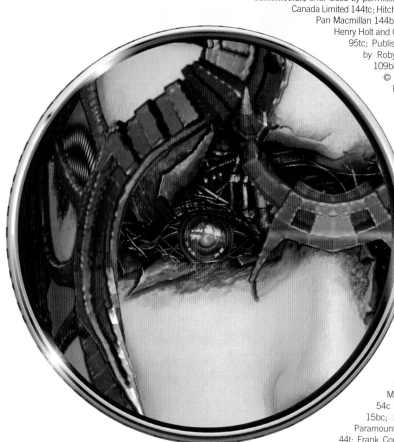

PICTURE CREDITS: Bridgeman Images and: © British Library Board. All Rights Reserved 6, 9, 25 (all), 30, 38tc, 38bl, 53bc, 61bc, 61tr, 61br; Bibliotheque des Arts Decoratifs, Paris, France/Archives Charmet 32; Bibliotheque Nationale, Paris, France 19; Bibliotheque Nationale, Paris, France/Archives Charmet 37tc; Bibliotheque Nationale, Paris, France/Archives Charmet 37tl; National Air and Space Museum, Smithsonian Institution, Washington DC, USA 38tl; Photo © Collection Gregoire 61bl; Private Collection 14t, 17; Private Collection/© Look and Learn 43r; Private Collection/© The Advertising Archives 61tc; Private Collection/Archives Charmet 18r, 37r; Private Collection/Photo © Ken Welsh 35; Universal History Archive/UIG 38tr, 52t, 52b. **Archive.org**: 53bl. **Pulpcovers.com**: 48, 56tl, 61tl, 66, 67 (all), 74 (all), 87tc, 89. © **David Revoy**/Blender Foundation, Creative Commons Attribution 3.0: 49. INeverCry/public domain: 29. **Library of Congress**: 31, 34, 60t. © **Mary Evans Picture Library**: 38br, 39, 50, 79bl, 79bc, 87 (all except tc), 95bl and: Iberfoto 18l; Courtesy Everett Collection 58t, 120tl, 135t; The National Archives, London, England 95bc; Ronald Grant Archive 111; © BBC/Courtesy Everett Collection 120tc; © Cinecom Pictures/Courtesy Everett Collection 144tl; ©MGM/Courtesy Everett Collection 152bc. Nemesis the Warlock™ Rebellion A/S, © **Rebellion A/S**, All Rights Reserved. Used with Permission: 7. Photo © **Brian Ameringen (www.porcupine. demon.co.uk)** and: Used by permission of McClelland & Stewart, a division of Penguin Random House Canada Limited 144tc; Hitch Hiker's Guide to the Galaxy copyright © Douglas Adams, publisher: Pan Macmillan 144bl; Publisher: Berkley/Penguin Random House LLC 79tc; Publisher: Henry Holt and Company 79tr; Reprint permission kindly granted by Robyn Asimov 95tc; Publisher: Rhapp & Whiting 109tc; Reprint permission kindly granted by Robyn Asimov 109tr; Publisher: Ace/Penguin Random House LLC 109bl. Photo © **Flame Tree Publishing** and: Childhood's End Copyright © Arthur C. Clarke, published by Pan Macmillan 95tr; Publisher: Panther/Author: E.E. Smith 109br; Publisher: Ace/Penguin Random House LLC 144br; The Fountains of Paradise Copyright © Arthur C. Clarke, publisher: Pan Macmillan 144bc. Photo © **John W. Knott, Jr., Bookseller (www.jwkbooks.com) and L.W. Currey, Inc. (www.lwcurrey.com)** and: Publisher: Methuen, © Estate of Olaf Stapledon 79tl; Reprint permission kindly granted by Robyn Asimov 95tl; Publisher: Walker & Co 109tl; Publisher: Putnam/Penguin Random House LLC 109bc; Publisher: St Martin's Press 144tr; Publisher: A.C. McClurg 56bl. Photo © **Phil Archer (www.philarcher. org)** and: Publisher: Ward, Lock & Co. Limited 38bc; Reprinted by permission of HarperCollins Publishers Ltd: © 1992 Kim Stanley Robinson 152tl and © 1993 Kim Stanley Robinson 152tc and © 1996 Kim Stanley Robinson 152tr and © 1991 Stephen Baxter 152bl. © **REX/Shutterstock**: 173b, 179 and: 20th Century Fox 36; 20th Century Fox Television/Kobal 160l; 20th Century Fox/Dreamworks/Kobal 167; 20th Century Fox/Gotham Group/Temple Hill/Kobal 175r; 20th Century Fox/Kobal 16l, 94, 97l, 97r, 124 (all), 132tl, 132c, 175l; Aaru Prods 120b; AIP/Kobal 37b; Alastair Muir 15br; Allied Artists/Kobal 100, 103t; Amazon/Big Light Prods./Kobal 115; Amblin Entertainment/Universal Pictures 137; Amblin/Universal/Kobal 138bc, 157; Andrew Cooper/Dreamworks/Warner Bros 51; Anglo Enterprise/Vineyard/Kobal 95br; Anthony Upton 162; Bad Robot 185; Bob Marshak/20th Century Fox/Kobal: 112l; CHRIS CAPSTICK 120tr; Darren Michaels/Columbia/Kobal 153; Design Pics Inc 8b; Disney/Kobal 54c & 55c; Dna/Film4/Kobal 4, 183; Dna/Kobal 139; Donald Cooper 15bc; Double Secret/Gekko/Stargate Sg-1/Kobal 152br; Dreamworks/Paramount 150l, 150r; Dreamworks/Paramount/Kobal 53t; First National 44t; Frank Connor/Lucasfilm/20th Century Fox/Kobal 1 & 130br; Granger 96; Hammer/Kobal 15tr; Hopscotch Features/Lakeshore/Kobal 16r; JoJo Whilden/Netflix/Kobal 184; Jonathan Olley/Lucasfilm Ltd/Kobal 180t; Kennedy Miller Prods./Kobal 136r; Ladd Company/Warner Bros/Kobal 114, 134; Lionsgate/Color Force/Kobal 174bc, 174br; Lionsgate/Kobal 174tl, 174tr, 174bl; London Films/United Artists/Kobal 79br; Lucasfilm/Bad Robot/Walt Disney Studios/Kobal 187; Lucasfilm/Fox/Kobal 11, 129 & 130tc, 130 (all); Mca TV/Kobal 116; Melies 43l; Mezhrabpom 45t; MGM/Kobal 70r, 88, 99r; MGM/Stanley Kubrick Productions 123t; Moviestore 15bl, 20, 42, 63t, 71l, 71r, 80, 117, 121, 135b, 138br, 156b, 160–61, 163tl, 163tc, 163bc, 171, 172t, 173t, 178, 181r, 186; Mutant Enemy/20th Century Fox TV 166; Nils Jorgensen 180b; Odd Lot/Kobal 141; Paramount/Gk/Kobal 62; Paramount Pictures/Bad Robot/Kobal 177bl; Paramount Television 156t; Paramount TV/Kobal 155, 118, 119, 176, 240t, 240bl, 240br; Paramount/Bad Robot/Kobal 177t; Paramount/Kobal 53br, 72, 73, 122, 138tl, 138tc, 138tr, 177br, 240bc; Revolution/Columbia/Tri Star/Kobal 163tr; Sci-Fi Channel/Kobal 110, 164l, 164–65; Scott Free Prod/20th Century Fox/Kobal 182; SNAP 15tc, 63b, 82c, 98l, 149; Snap Stills 143; Sony Pictures Entertainment 170; StudioCanal Films 123b; Toho/Kobal 101l, 101r; Twentieth Century-Fox Film Corporation/Kobal 181l; Universal 8t, 69, 81, 83, 131, 138bl; Universal/Kobal 14 & 15 main, 70l, 78, 82l, 151; Village Roadshow 172c; Warner Bros./Kobal 103c; Warner Bros/DC Comics/Kobal 133, 140, 163bl, 163br; Warner Bros/Hawk Films/Kobal 112r; Warner Bros/Kobal 98 –99, 180c; Warner Bros/Village Roadshow Pictures/Kobal 148, 158. **Shutterstock.com** and: agsandrew 108 ; Angela Harburn 23; Atelier Sommerland 10b, 2 & 3 @ 22, 26t, 56 main; breakermaximus 75; camilkuo 68, 136l; diversepixel 44 b & 45b; Fat Jackey 132t; Ociacia 21; RomanYa 28b, 28t; Rustic 26 b & 27, 58b & 59; sahua d 86; Slava Gerj 24; Sophon Mungmeetanawong 76 & 77; Tithi Luadthong 10t, 33, 46 & 47, 54b & 55 main & 57, 91, 92–93, 106 & 107, 113, 125, 128, 142, 145; Vadim Sadovski 102; Lobintz, Tithi Luadthong, IM_photo, camilkuo: background illustrations.

THE ASTOUNDING ILLUSTRATED HISTORY OF
SCIENCE FICTION

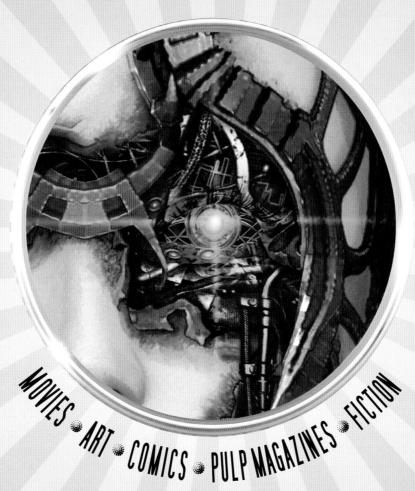

MOVIES • ART • COMICS • PULP MAGAZINES • FICTION

DAVE GOLDER, JESS NEVINS, RUSS THORNE, SARAH DOBBS

CONSULTANT EDITOR: DAVID LANGFORD • FOREWORD BY PAT MILLS

FLAME TREE
PUBLISHING

CONTENTS

LEFT: Alicia Vikander and director Alex Garland look at a humanoid robot face mounted on the wall in *Ex Machina* (2015)

FOREWORD

When I created the science fiction comic *2000AD* in 1977, satire and subversion were its themes. They were natural themes to me because I've always taken *The Matrix*'s red pill and challenged fake realities. But I was aware, as I developed the character of the futuristic cop Judge Dredd, that the readers might ignore its satirical subtext and simply enjoy the character, the hardware and the future city. They might not appreciate that Dredd, himself, is actually a monster, albeit an ambivalent one. But it doesn't matter, because that drip-feeds into their subconscious anyway.

6

Ambivalence seems to go with science fiction. Dredd's Mega-City One is equally enigmatic. Carlos Ezquerra's original, Gaudi-esque city has a strong sense of *other*, of mystery and far future remoteness. In fact, that first vision of the city was *so* mysterious, I don't think any of us, as writers, have ever done justice to it, even to this day.

That's the beauty of mysteries: they may never be explained. Thus the warp-spasm in my Celtic fantasy saga *Slaine*. When Slaine undergoes a metamorphosis more astonishing than the Incredible

Hulk, I found artists who could visualise the outrageous descriptions in the medieval Celtic texts. But I always felt eclipsed myself by the original scribe's writings and I still struggle to understand the mystery and meaning behind such a fantastic transformation.

Inspiration for stories can come from anywhere: ancient sagas, artists like Gaudi, or magazines like the **National Geographic**. Looking at their photos of hideous microscopic bugs, micro became macro, and I had the basis for the Biogs, huge, gas-propelled aliens who fly through the atmosphere of Jupiter, the planet the legendary hero Dan Dare visits in his first *2000AD* adventure.

Organic spaceships have always fascinated me, and I once was privileged to have a real life close encounter of the

ABOVE: Illustration for Arthur Conan Doyle's 'Horror of the Heights' (1912)

third kind and saw an organic UFO. It was rather like an amoeba or a jelly fish, pulsing across the night sky. Conan Doyle wrote about them in **The Horror of the Heights** (1913), 'Conceive a jelly-fish such as sails in our summer seas, bell-shaped and of enormous size.' Google images from **Cosmic Pulse of Life** and you will see photos of these unexplained phenomena. They were awesome in their own way, although I remember thinking at the time they weren't as awesome as conventional UFOs.

But it's important to be different, which is why I'm most proud of the strip **Nemesis the Warlock**, where humans are the threat to the Galaxy and aliens are the victims. They're led by Torquemada, with his infamous battle cry Be Pure! Be Vigilant! Behave! (The main title of my new ebook: **2000AD and Judge Dredd: The Secret History**.)

Torquemada's aim is to ethnically cleanse the Galaxy of alien life and make planets suitable for colonization. The fact that aliens always seem to be the threat in science fiction suggests some writers may have taken **The Matrix**'s blue pill. Because humanity's dark history surely indicates genocidal cleansing would occur if colonists discovered intelligent life on other planets.

Science fiction is a valuable device to take us out of our comfort zone and deprogram fake realities, and this book is a vital part of that deprogramming.

Pat Mills, 2017

www.millsverse.com

TORQUEMADA
THE CHIEF TERMINATOR

7

ABOVE: Torquemada in the *Nemesis the Warlock* strip from *2000AD*

INTRODUCTION

When and where did science fiction begin? There are many hotly argued answers, as many as Douglas Adams's solution to the ultimate question of life, the universe and everything, which is of course 42. Ask a dozen SF critics to debate the issue and you get thirteen if not 42 contradictory opinions.

There are many different definitions of SF out there, often cunningly crafted to support a particular origin story for the genre. One neat piece of SF empire-building is the idea of Proto SF – the classics that some would define as *very nearly* science fiction. Plato's *The Republic* (380 BC or so) describes the first ideal state, or Utopia; the one that so many later utopian writers hypothesized. Sir Thomas More invented the actual word and satirized the idea in his *Utopia* (1516). Meanwhile, Grendel and his mum, the monsters in *Beowulf* (written between 975 AD and 1025), are obviously mutants, though probably not radiation-spawned. Dante's *The Divine Comedy* (written 1313–21) speculates on cosmology as well as theology: the logical escape route from the deepest pit of Hell is to carry on down and emerge on the other side of the hollow earth (a favourite SF notion of the nineteenth century).

The Science to Fiction Ratio

Should SF contain some science amid the fiction? Theodore Sturgeon thought so: 'A science fiction story is a story built around human beings, with a human problem, and a human solution, which would not have happened at all without its scientific content.' Perhaps the first fantastic novel to feature actual scientists is Jonathan Swift's *Gulliver's Travels* (1726). The famous parts, Gulliver's adventures with the tiny folk of Lilliput and the giants of Brobdingnag, are more satirical fantasy than SF, but Part Three introduces the flying island of Laputa (magnetically powered; there's science for you) and much merciless sending-up of eighteenth-century scientific research by the Royal Society.

Swift was a latecomer to the tradition of fantastic voyages, and Gulliver never ventured into space. Much earlier, Bishop Francis Godwin's *The Man in the Moone* (published 1638) featured a lunar voyage in a flying machine powered by wild geese. Cyrano de Bergerac's joke autobiography from 1657 uses an actual rocket to boost him to the Moon (where, somewhat less prophetically, he finds the Garden of Eden). Voltaire's *Micromégas* (1753) brings in interplanetary and even interstellar travel, with Earth visited – to satirical effect – by two giant aliens, from Saturn and a world circling Sirius.

Brian Aldiss's 1973 definition of the genre is: 'Science fiction is the search for a definition of man and his status in the universe which will stand in our advanced but confused state of knowledge (science), and is characteristically cast in the Gothic or post-Gothic mould.' The Gothic part may surprise readers

LEFT: Gulliver and the floating city of Laputa. ABOVE: *Bride of Frankenstein* (1935), inspired by Mary Shelley's novel (1818).

steeped in the slam-bang action of space opera, but is carefully designed to support Aldiss's choice for the first true SF novel: Mary Wollstonecraft Shelley's **Frankenstein, or The Modern Prometheus** (1818). The Monster, or Creature, has become such an icon of horror cinema that it's easy to forget that in the novel he has a fine Gothic literary style and that his first spoken words are the mild-mannered 'Pardon this intrusion'.

The Birth of Modern Science Fiction

Others prefer to date modern SF from **The Time Machine** (1895) by H.G. Wells, who didn't stop with that masterpiece but followed through strongly with **The War of the Worlds** (1898) and **The First Men in the Moon** (1901). By 1895, though, the Moon was well-visited territory: Jules Verne had already described a fly-by in **From the Earth to the Moon** (1865). In fact, Verne and Wells together are merely the visible tip of the vast iceberg of nineteenth-century 'scientific romance', much of it French and never or only recently translated. Even Wells's trademark Time Machine was anticipated by the Spanish time ship of Enrique Gaspar's **El anachronópete** (1887), a novella not translated until 2012. These are deep waters, Watson.

The distinction between scientific romance and science fiction may not be terribly clear, but is sometimes insisted on by those fans and critics – mostly American – who prefer to date the genre from April 1926 and the launch of the first true SF magazine, Hugo Gernsback's **Amazing Stories**. Or perhaps from shortly afterwards, when Gernsback switched from his awkward coinage 'scientifiction' to the now more familiar phrase contained in: 'Jules Verne was a sort of Shakespeare in science fiction.' (**Amazing Stories**, January 1927.) Scientifiction was defined as 'a charming romance intermingled with scientific fact and prophetic vision'. John W. Campbell of **Astounding SF** more or less agreed: 'To be science fiction, not fantasy, an honest effort at prophetic extrapolation from the known must be made.'

Other terms for our favourite genre have been offered. The most enduring may be Robert A. Heinlein's suggestion of 'speculative fiction'. This has the advantage of including the traditional SF sub-genre of alternate history, which often – as in Keith Roberts's **Pavane** (1968) or Len Deighton's **SS-GB** (1978) – avoids scientific gadgetry like time machines but speculates in detail about what might have happened if history took a different course. Leading critic John Clute likes the European term **fantastika**, which covers fantasy as well as science fiction, and avoids any difficulty with the blurry SF/fantasy borderline cases sometimes described as 'science fantasy' – for example, Roger Zelazny's **Lord of Light** (1967) or Ursula K. Le Guin's **The Lathe of Heaven** (1971). Another critic, Darko Suvin, has memorably called SF a literature of 'cognitive estrangement'; unfortunately not everyone is sure what this means.

The Problem With Labels

Then there are technothrillers, featuring SF gadgetry but not in an SF way – more what Alfred Hitchcock called a McGuffin, the thing everyone chases after or fights over. Examples include the deadly electron-cloud weapon in

9

Leslie Charteris's **The Saint Closes the Case** (1930), and the nuclear missile in Ian Fleming's James Bond adventure **Moonraker** (1955). Fun books, but with a thriller rather than an SF buzz.

Definitions of what is **not** SF are frequently heard in literary circles. Robert Conquest summed up this tendency in **Spectrum II** (1962), second in an SF anthology series he co-edited with Kingsley Amis:

'SF's no good,' they bellow till we're deaf.
'But this looks good.' – 'Well then, it's not SF.'

Thus Anthony Burgess, who should have known better, reviewed Brian Aldiss's undeniably SF novel **Enemies of the System** (1978) and concluded: 'It contrives to be rich, allusive, full of real people, and unfailingly interesting. It is not, then, real SF.' Margaret Atwood has claimed that her 2003 **Oryx and Crake** – set in a future dystopia menaced by hybrid animal products of rampant genetic engineering – can't possibly be SF, because to her SF means 'talking squids in outer space'. Kurt Vonnegut had similar feelings after publishing **Player Piano** back in 1952: 'I have been a soreheaded occupant of a file drawer labeled science fiction ever since, and I would like out, particularly since so many serious critics regularly mistake the drawer for a urinal.' Such golden showers from serious critics are regularly reported in the 'As Others See Us' department of the long-running SF newsletter **Ansible**.

Make of It What You Will

Another way to brush SF under the carpet is to float the idea of a whole new literary genre, such as Climate Change Fiction or cli-fi (ugh). This is often promoted as an amazing new twenty-first-century thing, and never mind the SF treatments of rising sea-levels in J.G. Ballard's **The Drowned World** (1962) or George Turner's **The Sea and Summer** (1987).

In the media world, the battle isn't so much over origins, as about when cinema or TV SF first became seriously good. Was it with **Frankenstein** (1931), **Forbidden Planet** (1956), **Doctor Who** (1963), **Star Trek** (1966), **2001: A Space Odyssey** (1968), or – bringing space opera to life at last – **Star Wars** (1977)? Again, there are at least 42 different opinions.

Perhaps the roomiest of all SF definitions came from Damon Knight, a pioneering SF critic whose **In Search of Wonder** (1956) is still readable, insightful and funny, and declares that science fiction 'means what we point to when we say it'. We are the readers after all, we are in charge; but if we'd rather trust the publishers, there's always Norman Spinrad's uncompromising verdict: 'Science fiction is anything published as science fiction.'

Whatever you prefer to point to when you say SF, the amazingly erudite contributors to this book are waiting to tell you more.

ABOVE AND LEFT: What do we think of when we think of SF?

ABOVE: Epic space opera *Star Wars* (1977) helped to create a resurgence of interest in SF cinema

I: SCIENCE FICTION UNBOUND

Pre-1550 AD   **1600**   **1800**

380 BC • *The Republic* • Plato
Philosophy

c. 1495 • One of the first recorded humanoid robots is designed • Leonardo da Vinci
Science & Technology

1516 • *On the Best State of a Republic and on the New Island of Utopia* • Thomas More
Philosophy

1522 • The Magellan-Elcano circumnavigation of Earth is completed • Ferdinand Magellan
Science & Technology

1543 • *On the Revolutions of the Heavenly Spheres*, a seminal book in the scientific revolution which provides a heliocentric model of the Solar System • Nicolaus Copernicus
Science & Technology

1627 • *New Atlantis* • Francis Bacon
Novel

1657 • *The Other World: Comical History of the States and Empires of the Moon* • Cyrano de Bergerac
Novel

1665 • *Philosophical Transactions of the Royal Society*, the first exclusively scientific journal • The Royal Society
Science & Technology

1666 • *The Blazing World* • Margaret Cavendish
Novel

1726 • *Gulliver's Travels* • Jonathan Swift
Novel

1752 • 'Micromégas' • Voltaire
Short Story

1816 • Invention of the first working electric telegraph • Francis Ronalds
Science & Technology

1816 • 'The Sandman' • E.T.A. Hoffmann
Short Story

1818 • *Frankenstein, or the Modern Prometheus* • Mary Shelley
Novel

1820 • *Symzonia: A Voyage of Discovery* • Adam Seaborn
Novel

1822 • The difference engine, the first programmable computer, is created • Charles Babbage
Science & Technology

1826 • *The Last Man* • Mary Shelley
Novel

1835 • 'The Unparalleled Adventure of One Hans Pfaall' • Edgar Allan Poe
Short Story

1844 • Telegraph invented • Samuel Morse
Science & Technology

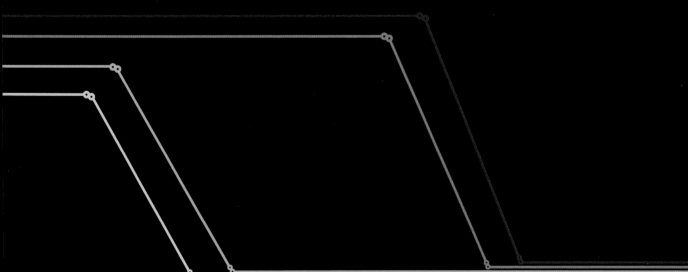

Chronology of selected events in the history of science fiction, from early influences to modern media.

Philosophy | Science & Technology | Novels | Short Story | World Events | Movies | Magazines | Comics | Play | Pulp Magazines | Radio | Small Publishers | TV | Video Games

1850   **1870**   **1880**

1851 • First use of the term 'science fiction' in *A Little Earnest Book Upon a Great Old Subject: With the Story of the Poet-Lover* • William Wilson
Critical Book

1859 • *On the Origin of Species by Means of Natural Selection, or the Preservation of Favoured Races in the Struggle for Life* • Charles Darwin
Science & Technology

1861 • Start of the American Civil War • USA
World Event

1864 • *Journey to the Centre of the Earth* • Jules Verne
Novel

1865 • *From the Earth to the Moon* • Jules Verne
Novel

1865 • End of the American Civil War • USA
World Event

1870 • *Twenty Thousand Leagues Under the Sea* • Jules Verne
Novel

1871 • *The Coming Race* • Edward Bulwer-Lytton
Novel

1872 • *Erewhon, or Over the Range* • Samuel Butler
Novel

1873 • *Around the World in Eighty Days* • Jules Verne
Novel

1874 • *The Mysterious Island* • Jules Verne
Novel

1874 • 'The Tachypomp' • Edward Page Mitchell
Short Story

1876 • First functioning telephone • Alexander Graham Bell
Science & Technology

1877 • Invention of the phonograph • Thomas Edison
Science & Technology

1880 • *Across the Zodiac* • Percy Greg
Novel

1881 • 'The Crystal Man' • Edward Page Mitchell
Short Story

1881 • 'The Clock that went Backward' • Edward Page Mitchell
Short Story

1883 • *The Twentieth Century* • Albert Robida
Novel

1885 • *After London* • Richard Jefferies
Novel

1886 • *Strange Case of Dr Jekyll and Mr Hyde* • Robert Louis Stevenson
Novella

1886 • *Robur the Conqueror* • Jules Verne
Novel

1886 • *L'Ève Future* • Auguste Villiers de l'Isle-Adam
Novel

1887 • *The Republic of the Future: Or, Socialism a Reality* • Anna Bowman Dodd
Novel

1888 • *Looking Backward: 2000–1887* • Edward Bellamy
Novel

1890 • *News from Nowhere* • William Morris
Novel

1894 • *Journey to Mars* • Gustavus W. Pope
Novel

1894 • Experiments in wireless telegraphy are conducted which would lead to the invention of the radio • Guglielmo Marconi
Science & Technology

IT'S ALIVE! IT'S ALIVE!

I f you'll forgive us a hint of nineteenth-century melodrama, Mary Shelley's *Frankenstein* (1818) was the spark that brought modern science fiction to life. Like electricity – that recently harnessed form of energy that brings the corpse-cobbled monster to life in Shelley's novel – it was a spark that took a surprisingly long time to make its influence felt.

While the nineteenth century was a time of great scientific, technological and social advances, electricity was surprisingly slow to catch on. Shelley may have been fascinated by tales of Luigi Galvani using electric shocks to make dissected frogs' legs twitch (a process called galvanism), but when Babbage came to build his proto-computer in the middle of the century, he didn't plug it in to get it working, he turned a crank handle. It wasn't until the late nineteenth century, with the War of the Currents between Thomas Edison's Edison Electric Light Company (Team DC) and the Westinghouse Electric Company (Team AC), that electricity began to light up the world in a big way. Meanwhile, science fiction was coming of age thanks to the public embracing of the work of two giants of science fiction, Jules Verne and H.G. Wells.

What's in a Name?

Frankenstein's monster is never named in the novel, and neither did Mary Shelley give a name to this new genre she was unknowingly creating. Indeed, given the novel's origin – a competition between her, her husband, the poet Percy Bysshe Shelley, Lord Byron and John Polidori to see who could write the best horror story when inclement weather ruined their 1814 holiday in Geneva – she probably regarded it as a gothic melodrama.

The term science fiction wouldn't actually be coined until 1851 by a literary critic called William Wilson in his marvellously titled *A Little Earnest Book Upon a Great Old Subject: With the Story of the Poet-Lover*. Even then it didn't catch on, and it wasn't until the 1920s and 1930s that the phrase came into common usage.

You Don't Have to be Mad to Work Here

Frankenstein is often cited as the blueprint for all mad-scientist novels, but again, the term 'scientist' hadn't even been created when the novel was published. Reverend William Whewell came up with that one in 1834. He went for the double and coined 'physicist' in the same paragraph. Both terms reflected the emergence of a new kind of man of science in that era – the full-time professional. In Shelley's day, scientists were 'professors of natural science'; not that what Dr Frankenstein was doing was in any way natural.

Issues of terminology aside, Dr Frankenstein was clearly the blueprint for the mad scientist: not so much evil as misguided; rash and touched with hubris; a man

ABOVE: Illustration from Mary Shelley's *Frankenstein* (19th century edition) by Theodor M. von Holst

ABOVE: Frankenstein has inspired many adaptations throughout the years, from a multitude of movies to plays and even ballets

who overreaches himself, with disastrous results. He dares to play God, hence the novel's subtitle **The Modern Prometheus**, referring to the Titan from Greek mythology who stole fire from the Gods and gave it to mankind, earning himself eternal punishment. Frankenstein stitches together a creature from corpses and resurrects it with (presumably) electricity. (Presumably, because the paragraphs concerning the animation of the creature are actually vague on the matter, though earlier mentions of Frankenstein's interest in electricity and galvanism suggest this is what Shelley had in mind.)

Doctor Hubris

The resulting creature is not the shambling, groaning, DIY disaster familiar from countless movies, but an erudite soul who even teaches himself to read. But his appearance is so monstrous that even Frankenstein cannot bear to look on him, and he rejects his creation. The creature wanders off into the world where he's feared and scorned by all he meets, which doesn't do much for his mental state. After an attempt to force Frankenstein to make him a mate goes hideously wrong, the creature becomes a killer. He becomes the monster people made him, both literally and figuratively.

These days, the mad scientist is such a staple of science fiction – and Frankenstein is so clearly a major origin of the trope – you would assume he would have immediately inspired a whole slew of imitators. However, while the mid-nineteenth century had its fair share of literary nutty professors, it wasn't until Robert Louis Stevenson's **Strange Case of Dr Jekyll and Mr Hyde** and H.G. Wells's **The Island of Dr Moreau** (1896) and **The Invisible Man** (1897) that the mad scientist returned to the fore.

LEFT: An example of the mad scientist trope is H.G. Wells's The Invisible Man, 'seen' here in *The League of Extraordinary Gentlemen* (2003). ABOVE: Artwork from the movie *I, Frankenstein* (2014),

The End of All Things

Mary Shelley's considerably less well-regarded follow-up to **Frankenstein**, **The Last Man** (1826), is an oddly meandering novel which bizarrely doubles as a fanciful biography of her husband Percy, who's recast as a possible President of England in a post-monarchy future. He's not the last man, though, instead dying from a plague that wipes out the planet's human population. It's a dry novel, with none of the iconic resonance of its predecessor.

Filling the Void

So if **Frankenstein** wasn't the immediate cultural phenomenon that you might have expected, what was happening in the realm of science fiction for most of the Victorian era? The development of the application of electricity wasn't entirely static (sorry); Michael Faraday was discovering the principles behind the electric motor, the transformer and the generator through the 1820s and 1830s. But science fiction literature had other discoveries and breakthroughs to fuel writers' imaginations, even if not all of them were scientifically sound.

One particularly spurious theory was Symmes Holes, a theory put forward by John Cleves Symmes Jr. in 1818, proposing that the Earth was hollow and there were openings at the North and South Pole, which enabled access to the interior of the globe. A novel based on the idea swiftly followed: **Symzonia: A Voyage of Discovery** (1820) is purportedly by one Adam Seaborn. It has been suggested that this was a pseudonym for Symmes himself; although Symmes' theories are satirized within the novel, which may make him an unlikely author.

Not the Hole Truth

The Hollow Earth theory was debunked pretty quickly – many regarded Symmes as a crank – although not before the United States Government granted funds to mount an expedition to the South Pole to locate a Symmes Hole in 1838–42. It failed. The idea, though, proved too enticing for authors of scientific romances to ignore.

In the Fountain of Arethusa (1848) by Robert Eyres Landor, explorers discover a utopia beneath the Earth with its own sun. The unlikely entrance is via a river in Derbyshire. **The Coming Race** (1871) by Edward Bulwer-Lytton concerns a subterranean world where humans have evolved into a superior race (more equality for women, for one thing). Their society is powered by 'Vril' – an atmospheric force that's part electrical, part spiritual. The book was a hit at the time and one of its legacies is still around today – it inspired the 'Vril' in 'Bovril'.

The Hollow Earth genre proved remarkably resilient and would reach its apogee in the early twentieth century with Edgar Rice Burroughs' Pellucidar series; but more on that in the next chapter (**see** page 57).

New Frontiers

Exploring 'strange new worlds' has always been part of science fiction's DNA, even proto-science fiction – Cyrano de Bergerac wrote about sending a rocket to

ABOVE: Frontispiece for Cyrano de Bergerac's *The Comical History of the States and Empires of the World of the Moon* (1687 edition) by Frederick Hendrick van Hove

17

Egyptians, who all have shaved heads, because phrenology (the way bumps on the skull reveal a person's nature) is all the rage. Even the legendary Edgar Allan Poe, to whom we'll return in a while, turned to balloon technology to transport his eponymous explorer to the Moon in 'The Unparalleled Adventure of One Hans Pfaall' (1835), but this was a tale told for comic effect, so we'll forgive him; though not the 1965 US magazine that retitled the story 'Hans Off in Free Pfall to the Moon'.

Travelling in Style

A more practical form of transport was a copper cube coated in an anti-gravity substance in Joseph Atterley's **A Voyage to the Moon** (1827); while Jules Verne proposed shooting astronauts into space from a giant cannon in **From the Earth to the Moon** (1867). Anti-gravity (this time created via magnetics) rears its head again in J.L. Riddell's **Orrin Lindsay's Plan of Aerial Navigation** (1847). In Chrysostom Trueman's **The History of a Voyage to the Moon, With an Account of the Adventurers' Subsequent Discoveries** (1864) the gravity-defying ore is called 'repellante' and mined in Colorado.

the Moon in his **Comical History of the States and Empires of the Moon** (published posthumously in 1657). But it was in the nineteenth century that fictional space travel really came of age, with authors putting their minds to the mechanics of travel to other worlds as well as simply what we might find there. Even if the mechanics of travel did involve an unfeasible number of balloons.

One example is John Trotter's **Phrenologasta** (1829), in which the hero uses a balloon to get to the Moon, where he discovers a race descended from

The anti-gravity effect in Percy Greg's **Across the Zodiac: The Story of a Wrecked Record** (1880) is christened 'apergy', but that's less interesting than the fact that the book correctly predicts the weightlessness of space travel and also contains the first recorded use of the word astronaut. H.G. Wells was, unusually for him, a Johnny-come-lately with his 'discovery' of the gravity-busting 'cavorite' in **The First Men in the Moon** (1901).

LEFT AND OPPOSITE: Illustrations from Jules Verne's *From the Earth to the Moon* by Emile Antoine Bayard. ABOVE: Illustration from *From the Earth to the Moon* by Henri de Montaut.

19

THE ROBOT REVOLUTION

Although the development of electricity went into a bit of a holding pattern, Victorian writers still embraced the concept of mechanical men, or automata (not robots back then – that term was coined in 1920, as we'll learn in the next chapter). While Mary Shelley used electricity to reanimate her creature, no one appeared to think that mechanical people would benefit from a few volts to get them going. Instead most Victorian automata were either clockwork or steam-powered; it seems Victorians did, in fact, invent steampunk.

The century's first great mechanical man was actually a woman; Olimpia in E.T.A. Hoffmann's short story 'The Sandman' (1816). She is so lifelike that an impressionable young man called Nathaniel falls in love with her, a love that eventually sends him mad when he sees her eyes lying on the ground. If you're of a more highbrow persuasion, then 'The Sandman' will probably make more of an impact than **Frankenstein**; it has inspired no fewer than six ballets and operas, including Act I of Jacques Offenbach's **The Tales of**

Hoffman (1881). While Olimpia feels more like she comes from a fantasy or faery-tale tradition (certainly much more so than **Frankenstein**'s monster), it's difficult to shake the feeling that she's an ancestor of the android Maria in Fritz Lang's **Metropolis** (1927).

More Metaphorical Mechanics

Another, perhaps surprising, trend in nineteenth-century science fiction was the way celebrated mainstream authors were more than happy to add to the warp and weft of the genre. Maybe this was due to the fact that it hadn't yet been 'labelled' and wasn't seen as a facile pursuit by the literati. However, when they did dabble, authors like Charles Dickens and Herman Melville tended to do so for comic or metaphorical reasons. It wasn't **real** science fiction.

Both of those authors did indeed contribute automata tales to the **oeuvre**. Melville wrote the short story 'The Bell Tower' (1855), in which an artist builds a machine-man to strike the hour on a large bell in a small village, but the machine-man ends up killing its creator. Seems Melville was soundly in the technofear camp.

Dickens, meanwhile, populated a small British village with an automated police force in an edition of his serialized satirical magazine column, 'The Mudfog Papers' (1838). Apparently, they could take a battering from up to eight noblemen, for whom the experience would be as satisfying as laying into the real thing.

ABOVE: The iconic robot from *Metropolis* (1927), directed by Fritz Lang

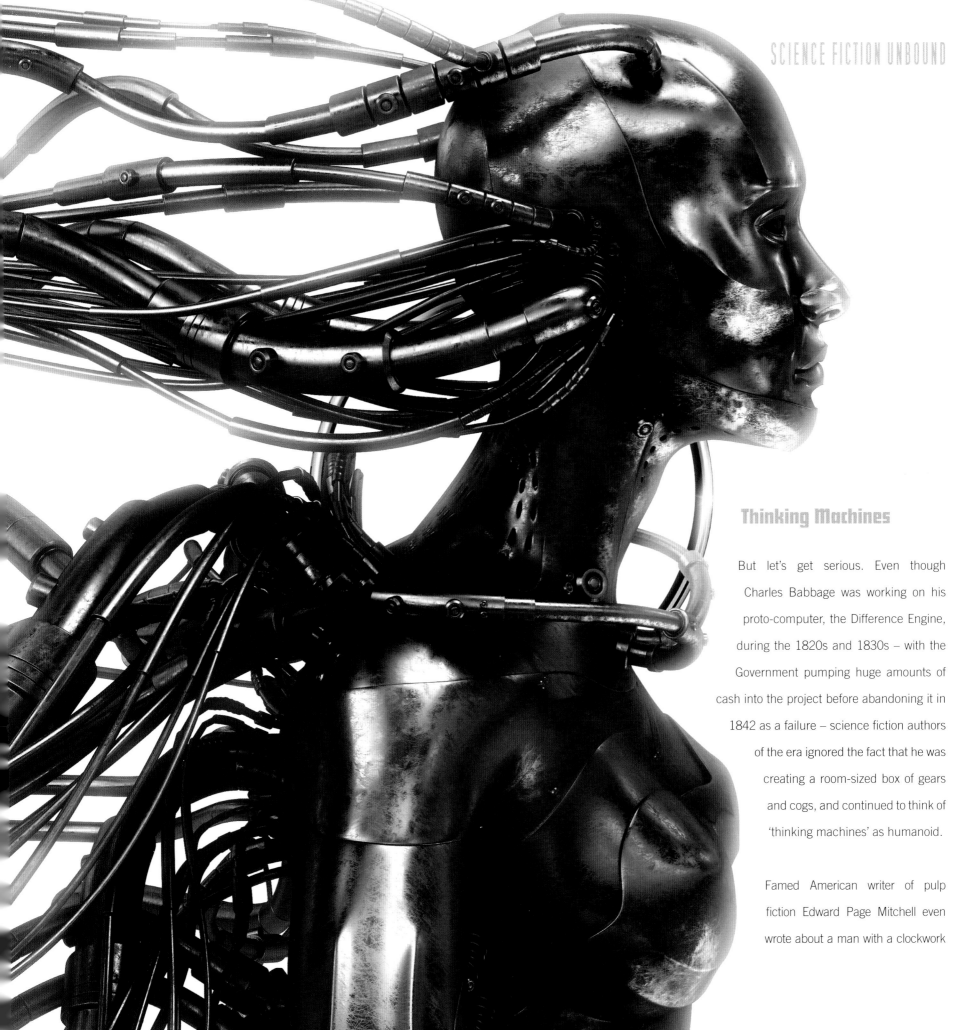

Thinking Machines

But let's get serious. Even though Charles Babbage was working on his proto-computer, the Difference Engine, during the 1820s and 1830s – with the Government pumping huge amounts of cash into the project before abandoning it in 1842 as a failure – science fiction authors of the era ignored the fact that he was creating a room-sized box of gears and cogs, and continued to think of 'thinking machines' as humanoid.

Famed American writer of pulp fiction Edward Page Mitchell even wrote about a man with a clockwork computer superior to the Difference Engine in 'The Ablest Man in the World' (1879), transforming him from an idiot into a genius who runs the Russian Empire. Maybe he was predicting how the microchip would miniaturize computers!

Jules Verne, though, seems to have been taking note that thinking machines might be more utilitarian in design. In **Paris in the Twentieth Century** (1863), he imagined a future Paris of 'calculating machines' that looked like 'huge pianos' operated from a 'keyboard' and hooked to 'facsimile' machines.

Bow to Your Robot Overlords

It seems fear of man being replaced by machine fuelled much nineteenth-century technophobia fiction – automation was as much an issue then as it is now. In a three-chapter section of his popular utopian novel **Erewhon** (1872) called 'The Book of the Machines', Samuel Butler was the first author to suggest that machines might develop consciousness through a form of Darwinian selection.

Critics assumed he was having a jolly jape, but in the preface to the second edition Butler wrote: 'I regret that reviewers have in some cases been inclined to treat the chapters on Machines as an attempt to reduce Mr Darwin's theory to an absurdity. Nothing could be further from my intention, and few things would be more distasteful to me than any attempt to laugh at Mr Darwin.'

Less scary were the domestic automata in Edward Bulwer-Lytton's **The Coming Race** (1871) and M.L. Campbell's 'The Automatic Maid-of-All-Work'

(1893), a rather tiresome comedy about an overenthusiastic mechanical home help who wrecks the house.

Mean Steam Machines

No recap of the century's mechanical marvels would be complete without Edward S. Ellis's **The Huge Hunter**, or **The Steam Man of the Prairies** (1865), and **Frank Reade and His Steam Man of the Plains** (1876) by Harold Cohen under the pen name Harry Enton; two characters so similar it was lucky they launched before the age of copyright litigation. Both were aimed squarely at the emerging dime novel market, which was making literature available to the masses – another great social innovation of the age – and cheerily lowbrow; a precursor to the pulp novels and magazines of the next century.

The Huge Hunter featured a 10-foot tall, steam-driven man of iron with a literal stovepipe hat, who pulled carriages across the Wild West, like a railway locomotive on legs. **Frank Reade** was an unashamed rip-off, and became science fiction's first great franchise. The first novel was serialized in **Boys of New York** magazine, then Cohen followed it up with a number of sequels about Frank's various other steam-powered inventions. In 1882, Frank was replaced by Frank Reade Jr. – and author Cohen replaced by Luis P. Senarens writing under the cunning pseudonym Noname – for an even more juvenile set of novels. Then 1892 saw the launch of **The Frank Reade Library**, a weekly (eventually biweekly) magazine at first reprinting old stories but later also commissioning new material.

ABOVE: Authors were fascinated with the idea of automata

MORE TIME & SPACE

The game-changing scientific watershed of the nineteenth century was the publication of Charles Darwin's *On the Origin of Species* (1859), or, to give it its full title (because Victorians never took a book seriously if its title wasn't a short story) *On the Origin of Species by Means of Natural Selection, or the Preservation of Favoured Races in the Struggle for Life*. Darwin's theories on evolution may have alarmed fundamentalists who didn't like the idea that they were half-cousins to orangutans, but they were also a mind- (and time-) expanding experience for those ready to embrace them.

Religious fundamentalists were already up in arms about palaeontologists' claims that the world was much older than the Bible would have us believe. Over the course of the nineteenth century, the Earth aged from a youthful 6,000 years to millions of years. (These days the figure is somewhere in the region of 4.5 billion years.) Darwin's theories, as H.G. Wells later attested, questioned the notion of a defined beginning to evolution and the idea that man was its pinnacle. Suddenly the past was a much broader canvas to explore and the future wasn't just a case of 'What will we do?' but also 'What will we become?'

In other words, time travel just became a lot more exciting.

Tentative Temporal Steps

We'll be dealing with that monolith of time travel, *The Time Machine* – a book which is pretty much a love letter to Darwin – in the next chapter (*see* page 51), but H.G. Wells had an earlier stab at the genre with his short story 'The Chronic Argonauts' (1888). Its *Jason and the Argonauts*-inspired title suggests that Wells was thinking of time as a new dimension through which epic voyages could be made. The tale is whimsical and not particularly memorable (though its protagonist bears the near unforgettable, and near unpronounceable, name Dr Moses Nebogipfel), but it's an interesting curtain-raiser for the next stage in Wells's career.

However, Wells was beaten to the post when it came to the first time machine in literature. While there had been previous time travel tales, they usually involved travel via dreams or falling asleep – Washington Irving's *Rip Van Winkle* (1819), Dickens' *A Christmas Carol* (1843) and Poe's *A Tale of the Ragged Mountains* (1844) to name but a few.

The first actual time machine, though, was (fittingly) a clock in Edward Page Mitchell's 'The Clock That Went Backward' (1881), a story that also contained fiction's first time paradox (somebody becoming their own ancestor). So, who was this ground-breaking fellow? We'll be coming back to him later.

Astronomy in the Nineteenth Century

Nineteenth-century authors seemed reluctant to move beyond the Moon when it came to space exploration, but this may be a reflection of the rather esoteric nature of developments in astronomy during Victorian times. There were few big discoveries

to fire the fictional imagination (most of the major planets in the solar system had already been discovered) as astronomers concentrated instead on using new developments in maths, physics, chemistry and geology to understand the make-up of celestial bodies and the origins of the universe. They were now interested in finding out exactly what a star, comet or planet consisted of and how each was formed. It just wasn't very … dramatic.

However, the careful, ground-laying work they were doing would lead to major discoveries in the twentieth century that would certainly impact on science fiction.

First Contact

This lack of interest in voyaging to alien worlds was reflected in a distinct lack of interest in aliens in nineteenth-century science fiction. The idea of life on other planets was far from new: ancient Greek philosophers Epicurus and Plutarch both wrote enthusiastically on the subject, though the other great thinkers of the classical age, Plato and Aristotle, both poured scorn on the notion. But during the nineteenth century, if space travellers did meet beings on the Moon or Mars, they were invariably human, or very human-like, such as the mini-humans on Mars in Percy Greg's *Across the Zodiac* (1880) – a title also used for a similar book by Edwin Pallander (1896), or Gustavus W. Pope's *Journey to Mars* (1894) with its colour-coded humanoids.

Truly *alien* aliens didn't appear until astronomer Camille Flammarion's *Real and Imaginary Worlds* (1864), a kind of travelogue of the universe, which imagined sentient trees and tentacled seal-like creatures. Once again, we would have to wait for H.G. Wells to put really outlandish aliens on the map.

ABOVE: Nineteenth-century authors looked to the stars, but not much further than the moon

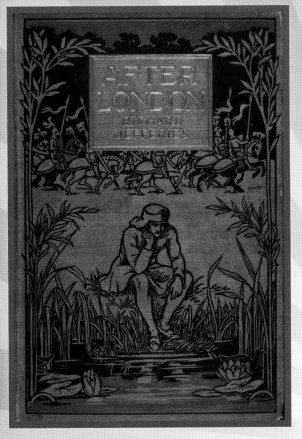

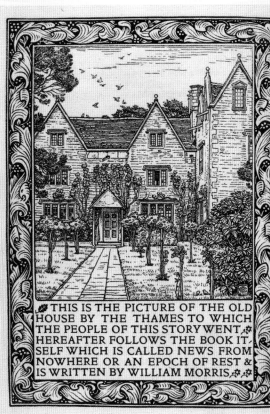

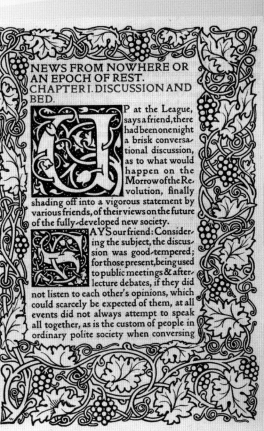

ABOVE: A selection of books from the nineteenth and early twentieth century

WAR – WHAT IS IT GOOD FOR?

Elsewhere, though, other advances in technology were certainly firing writers' imaginations, almost literally in the case of the weapons of war. The American Civil War (1861–65) was a turning point in the history of warfare, the conflict leading to a wide range of innovations, namely:

- The telegraph was invented by Samuel Morse in 1844. During the War, 15,000 miles of telegraph cable was laid purely for military purposes.
- Long-range weapons increased the range of rifles from 300 feet to 900 feet.
- The Minié bullet made shooting around five times more accurate.
  - The War saw the first engagement between two iron-clad warships.
    - The Gatling gun, which was invented by Richard Gatling, was the first 'repeating' weapon, the forerunner of the modern machine gun.

In addition, the Battle of Petersburg saw the first prolonged use of trench warfare, developing into a 292-day-long nightmare spanning 1864–65.

War was changing. It was getting uglier, bloodier, bigger. This, coupled with a global political situation where opposing empires were regularly involved in land-grabbing skirmishes, was fodder for the more pessimistic science fiction writer, inspiring no end of future wars and weapons of mass destruction.

Future War

R.F. Williams' *Eureka: A Prophecy of the Future* (1837) predated the American War, but reflected real-world concerns that Africa didn't seem content to roll over and let Great Britain stamp all over it. The book posited a future in which Britain is a backwater and the African Empire rules the world.

The British Empire is also a thing of the past in *The Air Battle: A Vision of the Future* (1859) by Hermann Lang, which proposes a war in the skies between Brazilia, Madeira and the Sahara. It's worth noting that while the Wright Brothers' first powered air flight was still over 40 years away, aeroplanes were very much part of the nineteenth-century zeitgeist thanks to the pioneering theoretical work of Sir George Cayley – 'father of the aeroplane' – in the last years of the eighteenth century.

Suburban Warfare

But the short story that really put future wars on the map was 'The Battle of Dorking' (1871) by George Tomkyns Chesney. This near-future tale saw

a ruthlessly efficient German army invade the UK and make mincemeat of the poorly trained British army. Chesney, who had served with the Bengal Engineers in British India, had an axe to grind about the state of the British defences, but his book was denounced by the then-Prime Minister, William Gladstone, and satirical magazine *Punch*. All of which no doubt helped it become a huge sales success.

ABOVE AND LEFT: Authors like Hermann Lang imagined wars fought in the skies

More War, Not Jaw Jaw

'The Battle of Dorking' inspired a whole new sub-genre, with many stories being little more than direct rip-offs (Horace Lester's *The Taking of Dover* (1888) – need we say more?) drenched in paranoia and fear; the foes had changed, the xenophobia remained the same. American novelist Pierton W. Dooner has Chinese immigrant workers overthrowing the USA in *Last Days of the Republic* (1880). *The Great War Syndicate* (1889) by Frank R. Stockton has war breaking out between the USA and Great Britain. The Germans were once again the bad guys in William Le Quex's *The Great War in England in 1897* (1894).

Bigger and Bloodier

As for the weapons themselves, for the majority of the Victorian era science fiction ordnance and firearms tended simply to be bigger, more powerful versions of real-world armaments. Jules Verne gave us the Fulgurator in *Facing the Flag* (1896), a weapon so powerful that 'the state which acquired it would become absolute master of earth and ocean'. In fact, it was basically the same as the exploding shell launched by the Zalinski dynamite gun (first demonstrated in 1883), only a few hundred times more powerful and self-propelling.

In *The Angel of the Revolution* (1893) George Griffith imagined a world war fought with airships and submarines, armed with unprecedentedly powerful explosives. T. Mullett Ellis's *Zalma* (1895) was a bit more prescient, foreshadowing the coming of bacteriological warfare. But as for more fanciful sci-fi weaponry – heat rays, death rays, lasers – they were all just a little in the future.

PERFECT WORLDS

A sub-genre that enjoyed an enthusiastic renaissance in the second half of the nineteenth century was the utopian novel. Utopia originated from Thomas More's work of that name published in 1516, in which he outlines a social, economic, political and religious structure for a 'perfect' island state – perfect for whom, being the main debate, since More's answer to many problems is slavery, but anyway....

Many other writers created their own utopias in the subsequent years – most famously Francis Bacon's *New Atlantis* (1627) and Margaret Cavendish's *The Blazing World* (1666) – but the massive and rapid social, technological and political changes of the nineteenth century breathed new life into the genre. Issues such as the increasing percentage of wealth that was being concentrated in an increasingly small number of hands, and social justice, spurred many authors to write about how society could be 'fixed'. It has been calculated that over 200 utopias were published from the middle of the century to the outbreak of the First World War.

ABOVE AND RIGHT: Imagined perfect cities of the future

One Man's Utopia is Another Man's Publishing Phenomenon

These utopias included **Three Hundred Years Hence** (1836) by Mary Griffiths, a feminist utopia in which a male time traveller awakes in a future of sexual equality. In **A Strange Manuscript Found in a Copper Cylinder** (1884) by James De Mille, a shipwreck survivor finds another world of sexual equality near the South Pole, while Mary E. Bradley's **Mizora: A Prophecy** (1881) goes even further, proposing a world where women rise up and dispense with men altogether. **Utopia** (1884) by Alfred D. Cridge travels to another planet that represents the best elements of Earth, while a visitor from Mars lays down his guide to social perfection in **A Cityless and Countryless World** (1893).

The flipside of utopia is dystopia, and Anna Bowman Dodd's **The Republic of the Future: Or, Socialism a Reality** (1887) acknowledges that striving for perfection could end up, well … a little dull. She predicts a world of mind-numbing monotony and regimentation.

The Utopian Blockbusters

Two specific utopian publications proved very popular and enduring, one even inspiring a political movement; not even George Orwell could boast that.

The title of Samuel Butler's **Erewhon** (1872) is – almost – nowhere backwards, and he sets his tale in the eponymous fictional land that appears to be utopian at first, but actually has many oddities that make you doubt the sanity of the place. For example, if you're ill, you're sent to prison; if you commit a criminal act, you are taken to hospital. Machinery is almost completely forbidden (there's a whole section called 'The Book of the Machines', which is a cautionary tale of machines gaining sentience).

In fact, Butler intended **Erewhon** to be a **Gulliver's Travels**-style parody of Victorian society. While there remain questions about Butler's skills as a satirist (his over-fondness of anagrams doesn't exactly scream 'rapier wit!'), his prescience about artificial intelligence is definitely to be admired.

Looking Backward

The other great utopian milestone of the late nineteenth century was **Looking Backward 2000–1887** (1888) by Edward Bellamy, a novel which had a huge influence, though not on science fiction.

In the book, lead character Julian West is transposed to the year 2000 by means of a hypnotic trance. He awakes to a collectivized America run along the principles of 'Nationalism'. Poverty and the evils of capitalism are things of the past. Everyone between the ages of 21 and 45 is conscripted into an 'industrial army' and given jobs that suit their skills, and they're all paid the same wage. (While all this is presented as utopian, Bellamy also predicts a machine that pipes music into everyone's homes, clearly unaware of the future horror of lift music.)

In terms of prose and ideas, there's little remarkable about **Looking Backward**, but the book proved immensely popular. It sold more than a million within a few years, and was translated and sold all over the world. Even more amazingly,

29

ABOVE: Book cover of the first edition of Erewhon by Samuel Butler (1872), published by Trübner & Co

over 160 'Bellamy Clubs' sprang up across the US, both to discuss his ideas and to lobby for Bellamy's nationalist concepts.

Hitting Back

The ultimate accolade for **Looking Backward**, though, was the number of authors who wanted to write rebuttals to it. **Caesar's Column, a Story of the Twentieth Century** (1890) by Ignatius Donnelly took Bellamy's ideals and re-imagined them as a dystopia.

Revered British designer William Morris reviewed **Looking Backward** and was not impressed. He questioned the validity of a society where there was no incentive to work, or to improve your lot in life: 'In short a machine life is the best which Mr Bellamy can imagine for us on all sides; it is not to be wondered at then that this, his only idea for making labour tolerable is to decrease the amount of it by means of fresh and ever fresh developments of machinery…. I believe that this will always be so, and the multiplication of machinery will just multiply machinery….'

As a response Morris wrote **News From Nowhere** (1891), which imagined a rather idyllic rural utopia, where no doubt the sun shone every day and little girls made daisy chains by babbling brooks. Rather fittingly for a work written by a designer, there was an emphasis on beauty. But however naïve and idealistic Morris's proposals may be, the book looks gorgeous, full of Morris's signature designs and artwork. It's still in print today and worth buying for the illustrations alone. Talking of which….

THE LOOK OF SF

Since the advent of cinema there's been a debate about the importance of spectacle in science fiction. With summer sci-fi blockbusters regularly relying on special FX rather than plots and characters, has visual science fiction become a form that appeals more on a visceral level than an intellectual one?

Back in the late nineteenth century, though, science fiction had a champion who appealed on both levels. The books of French illustrator Albert Robida were the blockbusters of the day, but, crucially, they were also bursting with imaginative ideas. He was Jules Verne in widescreen.

Born in 1848, Robida edited and published **La Caricature** magazine for 12 years from 1880, but the works we're most concerned with are his science fiction trilogy (which must surely count as the first sci-fi trilogy ever?):

• **Le vingtième siècle: roman d'une Parisienne d'après-demain** (**The Twentieth Century: The Tale of a Parisian Lady in the Day After Tomorrow**) (1883)

ABOVE: Flying machines in the shape of fish from *Le Vingtième Siècle* (1883) by Albert Robida

30

- *La guerre au vingtième siècle* (*War in the Twentieth Century*) (1887)
- *Le vingtième siècle: la vie électrique* (*The Twentieth Century: The Electric Life*) (1890).

Drawing the Future

The first book describes the transformation of Paris over the next century, and is a witty commentary on commercialism run wild. One illustration shows the Arc de Triomphe dwarfed by a vast hotel that has been built on an iron platform suspended above it. Another shows a rotating house extending above the surrounding rooftops.

The story – as much as there is one (this is an art book with text, to be honest) – centres on Hélène, an orphan adopted by the Ponto family, who experiences this new future Paris as a way of introducing it to the readers. She learns about the global telecommunications network; crystal screens; centralized food factories that pipe soup into people's homes; gender equality. The Moon has been dragged nearer the Earth seemingly just to make the night sky look prettier. Italy has been bought up and turned into a massive holiday-land.

It's all very whimsical and there's little in the way of social commentary or an understanding of science, but the beauty is in the art and the details. The visuals are simply gorgeous, bringing a near poetic beauty to a Victorian iron-and-rivets

aesthetic married to *fin de siècle* elegance and a Heath Robinson-esque love of quirky machinery.

Robida's Sequels

The first book was such a success that Robida created two sequels. **War in the Twentieth Century** (1887) tells of a war that begins in 1945. It stars Fabius Molinas, who's part James Bond, part Indiana Jones – a French soldier who can't help getting promoted for his derring-do. He goes on a globetrotting tour of fanciful conflicts that involve chemical warfare (mines loaded with 'poison gas, malignant fever bacilli, glanders, dysentery, measles and other maladies'), submarines, airship battles, massive cannons and a platoon of cyclists! This time there was more emphasis on the images than the text.

The Electric Life (1890) then moved the action to 1955 for an examination of how electricity was set to change the world (yes, finally writers were waking up to its potential). Robida writes about an electric-powered rapid transport system; a communication device similar to a telephone; a television-like piece of equipment with a large ovoid screen called the téléphonoscope (it also has VCR-style capabilities!); personal aircraft; and a military vehicle reminiscent of a modern submarine.

It's not much of a stretch to claim that Robida was probably more successful in predicting the course of the twentieth century than H.G. Wells. And he was funnier, too.

31

ABOVE: An airship of people needing medical care from *Le Vingtième Siècle* (1883) by Albert Robida

KEY FIGURES OF THE ERA

To finish off this look at the years between 1818 and 1894 (the reasons for this apparently arbitrary cut-off point will become clear in the following chapter), let's take a closer look at three major figures in science fiction during this time. You're bound to have heard of two of them (though one of them may leave you thinking, 'I didn't know he did sci-fi...'), whereas the other is a largely forgotten prophet, whose reputation was only partially restored when an anthology of his work – much of which was originally published anonymously – was belatedly published in 1973.

The Lost Prophet: Edward Page Mitchell

While Jules Verne and H.G. Wells are regularly cited as pioneering science fiction authors who originated many of the ideas we take for granted in the genre, there was one prolific nineteenth-century writer who can claim more 'sci-fi firsts' than either of

them. And we use the lowbrow term 'sci-fi' deliberately, because you could call this man a hack.

But What a Hack

Edward Page Mitchell was a newspaper man and would eventually become editor of **The Sun** (the New York one, not the UK one) in 1897. He started his career as a journalist on **The Daily Advertiser** in Boston, Massachusetts. His first published short story was 'The Tachypomp' (1874) for **Scribner's Monthly**, but after that all his fiction was published in **The Sun**, starting with a ghost story called 'Back From That Bourne' (1874), which was presented as a faux news story.

This led to more short stories for **The Sun**, and though he had been interested in the supernatural all his life, Mitchell was soon turning more and more towards science fiction. And he proved to have an incredibly fertile imagination.

The Ideas Generator

Mitchell wrote 'The Crystal Man' (1881), which featured a man made invisible by scientific means, before H.G. Wells wrote **The Invisible Man** (1897). He had a man use a machine to travel through time in 'The Clock That Went Backward' (1881) before Wells wrote 'The Chronic Argonauts' (1888). He was the first author to write about faster-than-

ABOVE: Central aircraft station at Notre-Dame from *Le XXeme siecle, La Vie Electrique* (*c.* 1890) by Albert Robida

light travel in 'The Tachypomp' (1874), albeit by the unlikely means of running successive trains on top of one another. He wrote about a thinking computer and a cyborg in 'The Ablest Man in the World' (1879). He even dreamt up a form of matter transmission for 'The Man Without a Body' (1877), while 'Exchanging Their Souls' (1877) is one of the earliest fictional accounts of mind transfer.

Other subjects Mitchell covered – if not originated – include travel by pneumatic tube, electrical heating, food-pellet concentrates and suspended animation by freezing (cryogenics). He also daringly predicted votes for American women, while his suggestion that the future would see newspapers being sent to people's homes by electrical transmission for them to print out could be seen as an embryonic version of the Internet.

A Nice Little Earner

Mitchell churned out these imaginative little tales for 12 years. After his last story for **The Sun**, 'The Shadow on the Fancher Twins' (1886), he seems to have turned his back on fiction entirely and returned to journalism. He probably never realized what a trailblazer he was; he was certainly never worried about his work being credited. His stories were probably just a way to make some extra money on the side.

He may have remained forgotten if not for some literary excavation work by Sam Moskowitz, who identified Mitchell as the author of the works and collected them together in **The Crystal Man: Landmark Science Fiction by Edward Page Mitchell** (1973).

ABOVE: Edward Page Mitchell wrote about a time machine in his story 'The Colck that Went Backward' (1881), written before H.G. Wells's *The Time Machine*

EDGAR ALLAN POE

Edgar Allan Poe was America's master of mystery and macabre during the middle of the nineteenth century. A poet, critic, author and editor, he was revered as one of the period's greatest practitioners of the short story. He also had a morbid fascination with death, and could probably lay claim to being the first ever goth. Much of his output was certainly gothic.

But Poe also dabbled in science fiction in the way some of his characters dabbled in the dark arts.

But is it Science Fiction?

Depending on how loose your definition, up to a fifth of Poe's work could be considered science fiction. Indeed, some of his more avid devotees lay claim to Poe being the well-spring for modern science fiction ('Poe is the source,' said American science fiction author and poet Thomas M. Disch), though there may be a little bit of national pride coming into play there.

It's fair to say that Poe's science fiction wasn't innovatory or revolutionary. Much of it was leavened with supernatural, mystical or whimsical elements. And it had little to do with science. But – and it is a big but – it had impact;

an impact which resonated with readers then, and still has the power to beguile today.

Poe With the Flow

Take, for example, an early long poem of Poe's called 'Al Aaraaf' (1829), with God giving instructions to stars to cut humankind off from the rest of the universe to stop its sins from spreading. Partly inspired by the Qur'an and partly inspired by astronomer Tycho Brahe's discovery of a supernova back in 1572 (which was visible for about 17 months), it was a true sci-fi/quasi-religious hybrid.

As was the short story 'The Conversation of Eiros and Charmion' (1839), which was a disaster movie in the making – a comet passes near Earth, causing environmental disasters and apocalyptic fires – with a religious twist. It is framed by a conversation between the two title characters, both spirits: Eiros, who died in the disaster, explaining what happened to Charmion, who died 10 years before. At the end they basically congratulate God on being mighty enough to move comets round and destroy planets. 'Well, yeah, I may have died horribly in flames but you have to admire His handiwork,' to paraphrase Poe's considerably more flowery prose.

Eureka!

Poe's marrying of science fiction and religion reached its apogee with the publication of his last major work, *Eureka: A Prose Poem* (1849), a sprawling

ABOVE: Photograph of Edgar Allan Poe, who wrote several stories which could be cnsidered science fiction

beast which combines contemporary astronomical theories in a cosmos ruled by a divine oneness. A kind of 'let's throw everything at the wall and see what sticks' affair, it does feature an embryonic version of the Big Bang theory. It also suggests that there'll be a Big Crunch, and that there's something big at the centre of the universe that's attracting everything to it, which is probably God. Oh, and Venus is self-illuminating and evolution is somehow connected to new planets being created.

Even in its day, **Eureka: A Prose Poem** must have come across as outrageously fanciful. Thankfully, when in a less spiritual frame of mind, Poe could produce some effective little science fiction shockers.

Life, Death and More Death

The Facts In the Case of M. Valdemar (1845) is a rum tale about a man being put into a hypnotic trance at the point of death and becoming, basically, a zombie. It was originally published in the **Broadway Journal**, without any indication it was fiction, and many readers were hoodwinked into thinking the events were real. Poet Elizabeth Barrett Browning commended Poe on his talent for 'making horrible improbabilities seem near and familiar'.

Mellonta Tauta (1849) is set in 2848 and told as a series of letters from a woman called Pundita, written to a friend to relieve the boredom of a long-distance balloon flight. The letters feature comparisons between science, philosophy and customs of their time and those of a thousand years before, with Pundita making some ludicrous assumptions about Poe's time period.

Eventually the balloon crashes into the Atlantic, so Pundita's final letter has to be sent in a bottle.

Ballooning to the Moon

Poe's most enduring contribution to the SF genre, though, was a comedy. 'The Unparalleled Adventure of One Hans Pfaall' (1835) is the tale of a lunar journey which may very well have been inspired by a similar journey to the Moon in **Baron Munchausen's Narrative of His Marvellous Travels and Campaigns in Russia** (1785), by Rudolf Erich Raspe. Munchausen's 'account' is similarly full of outrageous lies and Hans Pfaall is also outed as a hoaxer.

The story is told as a letter written by Hans Pfaall, a resident of Rotterdam who claims he built a hot-air balloon from newspapers and filled it with a substance lighter than air, which took him on a journey to the Moon. The journey took him 19 days, and he describes how Earth looks from space as well as his descent towards the fiery, volcanic surface of the Moon. Pfaall teases his audience with tales of lunar inhabitants that he will only divulge if the people of Rotterdam will pardon him for a few murders he committed before he left. But then they start noticing evidence that Pfaall might be telling porkies; and the reader starts to wonder if there's a hidden message in the fact that the balloon launched on April Fool's Day, and that Pfaall sounds like 'laugh' backwards.

Hoax or not, the lunar voyage itself is written with great gusto and is enormous fun.

35

ABOVE: Illustration by George Cruikshank for the poem 'The Monstre Balloon' (19th century)

THE EXTRAORDINARY VOYAGES OF JULES VERNE

36

Without a doubt, the pre-eminent science fiction author of the middle of the nineteenth century is Jules Verne, a name forever associated with intrepid explorers venturing to realms unknown in amazing craft – or *les voyages extraordinaires*, as they were known.

Verne was born in Nantes, the son of a lawyer. Aged 11 he tried to run away by boarding a ship to India but was intercepted by his father. In a story that's probably as apocryphal as that of Washington chopping down a cherry tree, young Jules is supposed to have said: 'I will no longer travel except in my dreams.'

His father wanted Verne to become a lawyer too, but Verne was fixated on becoming a writer. He didn't find immediate success. He took a job as a stockbroker in Paris for eight years while he was plugging away at his writing. He finally made a breakthrough in 1862, when publisher Pierre-

Jules Hetzel accepted his manuscript *Five Weeks in a Balloon* (1862) – a rip-roaring adventure about a balloon flight across Africa, exploring parts of the continent still a mystery to most Europeans, complete with secret tribes, condor attacks and daring rescue missions. It wasn't sci-fi, but it was a blueprint for the sci-fi to follow.

These Are the Voyages

Hetzel immediately snapped up Verne on a contract to write further adventures under the title 'voyages extraordinaires'. The relationship had a rocky start, though, when Hetzel rejected Verne's second submission, *Paris in the Twentieth Century*, telling the young writer he'd taken on an impossible task. The book was eventually disinterred and published in 1994, but the experience seems to have shaken Verne's confidence in straying too far from the *Five Weeks in a Balloon* formula.

So next up was *Journey to the Centre of the Earth* (*Voyage au centre de la Terre*, 1864), with the word 'voyage' prominent in the French title as if to re-affirm the mission statement. This was a return to the Hollow Earth genre, but Verne took a slightly different angle on the idea. Whereas traditionally these tales had concentrated on the wonderful worlds to be found beneath the Earth's crust, Verne was more interested in the details of the journey itself. This kind of detail-heavy info-dumping – which gave the extraordinary elements a more authentic documentarian feel – became a hallmark of Verne's prose.

ABOVE: Pat Boone in *Journey to the Center of the Earth* (1959)

ABOVE: Illustration for Jules Verne's *Robur the Conqueror* by Hippolyte Leon Benett; illustrations for *20,000 Leagues Under the Sea*; movie poster for *Master of the World* (1961)

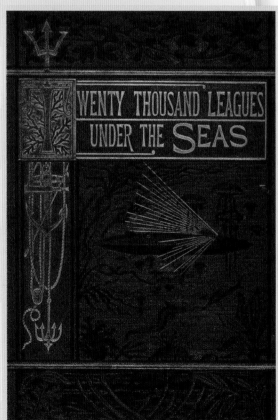

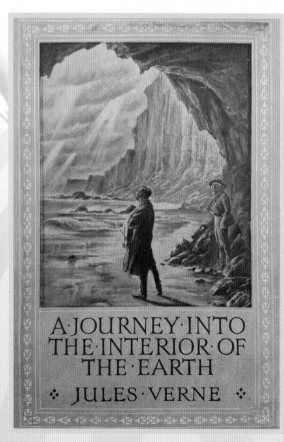

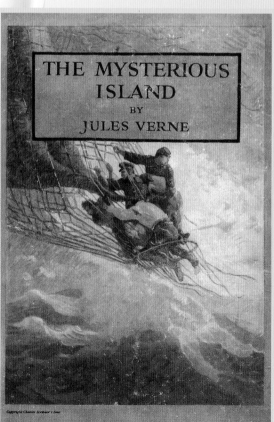

ABOVE: A selection of classic Jules Verne book covers

Hard SF

Next up was Verne's most 'hard SF' novel, *From the Earth to the Moon* (1865), which once again had more interest in detailing the building of the rocket and mechanics of the launch than a flight to the Moon. In fact, the book ends just after the launch (with some question about whether the ship itself may have blown up), so it's probably a good thing Verne was working in a pre-trading standards era.

Considering the mission is put together by the Baltimore Gun Club, a listless bunch of arms enthusiasts at a loss what to do after the end of the Civil War, it's little surprise that the launch method is via a giant cannon. As many critics have pointed out, the astronauts' main problem would have been surviving being crushed by the massive acceleration.

A sequel five years later, *Around the Moon* (1870), revealed the astronauts had lived and presented a typically fascinatingly detail-packed account of the voyage. Both books are full of all the (then) latest scientific knowledge about the Moon.

A League of His Own

Verne's masterpiece came not long after, and this time the realm he was exploring was the ocean: *20,000 Leagues Under the Sea* (1869) features the mysterious Captain Nemo and his marvellous submarine, the *Nautilus*.

The idea of a submarine was nothing new in literature, but the grandeur and marvel of the *Nautilus* really captured the public's imagination as it went on its elegant cruise.

Nemo re-emerged (oddly with an altered backstory) in *The Mysterious Island* (1874), which also featured a character from another previous Verne novel, *In Search of the Castaways* (1865). Verne had unknowingly created a prototype of the shared universe so beloved in modern movies (the Marvel Universe, the DC Universe, the Universal Monsters Universe, etc).

Verne wrote dozens more novels before his death, some with SF elements. A meteor collision sends a sizeable chunk of North Africa into space in *Off on a Comet* (1877). *The Bégum's Five Hundred Million* (1879) features two warring communities in the USA building giant weapons to destroy each other in a thinly disguised France versus Germany parable. *Robur the Conqueror* (1886) is practically a remake of *20,000 Leagues* but set in the air, and also generated a sequel, *Master of the World* (1904).

The Verne Effect

Jules Verne has his critics. His linear, globetrotting plots have been dismissed as SF tourism, and it's true that his characters are rarely changed by the extraordinary event they go through (unless they die, that is). But Verne was the early master of science fiction as spectacle; it was just that he painted his pictures with words.

ABOVE: Illustration from *Journey to the Centre of the Earth* (c. 1870) by Edouard Riou

2: NEW FRONTIERS

1895

1895 • *The Time Machine* • H.G. Wells
Novel

1895 • First screening of motion pictures, using the Cinématographe • Auguste & Louis Lumiére
Science & Technology

1895 • *La Charcuterie mécanique* • Auguste & Louis Lumiere
Movie

1896 • *The Island of Doctor Moreau* • H.G. Wells
Novel

1896 • *The Argosy* publishes its first fiction-only issue • Frank Munsey
Magazine

1897 • *The War of the Worlds* • H.G. Wells
Novel

1897 • *The Invisible Man* • H.G. Wells
Novella

1897 • *Dracula* • Bram Stoker
Novel

1898 • *Edison's Conquest of Mars* • Garrett P. Serviss
Novel

1900

1900 • *The Struggle for Empire* • Robert William Cole
Novel

1901 • *The First Men in the Moon* • H.G. Wells
Novel

1902 • *A Trip to the Moon* • Georges Méliès
Movie

1903 • First controlled, propelled aircraft flight • Orville & Wilbur Wright
Science & Technology

1905 • *On the Electrodynamics of Moving Bodies*, the first publication of the theory of special relativity • Albert Einstein
Science & Technology

1905 • *Sultana's Dream* • Rokeya Sakhawat Hussain
Novel

1905 • 'With the Night Mail' • Rudyard Kipling
Short Story

1907 • *Before Adam* • Jack London
Novel

1908 • *The Iron Heel* • Jack London
Novel

1909 • 'The Machine Stops' • E.M. Forster
Short Story

1910

1910 • *Frankenstein* • J. Searle Dawley
Movie

1910 • *The Death of the Earth* • J.-H. Rosny
Novel

1910 • *The Sleeper Wakes* • H.G. Wells
Novel

1912 • *Under the Moons of Mars* • Edgar Rice Burroughs
Novel

1912 • *The Lost World* • Arthur Conan Doyle
Novel

1912 • 'As Easy as A.B.C.' • Rudyard Kipling
Short Story

1912 • *The Scarlet Plague* • Jack London
Novel

1914 • Start of the First World War • Worldwide
World Event

1914 • *At the Earth's Core* • Edgar Rice Burroughs
Novel

Chronology of selected events in the history of science fiction, from early influences to modern media.

Philosophy Science & Technology Novels Short Story World Events Movies Magazines Comics Play Pulp Magazines Radio Small Publishers TV Video Games

1915　　　　　　　**1920**　　　　　　　**1923**

1915 • *Herland* • Charlotte Perkins Gilman
Novel
1915 • *The Man Who Rocked the Earth* • Arthur C. Train
and Robert W. Wood
Novel
1916 • *20,000 Leagues Under the Sea* • Stuart Paton
Movie
1917 • America enters the First World War • USA
World Event
1918 • *The Land That Time Forgot* • Edgar Rice Burroughs
Novel
1918 • End of the First World War • Worldwide
World Event
1919 • First issue of *The Thrill Book* • Harold Hersey
Magazine
1919 • Publication of the first account of 'splitting' an atom •
Ernest Rutherford
Science & Technology
1919 • *The First Men in the Moon* • Bruce Gordon,
J.L.V. Leigh
Movie

1920 • *Strange Case of Dr Jekyll and Mr Hyde* •
John S. Robertson
Movie
1920 • *A Voyage to Arcturus* • David Lindsay
Novel
1920 • *Rossum's Universal Robots* • Karel Capek
Play
1921 • *The Verge* • Susan Glaspell
Play
1922 • *The Girl in the Golden Atom* • Ray Cummings
Novel

1923 • The first issue of *Weird Tales* • J.C. Henneberger,
J.M. Lansinger
Pulp Magazine
1923 • *The Clockwork Man* • E.V. Odle
Novel
1923 • *Aelita* • Alexei Tolstoy
Novel
1924 • *We* • Yevgeny Zamyatin
Novel
1924 • *Aelita* • Yakov Protazanov
Movie
1924 • *The Last Man on Earth* • John G. Blystone
Movie
1924 • The first findings of galaxies outside the Milky Way are
published in *The New York Times* • Edwin Hubble
Science & Technology
1925 • *The Monster* • Crane Wilbur
Play

NEW VISIONS

Choosing to kick off this chapter in 1895 – just short of a new century – may seem a random decision, but cultural revolutions rarely happen on round numbers. You may recall 1977 was a watershed year both for movies – with *Star Wars* – and music – with punk.

42

So 1895 was a turning point in science fiction for two major reasons: it saw the birth of cinema, a medium that would have a game-changing effect on the genre, and the publication of H.G. Wells's **The Time Machine**, a novel that began a decade-long golden period for the author's SF.

Because, while it's traditional to lump Verne and Wells together – they were both Victorian science fiction writers – there are more differences than similarities. They never met. They were from different generations (Verne was 38 when Wells was born in 1866). Verne was what today we would call a geek – interested in the hardware and the nitty gritty of the science. Wells was the intellectual, a satirist, social realist and political commentator, who could wrap all that in a rattling good yarn. Verne's characters were rarely affected by the events they lived through. Wells's characters were often profoundly changed by them.

That's not to say Wells's science fiction operated on a purely allegorical level; his concepts were as hard SF as Verne's, maybe harder, and his ideas could be even more prescient. But Wells at his best wrote science fiction that actually mattered.

Life in the Fin de Siècle World

So what kind of a world was Wells writing in? The late nineteenth and early twentieth century was a time of radical change. Electricity, that great subplot of these first two chapters, was finally coming into its own; it had been a major theme at the 1893 World's Fair, and homes, businesses and street lamps were beginning to adopt electricity over gas. And although the Edison Electric Light Company's DC was losing the War of the Currents to Westinghouse's AC, the inventor extraordinaire Thomas Edison had won the PR battle and was pretty much legend in his lifetime. He even became a sci-fi pulp hero of sorts, starring in books such as **L'Éve Future** (1886) by Auguste Villiers de l'Isle-Adam, in which Edison creates a robot woman, and **Edison's Conquest of Mars** (1898) by American astronomer and writer Garrett P. Serviss.

Lights, Camera, Action!

Edison's work in the field of electronics and lighting paved the way for the invention of cinematic projection, enabling French brothers Auguste and Louis Lumière to design and build the first motion-picture camera. Although others

ABOVE: Rod Taylor in *The Time Machine* (1960), directed by George Pal

had developed similar inventions around the same time, what the Lumières invented was special: a portable motion-picture camera, film-processing unit and projector in one: the cinematographe.

In 1895, the brothers demonstrated the first photographic moving pictures projected on to a screen for a paying audience, which was treated to ten 50-second films, including **Sortie des Usines Lumière à Lyon** (**Workers Leaving the Lumière Factory in Lyon**), officially the world's first commercial motion picture.

Developments in cinema were rapid, with the subject matter developing from short documentaries to long, elaborate dramas in just a few years, with the first science fiction 'epic', director Georges Méliès' **A Trip to the Moon**, premiering in 1902.

Death Rays

Before **A Trip to the Moon**, Méliès, a director who specialized in creating illusions in cinema, had made a couple of shorts which could be considered 'fringe' science fiction. **Gugusse et l'automate** (1897) featured a clown fascinated by an automaton, while **Les rayons Röntgen** (1898) saw a man being X-rayed and his skeleton making a run for it. X-rays were currently en vogue after having been discovered by Wilhelm Röntgen in 1895. They really caught the public's imagination, not to mention the imaginations of writers and filmmakers. **The X-Rays** (1897) was a British short about a courting couple who become skeletons.

The word 'ray' also was further co-opted by science fiction with the discovery of radioactive emissions by Antoine Henri Becquerel in 1896. He called

ABOVE: The first science fiction epic, Georges Méliès' *A Trip to the Moon* (1902). RIGHT: The Martian invasion from H.G. Wells's *The War of the Worlds*

them 'rays' and the word swiftly took on a negative meaning in the public consciousness. Thus the 'death' ray so beloved of science fiction was born, making its first appearance as the Martians' heat-rays in Wells's **The War of the Worlds** (1898).

Endless Energy

This was also the dawn of the atomic age. The double whammy of Albert Einstein announcing that E=mc2 in 1905 and Ernest Rutherford's further research into radioactivity – culminating in the splitting of the atom in 1919 – sent SF practitioners into overdrive. Suddenly atomic power was the answer to everything and the end of everything. So while Garrett P. Serviss wrote about an atomic-powered spaceship in 'A Columbus of Space' (1909) for pulp magazine **All-Story**, Wells was writing about atomic war in **The World Set Free** (1914). In **The Man Who Rocked the Earth** (1915) Arthur C. Train and Robert W. Wood give a remarkably prescient description of a nuclear explosion 30 years before the United States detonated the first atomic bomb.

But that was writers taking only the headlines from Einstein's theory of relativity – 'energy and mass are equivalent and transmutable!' Some of the more intriguing things he had to say about the nature of space-time took a lot, lot longer to permeate the genre, especially when it came to time dilation.

NEW EMPIRES, NEW FRONTIERS

The period saw the end of an era of imperial expansion and exploration too. Little of our planet's land surface remained undiscovered. In the USA, the western frontier was a frontier no longer. But as Americans and Europeans in the real world were being denied their favourite colonial pastimes – claiming land, shooting big animals and showing natives the benefits of civilization down the barrel of a gun – science fiction writers filled the void with ever-more fanciful tales of lost worlds and new planets to conquer.

The most obvious examples of surrogate-colonialism were the Professor Challenger tales of Sir Arthur Conan Doyle, including **The Lost World** (1912) with its discovery of a plateau in the Amazon where dinosaurs still roam, and the Pellucidar stories of Edgar Rice Burroughs, a Hollow Earth scenario, which began with **At the Earth's Core** (1914).

ABOVE: *The Lost World* (1925) was based on Arthur Conan Doyle's novel (1912) about discovering dinosaurs

The Final Frontier, First Time Around

Meanwhile another of Burroughs' series, the Mars-based Barsoom stories (1912–41) starring transposed American Civil War soldier John Carter, was at the forefront of a new urge in science fiction to explore strange new worlds after the resolutely Earthbound nature of the genre in the nineteenth century. Mars also proved enticing for Russian novelist Alexei Tolstoy (a remote relative of Leo of **War and Peace** fame), who sent his hero to the red planet in a rocket to discover an evil and somewhat capitalist-inspired empire in **Aelita** (1923).

Space opera (which actually wouldn't earn its name until 1941) was also in an embryonic stage. Robert William Cole's **The Struggle for Empire** (1900) features an intergalactic war in 2236 between Earth (now ruled by the British) and Sirius, made possible by 'interstellar ships'.

New Galaxies to Explore

Just as our concept of time had expanded in the nineteenth century thanks to Darwin, our concept of space was expanding in the twentieth thanks to the likes of astronomers such as Edwin Hubble. His observations, made in 1922–23, proved conclusively there were entire galaxies outside our own Milky Way. Science fiction writers were eager to play in this mind-bogglingly vast new playground, even if real scientists insisted on ruining the fun by pointing out the bit in Einstein's theories about faster-than-light travel being impossible; in other words, the shortest time it would take you to reach the nearest next galaxy would be 25,000 years.

Ignore It and It'll Go Away...

Early SF authors largely tended to simply ignore this annoying detail, including E.E. 'Doc' Smith, whose galaxy-trotting Skylark series kicked off with **The Skylark of Space** (1928). David Lindsay's **A Voyage to Arcturus** (1920) – a highly regarded fantasy/sci-fi hybrid – had its hero transported to the eponymous solar system naked in a 'torpedo of crystal' propelled by Arcturian back-rays.

In later years, as the **hoi polloi** became more science literate, subsequent authors came up with all sorts of cheats to get round Einstein's inconvenient truth: hyperspace, wormholes, black holes, matter transmission and even an Infinite Improbability Drive, as seen in Douglas Adams's **The Hitchhiker's Guide to the Galaxy** (1978).

ABOVE: *Aelita* (1924), based on the novel by Alexei Tolstoy (1923), had wonderfully outlandish costumes designed by Aleksandra Ekster

45

RE-BOOTING AFTER THE WAR

The single most devastating and significant event of this era, though, was the First World War, or the Great War as it was referred to at the time. There was little great about it. This was one of the darkest chapters in world history. Not simply because of the sheer, horrifying number of people who died, but the utter, abject misery the fighters were subjected to in trench warfare at the Front.

46

Pat Mills, Judge Dredd co-creator and writer of critically acclaimed First World War comic strip 'Charley's War', once told the BBC: 'To me, the First World War was the world's first science fiction war.' He wasn't being glib. The War saw military engagement transformed. Tanks were deployed for the first time. The Germans used Zeppelins for aerial reconnaissance. Flamethrowers and poison gas were terrifying new weapons. Fighter planes were fitted with interrupter guns, making aerial combat possible. Aircraft carriers roamed the seas like iron titans.

Suddenly the technology that was building a better future in the nineteenth century was now creating a more miserable one. Science fiction reflected this with an increasingly dystopian view of the future and discovering ever more ugly weapons and ways for humans to kill each other.

Delayed Reaction

It's worth noting, though, that in the immediate aftermath of the First World War, science fiction went a little bit quiet. Immediately prior to the War there was a mini-trend for what would now be called apocalyptic or post-apocalyptic novels. In Garrett P. Serviss's **The Second Deluge** (1912) Earth passes into the Aquas Nebula, resulting in global floods and the building of – you guessed it – an ark. In the Belgian novel **The Death of the Earth** (1910) by J.-H. Rosny our world becomes a dying desert planet. Jack London's **The Scarlet Plague** (1912) takes place 60 years after a deadly epidemic has swept the globe.

But the reality of the First World War seems to have left science fiction authors shell-shocked, perhaps wondering if they could ever imagine anything more terrible, perhaps just fearful of appearing to be trivializing the War. It took until the second half of the 1920s for post-apocalyptic novels to return in a big way. Even Wells – who immediately prior to the War had written **The World Set Free** (1914) about a nuclear war – didn't write another hard science fiction novel until **Men Like Gods** (1923), and that was, perhaps tellingly, a utopian novel set in a parallel universe.

Return of the Robots

Robots were still a theme of science fiction in this era, and at last they had a name, ironically derived from a play that doesn't feature robots as we understand them. In 'R.U.R.' (1920) by Czech writer Karel Čapek, those initials stood for Rossum's Universal Robots, a company which manufactures artificial people, or 'roboti', from synthetic organic matter; they're closer to clones than what we know as robots. However, they are very much robots in one way: they rise up and overthrow their human masters. In Czech, **robota** means forced labour.

Fear of artificial intelligence was also the theme for a novel by another one of those 'highbrow' authors who decided to have a go at science fiction – E.M. Forster of **A Room with a View** (1908) fame. And a very good go of it he made, too. 'The Machine Stops' (1909) is a compelling novella set in a future Earth controlled by a machine whose influence stretched across the entire globe. It basically nursemaids every human on the planet, taking care of their every need, except sex. People live alone and mostly communicate through the Machine rather than face to face – an anticipation of the internet age! So when the Machine breaks down, the humans don't have a clue how to survive. It makes you wish Forster had written more science fiction.

Like Clockwork

E.V. Odle's **The Clockwork Man** (1923) was a rather more whimsical 'mechanical man' tale, but is worth mentioning for a couple of reasons. Several thousand years from now, advanced humanoids known as the Makers implant clockwork devices into people's heads that enable them to move through time and space. In other words, the story involves travelling cyborgs, long, long before **The Terminator** (1984). When one of these Clockwork Men accidentally ends up in an English rural village, much hilarity ensues. Well, maybe not so much hilarity, as mild amusement. Still, you could also cite this as an early example of a sub-genre of very English comedy science fiction that eventually led to **The Hitchhiker's Guide to the Galaxy** (1979).

ABOVE: Robots and intelligent machines were a popular science fiction theme, inspiring authors like E.V Odle in *The Clockwork Man* (1923)

HACK TO THE FUTURE

Although the dedicated science fiction pulp magazine is a phenomenon that will come to fruition in the period covered in the next chapter, the groundwork was being laid in the first quarter of the twentieth century and its practitioners were honing their art.

Like the dime novels of the previous century, pulp magazines were making literature accessible to the masses. It needed to be, because the working classes were finally getting properly educated. In Britain the 1870 Education Act saw literacy boom. In America by 1910, 72 per cent of United States children were obliged to stay in school until at least 14. Suddenly, everybody was reading.

So the publishing industry needed to cater for them, which didn't just mean cheaper books (the paperback becoming more popular than the hardback) but also stories that were more accessible. Or lowbrow, depending on your point of view.

Pulp-able Hits

So magazines like **The Argosy** in the United States (first published 1886) and **The Strand** in the UK (first published 1891) provided readers with a constant stream of bite-sized fictions every month, from serialized reprints of more popular novels to all-new stories written at speed, usually by underpaid hacks who had to just 'knock 'em out'.

Not that there was a total lack of quality control from the editors, though some had higher standards than others. One who would go on to have very exacting standards in the 1930s was Hugo Gernsback, creator of the legendary **Amazing Stories** (launched 1926). In this period he was just starting his career, both as an editor – he founded the magazine **Modern Electrics** in 1908 – and as a writer, with **Ralph 124C 41+: A Romance of the Year 2660**, a 12-part serial that he ran in his magazine from April 1911. (The alphanumeric surname in the title is supposed to be read as, 'One to foresee for one'– which barely makes any more sense.)

Hacking Away for Years

Not all the hacks were without talent. Over his career Murray Leinster would write an unfeasible number of short stories and novels, as well as TV and film scripts. The amazing thing with a workload like this is that some of his stuff is very good, even award-winning.

After selling western, romance, crime and jungle-adventure short stories to various pulp magazines in the 1910s, Leinster published his first SF story, 'The Runaway Skyscraper', in a 1919 issue of **Argosy** – a wry little tale about a building falling into a crack in time. More sci-fi tales for **Argosy** followed in the 1920s ('The Mad Planet', 'The Red Dust', 'The Gallery Gods', 'Nerve') before his career really exploded in the 1930s.

ABOVE: 'The Mad Planet' by Murray Leinster, reprinted in *Fantastic Novels Magazine* (November 1948), cover art by virgil Finlay

ALIENATION

Aliens – properly alien aliens this time, not just slightly odd humans – finally came to the fore in this period, thanks to a three-pronged approach from H.G. Wells, Edgar Rice Burroughs and the pulps.

Wells, ever in the thrall of Darwin's theories on evolution and survival of the fittest, ran with the idea that different worlds' conditions would cause different beings to evolve. His Martians in **The War of the Worlds** (1898) look like disembodied heads nearly four feet across, with a v-shaped beak for a mouth, surrounded by two groups of tentacles. Victorian readers must surely have been overcome by a touch of the vapours at reading that.

Meanwhile, Burroughs' Tharks in his Barsoom series were six-armed, tusked, green-skinned Martians with that must-have accessory for all early aliens – antennae.

A Brash and Bold New Look

As for the pulps, if they were lucky to have artist Frank Rudolph Paul working for them, they could have aliens that looked as alien as you could wish for:

monkey-creatures with chitinous armour; giant reptiles with wing flaps; penguin/snake hybrids. He was pretty mean at rendering robots and spaceships too, and his contribution to establishing science fiction as a visual medium cannot be understated. He was a major collaborator with Hugo Gernsback on his pulp magazines in the 1930s and 1940s, and helped define a 'look' for the genre that still has an influence today. If a sci-fi film is described as having 'retro' stylings, that probably means it looks like Paul's work.

But Were They Aliens?

Once again we hit that stumbling block of all these 'aliens' existing before they were even called aliens.

According to many sources the first use of the word 'alien' to mean extra-terrestrial was in 1953, coined by John W. Campbell in his magazine **Analog Science Fiction and Fact**. However, other critics have noted that Edgar Rice Burroughs used the word 'alien' twice in **A Princess of Mars** (1917). John Carter, the Earth-born hero of the novel, describes an 'alien incubator' soon after his arrival on Mars. Later on, a Martian says to Carter: 'You are an alien.'

There are convincing arguments that in neither case is Burroughs using the term in the sense we mean it now (the first use is as an adjective not a noun); however, there's every chance that he did (that first alien could be a noun if you read it as the incubator for aliens). And with the Barsoom series so widely read and imitated by the creators of the pulps, it seems improbable that not one of them picked up on the term and copied it in some long-lost tale between 1917 and 1953.

ABOVE: Aliens became a popular science fiction theme during this period

H.G. WELLS & OTHER KEY PLAYERS

Most of the big names in science fiction are pretty much big names in literature, full stop – H.G. Wells, Edgar Rice Burroughs, Sir Arthur Conan Doyle and Jack London. Indeed, those last three are probably more famous for their non-science fiction – Tarzan, Sherlock Holmes and *White Fang* respectively. But all of them left an indelible mark on the historical landscape of the genre.

The Time of H.G. Wells

While Jules Verne brought a sense of wonder to science fiction, H.G. Wells brought a sense of humanity. A Darwinist through and through, Wells wasn't affronted by the idea that man was simply just another animal, destined to evolve into a form other than 'in God's image'; instead, he was fascinated by exploring the possibilities of evolution, socially as much as scientifically.

Wells also had a social agenda that complemented his Darwinist leanings. Born in 1866 in Bromley in Kent, he was the son of a shopkeeper and a maid. At one point the family was so poor, Wells was forced to become an apprentice draper, an experience he loathed. In other words, he had only

the tiniest toehold in the middle class at a time in England when class was everything. And the working classes did not become intellectuals and authors.

Wells's path to literary glory was, therefore, his own personal struggle to prove 'survival of the fittest'.

More Than Just a Science Fiction Writer

We said at the start of this section how Burroughs and Doyle are more famous for their non-science fiction. Wells would probably have liked to have been included in that list. Over his 60-year writing career he penned a vast variety of fiction, non-fiction and journalism, including over 50 novels. Of those novels, only around a third are science fiction (depending on the looseness of your definition) and most of the ones he's most famous for were published over a nine-year period, 1895–1904.

Perhaps tellingly, the title of the other novels he wrote in that period – two fantasies, ***The Wonderful Visit*** (1895) and ***The Sea Lady*** (1902), a comedy, ***The Wheels of Chance*** (1896), and the drama ***Love and Mr Lewisham*** (1900) – would merit only a shrug if you asked most people today who authored them.

The Forgotten Wells

That's not to say that none of Wells's non-SF has resonance. But other than ***Kipps*** (1905), ***Tono-Bungay*** (1909) and ***The History of Mr Polly*** (1910), most of his other work failed to make much of a dent on the zeitgeist. Even

ABOVE: Divers encounter weird creatures in H.G. Wells's 'In the Abyss' (1905), illustrated by Henri Lanos

weighty academic tomes such as *A Short History of Mankind* (1925) and *The Science of Life* (1930) – bestsellers in their day – are only read by Wells scholars today.

Sadly – outside his SF work – what Wells is now most notorious for are his views on eugenics, the 'science' of selective breeding now heavily associated with Hitler's death camps. Academics still argue the extent of Wells's support for the concept. In *Anticipations* (1902) he praises 'the nation that most resolutely picks over, educates, sterilizes, exports or poisons its People of the Abyss'. However, he distanced himself from the hard-line eugenics advocated by the likes of Francis Galton (who extrapolated the case for eugenics from Darwinism and who coined the term), favouring education over compulsion. But Wells did advocate the sterilization of genetic 'failures', and there's a very uncomfortable section on eugenics in *A Modern Utopia* (1905).

Wells's Golden Age

Controversies aside, that decade-long Golden Age for Wells is a landmark in the development of science fiction. Okay, Edward Page Mitchell may have beaten him to the punch with a few concepts (time travel, invisibility, etc.) but Mitchell never developed those ideas; they were one-gag conceits. Wells truly explored them and popularized them.

The Time Machine (1895) was Darwinism and Wells's own brand of socialism writ large on a canvas of eternity. The Time Traveller (he is never named) voyages to a future where man has evolved into two castes, the gentle and naive Eloi who live on the Earth's surface in an Eden-like idyll, while the monstrous Morlocks live underground and come to the surface at night to feed on the Eloi. This was a working-class revolution on an entirely different scale. The Time Traveller then goes further into the future to a time when humans have vanished from view and the world is populated by giant crabs scuttling listlessly on a dying planet, and then finally, tentacled blob-like creatures.

Mad Scientists and Aliens

Wells added to the mad-scientist genre with both *The Island of Doctor Moreau* (1896) and *The Invisible Man* (1897). The first is a ghoulish reimagining of the Garden of Eden with a vivisectionist twist. Dr Moreau creates animal hybrids shaped into human form on his secret island before the only female beast he creates tellingly brings about his downfall. In *The Invisible Man*, a scientist called Griffin turns himself both see-through and mad in a bleak warning about power corrupting; he's soon terrorizing a small village and promising a 'reign of terror'. Wells is making the point that morality 'vanishes' when you think you can get away with doing bad things.

The War of the Worlds (1898) grew out of the future war genre popularized by *The Battle of Dorking* (1871) but supercharged it with truly alien extra-terrestrials. Interestingly, Wells uses Verne's much criticized 'space cannon' technology to launch his Martians towards Earth; he presumably knew the science was dodgy, but the visual metaphor in a novel with 'war' in the title was presumably too much to resist.

51

ABOVE: Guy Pearce as the Time Traveller in *The Time Machine* (2002), directed by H.G. Wells' great-grandson Simon Wells

Growing Pains

The First Men in the Moon (1901) is Wells's take on the lunar voyage, his explorers using an anti-gravity substance called cavorite to get them into space. On the Moon, they face the insect-like Selenites in a story that feels more like a straight Vernian action adventure, but an enjoyable one, nonetheless.

In **The Food of the Gods and How It Came to Earth** (1904) Wells's bumbling scientists create a superfood that makes living things – plants, animals, eventually humans – grow to extraordinary size. This leads to a war with the giants, in which the giants are far more sympathetically portrayed than the devious humans.

And There's More

During this period Wells also wrote **When the Sleeper Wakes**, which was serialized in **The Graphic** magazine between 1898 and 1903, then significantly rewritten and republished as the novel **The Sleeper Wakes** in 1910. A man falls asleep for over 200 years, and when he wakes, he finds that the compound interest on his bank account has made him the richest – and most

powerful – man on the planet. While he was sleeping, a trust was created to administer his wealth and establish a vast political and economic world order. But the trustees (12 of them, like disciples, in a 'resurrection' analogy) are not happy they're no longer in control.

Wells also gave us his ideas on a perfect society in the rather dry **A Modern Utopia** (1905), a world high on happy gas in **In the Days of the Comet** (1906), and global aerial combat in **The War in the Air** (1908), partly inspired by Orville and Wilbur Wright's breakthroughs with powered flight in 1903.

Later Scientific Romances

Then there was a bit of a gap in Wells's SF, as he concentrated on his social-realist fiction. Radioactivity plays a cameo in the otherwise un-SF **Tono-Bungay** (1909), when a substance called 'quap' melts a ship, but it wasn't until the atomic war in **The World Set Free** (1914) that he again fully embraced the genre. In **Men Like Gods** (1923) a journalist is transported to a parallel Earth for yet another stab at utopia.

Later novels would include Wells's ambitious 'future history of mankind' (yes, more nuclear war) in **The Shape of Things to Come** (1933), **The Camford Visitation** (stuffy English education system given a lesson by visiting utopian) and **Star Begotten** (1937), based on the intriguing concept that the human race is being secretly altered by genetic modification to replace the dying Martian-kind on Mars. Even at the end it's all about evolution, even if it's a twisted version.

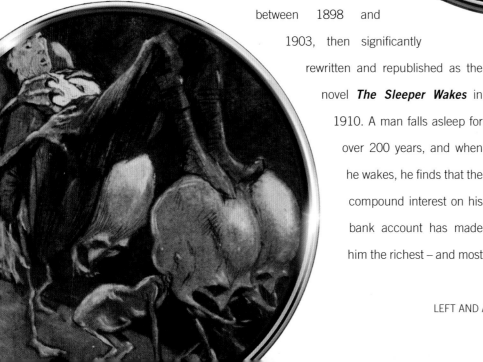

52

LEFT AND ABOVE: Illustrations from H.G. Wells's *The First Men in the Moon* (early 20th century) by Claude Shepperson

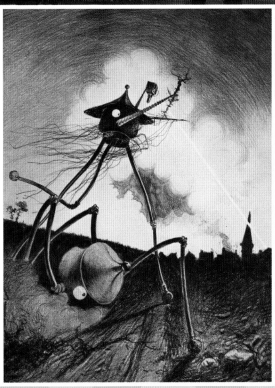

ABOVE: *The War of the Worlds* has been reimagined many times: A 2005 movie; *Amazing Stories* (August 1927) art by Frank R. Paul; Illustration (1906) by Henrique Alvim Corrêa; A 1953 movie

PULP HERO, EDGAR RICE BURROUGHS

54

Edgar Rice Burroughs never expected to be a celebrated writer. Having been booted out of the army because of a dodgy heart in 1897, he spent over a decade bouncing between various low-paid jobs, wondering why he never seemed to be getting anywhere in business. So, to earn some extra cash, he turned to writing, mainly because he'd read the stories in pulp magazines and reckoned he could do better.

In an interview with the **Washington Post** in 1929, Burroughs recalled developing the idea that 'if people were paid for writing rot such as I read in some of those magazines, that I could write stories just as rotten.... Although I had never written a story, I knew absolutely that I could write stories just as entertaining and probably a whole lot more so than any I chanced to read in those magazines.'

His readers agreed.

A Man Wakes Into a Barsoom

Burroughs sold his first story, 'Under the Moons of Mars', for serialization in **All-Story** magazine in 1912, writing under the name Norman Bean (he'd actually asked to be credited as Normal Bean but the typesetters made a mistake). At this point he still thought that he'd find a 'real' job that would make his fortune, and didn't want prospective employees knowing he was writing pulp fiction.

The serial, which was later published as a novel called **A Princess of Mars** (1917), was a runaway hit with readers and marked the beginning of the Barsoom series, Barsoom being Burroughs' name for Mars. Burroughs would go on to write seven sequels, all serialized in pulps before being published in novel form, the last being **Synthetic Men of Mars** (1940).

John Carter

A Princess of Mars introduced the star of the series, John Carter, a former Confederate soldier who literally wills himself to Mars when he hides in a magic cave while on the run from Apache Indians. Once there he discovers that the Martian gravity has turned him into that planet's version of Superman, allowing him to make extraordinary leaps with extraordinary agility. He falls in with a tribe of six-armed Green Martians and swiftly rises up the ranks, impressing them with his abilities. Then he becomes enmeshed in Martian politics between the Green and Red Martians. Oh, and there's a princess to rescue. And fall in love with.

ABOVE AND INSET RIGHT: Lynn Collins and Taylor Kitsch as Dejah Thoris and John Carter in *John Carter* (2012), directed by Andrew Stanton

ABOVE: Edgar Rice Burroughs' popular Barsoom series provided a romantic vision of Mars

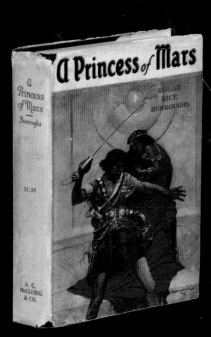

The parallels between the Martians and native American tribes are obvious, if unenlightened; the idea of the White Man arriving and immediately becoming the hero who sorts everything out is just a little condescending for modern sensibilities. However, as pulp adventure, the Mars series, which becomes more colourful, complicated and alien-packed as it goes on, was cracking stuff and clearly an inspiration for the escapades of Buck Rogers and Flash Gordon and so, in turn, **Star Wars**.

In fact, when the film **John Carter** was released in 2012, the publicity team was so worried that the movie looked like a rip-off of **Star Wars**, they made a big deal of promoting it as 'based on the stories that inspired **Star Wars**'. It didn't work.

Other Burroughs Series

Burroughs would go on to create a number of other sci-fi series. The Pellucidar series was a Hollow Earth affair, though this one saw the surface dwellers reaching the core not by means of a handy hole in the Earth's crust, but by burrowing there in the best piece of Verne tech that Verne never invented – the Iron Mole. Pellucidar itself was pretty much a prehistoric world with fur-wearing tribes and made-up dinosaurs.

Burroughs' serialized novel **The Land that Time Forgot** (1918), the two later instalments titled **The People that Time Forgot** (1918) and **Out of Time's Abyss** (1918), boasted proper dinosaurs, though.

The Amtor or Venus series – kicking off with **Pirates of Venus** (1934) – is pretty much a cover version of the Mars series but set on Earth's neighbouring planet in the opposite direction, with a hero whose first name is practically 'John Carter' distilled – Carson Napier.

Jungle Japes

While we said Burroughs was most famous for his non-SF creation, it's not entirely true to call the entire Tarzan series non-SF. The first Tarzan tale – **Tarzan of the Apes** (1912) was Burroughs' immediate follow-up to 'Under the Moons of Mars', once again for **All-Story**, and it was immediately an even bigger hit. The story has everything (well, everything except sci-fi): exotic locations, savage beasts, action, rescues, a love story and a big, tear-jerking twist at the end about Tarzan's origins.

But as Burroughs' 22 sequels rolled on, Tarzan's world became more and more sci-fi, with various lost worlds and lost races, dinosaurs (in **Tarzan the Terrible**, 1921), a miniaturized Tarzan (in **Tarzan and the Ant Men**, 1924), a crossover with Pellucidar (in **Tarzan at the Earth's Core**, 1929) and giant seahorses with unicorn horns (in **Tarzan and the Forbidden City**, 1938).

Edgar Rice Burroughs never did make it big in business, but he didn't use a pseudonym for his writing for long.

57

OPPOSITE: *A Princess of Mars* (1917), cover art by Frank E. Schoonover. TOP LEFT: *John Carter and the Giant of Mars* in *Amazing Stories* (January 1941), cover art by J. Allen St John

THE LOST WORLDS OF SIR ARTHUR CONAN DOYLE

We all know Sir Arthur Conan Doyle for creating Sherlock Holmes; that's elementary. But his other recurring creation was the hot-tempered, no-nonsense explorer Professor Challenger, the star of three very, very different novels and two short stories.

The most famous and enduring is the first, **The Lost World** (1912), in which the Professor and his team find a lost plateau in South America where dinosaurs still roam. The expedition returns to civilization with a pterodactyl with which to impress the scientific community, but it escapes. The story was the inspiration for a whole load of similar lost-world stories in the following years (including Burroughs' **The Land That Time Forgot**) and its structure is practically the blueprint for the film **King Kong** (1933).

Claustrophobic Sequel

A year later Challenger returned in **The Poison Belt** (1913), a sequel that was daringly unlike its predecessor. As opposed to the globetrotting adventure of **The Lost World**, much of this story is set in a drawing room. It's about Challenger and three colleagues from the Lost World expedition in a sealed room, sitting out the effects of the Earth entering a belt of poisonous ether. When the danger passes they venture out into the world to discover a big twist: the ether didn't kill anyone, only sent them to sleep, though that did cause a large number of deaths through accidents.

The third Challenger tale came many years later, by which time Doyle was well into his spiritualist stage. **The Land of Mist** (1926) was more concerned with life after death than real science; but then this was the author who fell hook, line and sinker for the infamously fake Cottingley Fairies photos. (These were five photos taken in 1920 by Elsie Wright and Frances Griffiths and cleverly doctored to show two young girls frolicking with little people at the bottom of the garden.)

That said, Challenger holds an important place in SF history as an example of the 'hero scientist' – as opposed to the mad scientist – who inspired grumpy, mature, eccentric boffins such as Bernard Quatermass and the original Doctor in **Doctor Who** (1963).

ABOVE: Arthur Conan Doyle's *The Lost World* (1912) was the blueprint for *King Kong* (1933)

58

LONDON CALLING

American Jack London was a prolific writer and wildly successful early twentieth-century author, who wrote across a multitude of genres, but who will always be known for two novels. Both were set during the Klondike Gold Rush and written from the point of view of animals: a dog called Buck in *The Call of the Wild* (1903) and the eponymous wolf in *White Fang* (1906).

But London wasn't shy of turning his attention to science fiction. Prehistory clearly had a fascination for him. 'A Relic of the Pliocene' (1901) is a fanciful tale about a modern-day man who meets a mammoth, while somewhat weightier was the novel **Before Adam** (1907) about a man who dreams about living life in prehistoric times.

'The Shadow and the Flash' (1903) is a tale about two brothers trying to achieve invisibility in different ways, while 'Goliath' (1910) concerns a deadly energy weapon. 'The Unparalleled Invasion' (1910) describes germ warfare against China and 'The Red One' is set on an island where a tribe worships an extra-terrestrial object.

Getting Political

Like Wells, London had socialist leanings, and his most interesting SF tale reflects that. *The Iron Heel* (1908) is a dystopian novel that describes the rise of an oligarchic tyranny in the United States with more emphasis on social than technological change. This oligarchy maintains power through a labour caste and a military caste, and by manipulating unions to shaft the workers.

Some have cited *The Iron Heel* as an influence on George Orwell's **Nineteen Eighty-Four** (1949). It's certainly a forerunner, but Orwell himself was less than complimentary in a 1940 review of a reissue: 'It is clumsily written, it shows no grasp of scientific possibilities, and the hero is the kind of human gramophone who is now disappearing even from Socialist tracts. But because of his own streak of savagery, London could grasp something that Wells apparently could not, and that is that hedonistic societies do not endure.' So, not all bad, then.

ABOVE: Jack London bookplate (1900–16), and front cover of *The Iron Heel* (1910 edition)

ABOVE: A selection of stories by Jack London, Fenton Ash, H.G. Wells and Rudyard Kipling

EARLY SCIENCE FICTION CINEMA

Meanwhile, at the cinema, science fiction was already proving a crowd pleaser. Cinema always wants to give audiences some new wonder to marvel at, and science fiction went hand in hand with one of cinema's greatest weapons of wonder: special effects. The early master of special effects was Georges Méliès.

The First Screen Wizard

Georges Méliès was born in Paris in 1861 and started making cardboard puppet theatres aged 10, and more sophisticated marionettes as a teenager. Continuing his passion for illusion, as a young man he fell in love with stage magic and began to learn about its secrets. When his father died, he sold his share of the family's shoe business to his brothers and bought a theatre, which he equipped specially for stage illusions.

On 27 December 1895, Méliès attended a private demonstration of the Lumière brothers' cinematograph and was dumbstruck by what he saw. He immediately offered to buy one of their cinematographs. Oddly, they turned him down. So he bought an animatograph from Robert W. Paul in London instead, and was soon showing daily films in his theatre.

The next logical step was making movies himself.

Making Effects Special

Méliès directed over 500 films between 1896 and 1913, ranging from one minute to 40 minutes. More importantly, he experimented. He created effects such as substitution splices, multiple exposures, time-lapse photography, dissolves and hand-painted colour – anything to create on-screen magic. It may look crude to us, but it was astonishing at the time to see a lady vanish or an object move of its own accord.

A number of Méliès' films were science fiction in nature, including **Under the Seas** (1907), a whimsical skit of **20,000 Leagues Under the Sea**, and **The Eclipse, or the Courtship of the Sun and the Moon** (1907), in which the two celestial bodies have a snog as they pass.

Méliès' Masterpiece

But Méliès' masterpiece was **A Trip to the Moon** (1902), an 18-minute showcase for special effects and dancing girls, boasting one of cinema's earliest iconic images: the (literal) face of the Moon with a space rocket crashed in its eye. It was a box-office blockbuster, with a reliance on spectacle and some very dodgy science (even for the time). So, mainstream

ABOVE: Ben Kingsley as Georges Méliès in the movie *Hugo* (2011), directed by Martin Scorsese

science fiction movies haven't changed much, have they? The film maintains its charm even today and is an undoubted landmark in cinema as a whole as well as in science fiction cinema.

Other Early Landmarks

Even back in the early days of science fiction cinema, adapting literary classics was the major trend: **20,000 Leagues Under the Sea** was filmed yet again in 1916, the first film to use underwater footage. The American Edison Studios made a 16-minute version of **Frankenstein** (1910), while another Mary Shelley book, **The Last Man**, was made into **The Last Man on Earth** (1924). Germany produced **Tales of Hoffman** in 1916, and a little later Britain filmed H.G. Wells's **The First Men in the Moon** (1919).

In 1920 not one but two American adaptations of the novella **Strange Case of Dr Jekyll and Mr Hyde**, the one starring John Barrymore (in a quite stunning performance) being far more renowned now than the one starring Sheldon Lewis. There was also a German version of the same story in 1920, **Der Januskopf** ('The Janus Face'), directed by F.W. Murnau of **Nosferatu** (1922) fame.

Russia got in on the act with a version of **Aelita** (1924), featuring some remarkable Martian sets by Isaac Rabinovich and Victor Simov, and outlandish costumes by Aleksandra Ekster.

65 Million Years in the Making

The Lost World (1925), an adaption of the Sir Arthur Conan Doyle Professor Challenger tale, is notable for the special effects work of stop-motion animator Willis O'Brien, who brought the film's dinosaurs to life one painstaking frame at a time. O'Brien went on to produce the special effects for **King Kong** (1933) and stop motion would remain the deluxe method for creating movie monsters (as opposed to puppets, costumes or optically enlarged lizards) until the dawn of CGI (computer-generated imagery).

For the most part, though, the development of science fiction movies up until this point had been a fairly **ad hoc**, random, disjointed affair – a period of experimentation and 'let's see what works'. That was about to change as some true cinematic visionaries began to assert their influence on the genre.

63

LEFT AND ABOVE: Litereary classics were often adapted for early cinema, such as with *Dr Jekyll and Mr Hyde* (1920)

3: THE RISE OF THE PULPS

1926

1926 • The first television demonstration • John Logie Baird
Science & Technology

1926 • The first issue of *Amazing Stories*, the first pulp magazine devoted entirely to science fiction • Hugo Gernsback
Pulp Magazine

1927 • *Metropolis* • Fritz Lang
Movie

1928 • *Armageddon 2419 A.D.*, first appearance of Buck Rogers in Amazing Stories • Philip Francis Nowlan
Pulp Magazine

1928 • *The Skylark of Space* • E.E. Smith
Novel

1928 • 'The Call of Cthulhu' • H.P. Lovecraft
Short Story

1929 • *Woman in the Moon* • Fritz Lang
Movie

1929 • First issue of *Air Wonder Stories* • Hugo Gernsback
Pulp Magazine

1929 • First issue of Science Wonder Stories • Hugo Gernsback
Pulp Magazine

1929 • *Mysterious Island* • Lucien Hubbard
Movie

1929 • *Buck Rogers* • John F. Dille
Comic

1929 • Wall Street Crash • USA
World Event

1930

1930 • First issue of *Astounding Stories of Super-Science* • William Clayton, Harry Bates
Pulp Magazine

1930 • First issue of *Wonder Stories* (merging of *Air Wonder Stories* and *Science Wonder Stories*) • Hugo Gernsback
Pulp Magazine

1930 • *Just Imagine* • David Butler
Movie

1930 • *Last and First Men* • Olaf Stapledon
Novel

1931 • *Frankenstein* • James Whale
Movie

1931 • *Jekyll & Hyde* • Rouben Mamoulian
Movie

1931 • 'Worlds to Barter' • John Wyndham (under 'John Beynon Harris')
Short Story

1932

1932 • First broadcast of *Buck Rogers in the 25th Century* • MBS
Radio

1932 • *Brave New World* • Aldous Huxley
Novel

1932 • *Public Faces* • Harold Nicolson
Novel

1933 • Adolf Hitler becomes Chancellor • Germany
World Event

1933 • *The Shape of Things to Come* • H.G. Wells
Novel

1933 • *King Kong* • Merian C. Cooper, Ernest B. Schoedsack
Movie

1933 • *The Invisible Man* • James Whale
Movie

1934 • First appearance of Flash Gordon • Don Moore, Alex Raymond
Comic

1934 • 'A Martian Odyssey' • Stanley G. Weinbaum
Short Story

1935 • First broadcast of *Flash Gordon* • MBS
Radio

1935 • *Bride of Frankenstein* • James Whale
Movie

1935 • *Mad Love* • Karl Freund
Movie

Philosophy · Science & Technology · Novels · Short Story · World Events · Movies · Magazines · Comics · Play · Pulp Magazines · Radio · Small Publishers · TV · Video Games

1936

1938

1940

1936

1936 • *Flash Gordon* • Frederick Stephani,
Ray Taylor (uncredited)
Movie Serial

1936 • *The Shadow Over Innsmouth* • H.P. Lovecraft
Novella

1936 • *At the Mountains of Madness* • H.P. Lovecraft
Novella

1937 • *Star Maker* • Olaf Stapledon
Novel

1937 • First broadcast of *Speed Gibson of the International Secret Police* • Virginia Cooke
Radio

1937 • John W. Campbell Jr becomes editor of *Astounding Science Fiction* • John W. Campbell Jr
Pulp Magazine

1938

1938 • First appearance of Superman in *Action Comics No. 1*
• Jerry Siegel, Joe Shuster
Comic

1938 • *The War of the Worlds* • Orson Welles
Radio

1939 • Start of the Second World War • Worldwide
World Event

1939 • *Lest Darkness Fall* • L. Sprague de Camp
Novel

1939 • Batman's first appearance in *Detective Comics No. 27*
• Bob Kane, Bill Finger
Comic

1939 • *Buck Rogers in the 25th Century* • Ford Beebe,
Saul A. Goodkind
Movie Serial

1939 • Arkham House founded • August Derleth and
Donald Wandrei
Small Publisher

1940

1940 • 'The Wheels of If' • L. Sprague de Camp
Short Story

1940 • First broadcast of *The Adventures of Superman* • WOR
Radio

1940 • *Fine Comics in Planet Comics*, the first exclusively science fiction comic book • Fiction House
Comic

1940 • *Dr Cyclops* • Ernest B. Schoedsack
Movie

1940 • *Slan* • A.E. van Vogt
Novel

1941 • Attack on Pearl Harbor • USA
World Event

1941 • *Latitude Zero* • Ishirō Honda
Radio

1941 • *Nightfall* • Isaac Asimov
Novella

1941 • *Dr Jekyll and Mr Hyde* • Victor Fleming
Movie

1941 • *Adventures of Captain Marvel* • William Witney,
John English
Movie Serial

1942 • 'Runaround', introducing the Three Laws of Robotics
• Isaac Asimov
Short Story

THE BEGINNING OF MODERN SF

Modern science fiction began in 1926 with the introduction of the *Amazing Stories* magazine, and by the end of 1941 it had become a thriving, vibrant popular culture genre in literature, movies, radio and comics. That 15-year period, in fact, can be divided into two discrete sets of years: 1926–30, when *Amazing Stories* and other science fiction pulps grew without serious hindrance, and 1931–41, when science fiction writers, publishers and readers faced the effects of the Great Depression.

Amazing Stories

The 1920s were generally boomtime in the United States, a decade of consumption, confidence and growth, when the economic status of ordinary Americans seemed to be permanently increasing. It was into this atmosphere, in 1926, that Hugo Gernsback introduced *Amazing Stories*, the first pulp magazine devoted solely to science fiction. There had been precursors, including two dime novels devoted to science fiction stories in the 1890s and 1900s, and *The Thrill*

Book (1919) and *Weird Tales* (from 1923), but *Amazing Stories* was the first pulp whose focus was purely science fiction. *Amazing Stories*' long-term effect was to establish science fiction as a separate, viable genre of modern publishing.

Amazing's presence on the stands, rather than what was inside its pages, inspired writers and publishers to contribute exclusively SF stories. Credit must be given to Gernsback for helming the creation and early years of *Amazing Stories*; without it, there would have been nothing for rivals and successors to imitate and better. But while much of what *Amazing* published might be generously described as mediocre, some stories of the 1926–30 period were not wholly without merit. Gernsback published stories by Ray Cummings and early works by Edmond Hamilton, among others. At any rate, *Amazing* remained the focus of attention of science fiction fans during that period.

Away from Amazing

Amazing was at the forefront of science fiction during that five-year period, but there were a great many other magazines publishing SF at that time. Science fiction at this time was a product of magazines rather than novels, while magazine SF appeared in two different types of magazines: the 'pulps', so-called because of the cheap wood-pulp paper they were printed on, and the 'slicks', printed on higher-quality paper. Science fiction appeared in pulps where the focus was science fiction, like *Amazing Stories*, but also in pulps of other genres (*Adventure*) or no genre (*Blue Book* magazine). In fact, during the 1926–30 period, more SF appeared in the slicks and other genres than in the SF pulps – a state of affairs that held true through to the end of 1941.

ABOVE: The first issue of *Amazing Stories* (April 1926), the first science fiction pulp magazine; cover art by Frank R. Paul

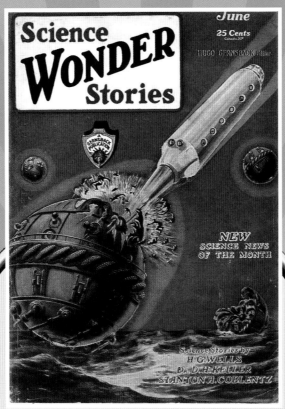

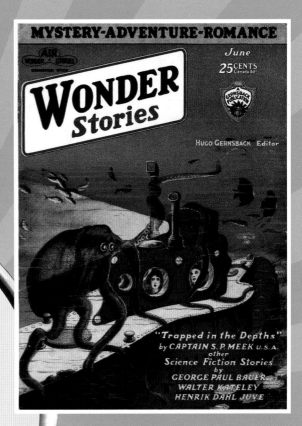

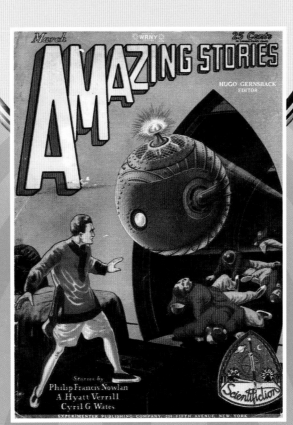

ABOVE: A variety of pulp magazines from 1928 to 1930

The stories themselves began to develop into two different directions. What appeared in the SF pulps during this time period can be thought of as 'genre SF', the kind of stories one thinks of when considering the classics: colourful, full of action and adventure, with an emphasis on technology, science and plot rather than style and characterization. The science fiction appearing in the slicks and the other pulps can be thought of as 'mainstream SF', the kind of science fiction that had been published in novels and magazines before the appearance of **Amazing Stories**. Mainstream SF was generally of better quality and was written by professionals rather than amateurs, but it was genre SF, written and read with the consciousness of science fiction as a separate genre, that consumers and producers of science fiction embraced and took their cues from.

Dozens of pulps were published during the 1926–30 period, but only a handful of those were SF pulps: **Air Wonder Stories** (1929–30), **Amazing Stories** (from 1926), **Amazing Stories Annual** (1927), **Amazing Stories Quarterly** (from 1928), **Astounding** (from 1930), **Science Wonder Quarterly** (1929–30), **Science Wonder Stories** (1929–30), **Wonder Stories** (from 1930) and **Wonder Stories Quarterly** (from 1930).

Genre Versus Mainstream SF

Genre SF was more identified with these magazines than with major writers during the period. The writers who would become prominent in the 1931–41 period, and would become identified with the genre SF movement, were only beginning to make their names known. Edmond Hamilton published throughout the period, but from 1926–28 his work was science fantasy rather than science fiction. It was only in 1928, with his 'Crashing Suns' serial, that he began writing the space operas for which he became famous. E.E. 'Doc' Smith didn't publish his own first space opera, *The Skylark of Space*, until 1928. H.P. Lovecraft published little throughout the period – one major story a year. *Armageddon – 2419 A.D.* by Philip Francis Nowlan (the first appearance of Buck Rogers) appeared only in 1928, with the sequel following the next year. John W. Campbell Jr. didn't make his debut as a fiction writer until 1930. These writers attracted attention, and in some cases fame – by the end of 1930 Hamilton and Smith were well known to fans of genre SF – but not to the point of overshadowing the magazines in which their stories appeared.

By comparison, mainstream SF was identified with a handful of writers. During the 1926–30 period mainstream SF was appearing in magazines as varied as *Adventure*, *Air Trails*, *All Story Weekly*, *Blue Book*, *Detective Story Magazine* and *Railroad Man's Magazine*. The science fiction of these pulps stands in stark contrast to the genre SF of the science fiction pulps. Mainstream SF was largely written by professional writers such as George Allan England, Robert M. Wilson, Johnston McCulley and J.U. Giesy, authors who wrote in numerous different genres and for numerous different magazines. The only writer of mainstream SF to specialize in science fiction was Ray Cummings, who had made a career of publishing science fiction in the mainstream pulps before Hugo Gernsback had conceived of *Amazing Stories*. Cummings was comparable in renown among science fiction fans to Edmond Hamilton during the 1926–30

period, but only ventured into genre SF with the appearance of *Astounding* in 1930. (His appearance in *Amazing Stories* in 1927 was a reprint.) Edgar Rice Burroughs, the most science fiction writer of this period, was likewise publishing in the mainstream pulps before turning his serials into novels.

Novels, Films and Comic Strips

Science fiction novels, hundreds of them, in fact, were published during the 1926–30 period. Some were by writers who were well known in other fields, like Fred MacIsaac and Arthur J. Burks. Novels were considered a more respectable medium than the pulps or the slicks, and fortunate was the magazine author who could turn his or her serial into a novel. But in the eyes of the fan, the genre's energy and momentum, its *élan vital*, was found in magazine science fiction, with the SF in novels distinctly less interesting.

The consumers and producers of pulp and slick science fiction were aware of the SF in the two other formats, movies and comic strips, but viewed them as less important and less relevant. Of the few science fiction movies appearing during the 1926–30 period, only three – *Metropolis* (1926; 1927 American release), *Mysterious Island* (1929) and *Just Imagine* (1930) – were notable to science fiction fans, and of the three only *Metropolis* was an original work, the other two being dramatizations of novels. The American reaction to *Metropolis* was lacklustre, as had been audiences' reactions in Germany, and while later critics and audiences have seen the film as a major work of science fiction of this period, that was certainly not the contemporary view.

69

ABOVE: Larry Crabbe as the eponymous hero in *Buck Rogers* (1939), directed by Ford Beebe

There was even less science fiction to be found in comic strips. The wave of science fiction comic strips in the first decade of the twentieth century – **Airship Man** (1902–03) by C.W. Kahles, **Hugo Hercules** by William H.D. Koerner and **The Explorigator** (1908) by Harry Dart – had stopped by 1910, and during the 1926–30 period the most popular and artistically successful comic strips – C. W. Kahles' **Hairbreadth Harry** (from 1906), **Wash Tubbs** (from 1924) by Roy Crane, **Connie** (from 1926) by Frank Godwin – were imitative and lacked fantastic elements. The exception was **Buck Rogers** by Philip Francis Nowlan, John F. Dille and Dick Calkins, starting in 1929 and based on Nowlan's **Armageddon – 2419 A.D.** and **The Airlords of Han** (1929). Buck Rogers, though crude as art, was an archetypal space opera and extremely influential on later science fiction strips, particularly **Flash Gordon**.

Outside Influences

Science fiction of the 1926–30 period was largely the product of what had preceded it. Both genre SF and mainstream SF took their cues from earlier SF and from the types of stories that were appearing in the other pulps and slicks. But science fiction was not a hermetically sealed world. The stories and the authors who wrote them were influenced, however subtly, by events in the outside world.

The single largest influence was the rate of technology's change and invention. Technology that had for previous generations been science fiction, like washing machines or x-ray generators, was suddenly a part of real life. Technology that had previously been available only to the wealthy, such as automobiles, was suddenly mass-produced. The effect of this new technology on science fiction

LEFT: Gil Gerard in the TV series *Buck Rogers in the 25th Century* (1979–81), inspired by the stories of Philip Francis Nowlan. ABOVE: *The Mysterious Island* (1929), directed by Lucien Hubbard

was in some cases only moderate; x-rays, newly available thanks to the Coolidge x-ray tube, became a common trope in science fiction stories of the time period, but colour movies and publicly broadcast radio stations remained rarities in science fiction. In other cases the effect of changing technology was more strongly felt. The trans-Atlantic flight in 1927 by Charles Lindbergh sparked a burst of interest in air travel. As ordinary Americans became aware that long-distance air travel was an imminent reality, the pulps responded with a wave of air adventure pulps, beginning in 1927. Science fiction pulps followed with a number of stories about air travel, such as 'Four Dimensional Transit' (1928) by Bob Olsen, and a pulp dedicated to science fiction air adventure, **Air Wonder Stories**, appeared in 1929.

Sometimes the technology doing the influencing was itself science fiction. Humanoid robots were exhibited in museums in the United States and Japan, and at the same time men and women dressed in robot suits toured these countries, promoting themselves as actual robots. These robots, both mechanical and fancy-dress, were presented as objects to be gawked at, spectacles to be enjoyed no different than a two-headed calf, but in the newspaper coverage of the 'robots', there was a considerable uncertainty about whether they should be viewed as pure entertainment or whether they were something the average citizen needed to be warned about. A typical headline was 'The Mechanical Man Has Come to Laredo!' This wariness about robots was replicated in the pulps of the period; for every story like 'The Psychophonic Nurse' (1928), by David H. Keller, in which the robot is a dutiful servant, there is one like 'The Robot Master' (1929), by O.L. Beckwith, in which only the negative potential of robots is to be seen.

ABOVE: The imagined New York of 1980 in *Just Imagine* (1930), directed by David Butler. RIGHT: Movie poster for *Metropolis* (1927), directed by Fritz Lang

THE LONG 1930S

I f 1926–30 were the years in which science fiction, genre and mainstream, was laying the groundwork for what was to follow, 1931–41 were the years in which science fiction took advantage of what had preceded it and established itself as a genre capable of anything, producing works of prodigious imagination and great artistic quality. This decade was known as the 'long 1930s', after the 'long nineteenth century', so complex and world-altering that it spanned the period from the French Revolution to the First World War and formed the foundation of the modern world. Big changes in science fiction were certainly afoot.

The world of science fiction, in the 1926–30 period, was one in which the genre was delineated; it was one in which science fiction was gathering its legs beneath it. The 1931–41 period was when SF made its great leap forward, displaying an imagination and thematic range that had not previously been seen. In the 1926–30 period the genre was wrestling with how to identify itself, and whether or not to use Gernsback's neologism 'scientifiction' as its self-descriptor. During the 1931–41 period the phrase 'science fiction' became generally accepted and fans and writers began to brandish it unabashed, as they knew they were a part of an established genre of literature.

The Dawn of a New Age

The question can be asked, of course, what set this span of years apart from what came before and after? The year 1931 stands out as the starting point for several reasons. It was when **Last and First Men**, Olaf Stapledon's landmark novel, was published in America, creating a sensation among writers and readers, and providing possible paths for science fiction to take; 1931 was the first year in which the Wall Street Crash of 1929 deeply affected publishing, both of magazines and books; 1931 was the year in which **The Shadow** debuted, creating the hero-oriented science fiction pulp form and providing a model for comic books to follow; 1931 was the year in which **Relativisme** by Andre Maurois was translated into English as **A Private Universe**, providing a model for other mainstream writers to use when writing science fiction; 1931 was the year in which the films **Frankenstein** and **Jekyll and Hyde** debuted, setting examples of successful science fiction for other films to emulate; and 1931 was the year in which a number of genre SF authors, who would later become famous, began publishing regularly and in earnest.

The Genre of SF

During the 1931–41 period magazine science fiction continued to be the genre driver. Science fiction in novels, films, comic strips and comic books was more influenced by what appeared in the pages of SF magazines rather than the other way round. But the genre of science fiction was not a unitary whole during these years. There were significant divisions within

ABOVE: Fredric March in *Dr Jekyll and Mr Hyde* (1931), directed by Rouben Mamoulian

ABOVE: Fredric March, Rouben Mamoulian and Miriam Hopkins on the set of *Dr Jekyll and Mr Hyde* (1931)

A NOVEL OF THE FUTURE COMPLETE IN THIS ISSUE!

STARTLING STORIES

NOV.

ARK OF SPACE

15¢

A THRILLING PUBLICATION

THE FORTRESS OF UTOPIA
By JACK WILLIAMSON

A MARTIAN ODYSSEY By STANLEY G. WEINBAUM

Apr. 16 Nine Varied Action Stories

ARGOSY

10¢

ISSUED WEEKLY

Ray Cummings'
The Insect Invasion

Western and Pirate Novelettes by
Robert Ormond Case and T.G. Roberts

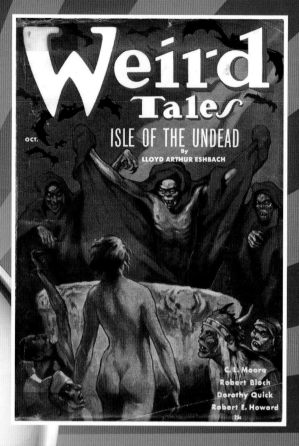

Weird Tales

OCT.

ISLE OF THE UNDEAD
By LLOYD ARTHUR ESHBACH

C. L. Moore
Robert Bloch
Dorothy Quick
Robert E. Howard

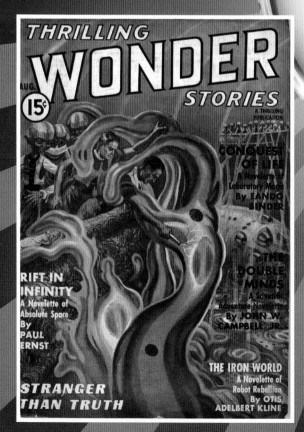

THRILLING

WONDER STORIES

AUG.

15¢

A THRILLING PUBLICATION

CONQUEST OF LIFE
A Novelette of Laboratory Magic
By EANDO BINDER

RIFT IN INFINITY
A Novelette of Absolute Space
By PAUL ERNST

THE DOUBLE MINDS
A Scientific Adventure Novelette
By JOHN W. CAMPBELL, JR.

THE IRON WORLD
A Novelette of Robot Rebellion
By OTIS ADELBERT KLINE

STRANGER THAN TRUTH

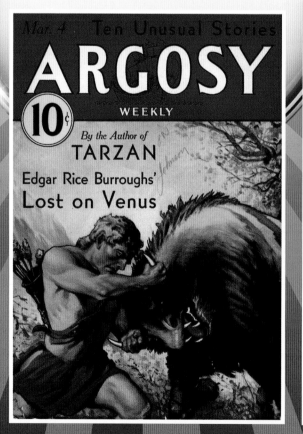

Mar. 4 Ten Unusual Stories

ARGOSY

10¢

WEEKLY

By the Author of
TARZAN

Edgar Rice Burroughs'
Lost on Venus

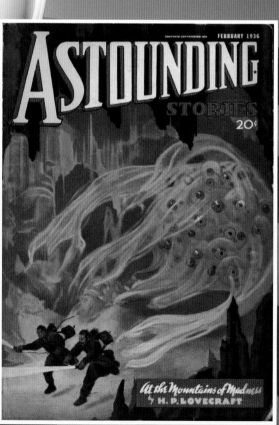

FEBRUARY 1936

ASTOUNDING STORIES

20¢

At the Mountains of Madness
By H. P. LOVECRAFT

all of these media and formats, so that any discussion of magazine science fiction – or science fiction in novels, film or comics – must begin with an examination of these divides.

The genre SF pulps versus mainstream SF pulps divide became, if anything, more pronounced during the long 1930s than it had been in the years before. Continuing the trend of the previous period, there was more science fiction published in the mainstream pulps and the slicks than in the SF pulps, despite the growing number of science fiction pulps to appear during the 1930s. There were eight science fiction pulps published in 1931, 12 in 1935, 19 in 1939 and 27 in 1941. By comparison, there were 192 total pulps published in 1931, 210 in 1935, 258 in 1939 and 264 in 1941, in addition to the dozens of slicks appearing at this time. Science fiction stories appeared in a large number of these, more than in the SF pulps.

But, as in the previous period, most of the science fiction community's attention during this time was on the Gernsback-Campbell continuum of pulps: *Amazing Stories*, *Amazing Stories Annual*, *Amazing Stories Quarterly*, *Air Wonder Stories*, *Science Wonder Stories*, *Wonder Stories*, *Science Wonder Quarterly*, *Wonder Stories Quarterly*, *Scientific Detective Monthly*, *Amazing Detective Tales* for Gernsback, through 1936; *Astounding* for John W. Campbell Jr. from 1937. But roughly 60 per cent of all science fiction published during the 1930s appeared outside the Gernsback-Campbell continuum, in the other science fiction pulps, in the mainstream pulps and in the slicks.

This may come as a surprise to aficionados of Golden Age science fiction: the names of the authors of science fiction outside the Gernsback-Campbell continuum are significantly less known in the SF community than the authors of science fiction inside the continuum. Nonetheless, the science fiction fans of the 1930s, when looking for SF stories, could look to *Adventure*, *Argosy*, *Blue Book* as well as *Dusty Ayres*, *Secret 6*, *Spider*, *Astonishing Stories*, *Planet Stories* and *Weird Tales*. Authors like Frank Triem, Robert J. Hogan and Donald Keyhoe, who were well known and respected as professional authors in other genres, also produced substantial quantities of science fiction during these years.

The Gernsback-Campbell Continuum

That being said, it was the science fiction within the SF pulps, and specifically within the Gernsback-Campbell continuum, that was the most popular with readers and which was most influential on the science fiction to follow.

The first half of the long 1930s belonged to Gernsback and his family of pulps, of which *Wonder Stories* is (deservedly) the best known. *Wonder Stories*, like Gernsback himself, has come to have a bad reputation for publishing clunky stories, whose emphasis on science and technology left behind traditional literary virtues like characterization and narrative style. However, during the 1931–36 period, under Gernsback (editor-in-chief), and David Lasser and Charles Hornig (managing editors), *Wonder Stories* was publishing the best genre SF. Notable writers to debut or appear in *Wonder Stories* during the 1931–36 period include: Laurence Manning, one of the best-known of the SF pulp authors, most of whose work appeared in the magazine during this period; Clifford Simak, Hugo and SFWA Grand Master award winner, whose genre SF debut was 'The World of the Red Sun' (December 1931); Clark Ashton Smith, enormously influential on later planetary romances and 'dying Earth' stories, whose best SF work appeared in **Wonder Stories** during this time; John Taine, better known as a novelist but whose 'The Time Stream' (December 1931–March 1932), a time travel epic of uncommon imagination and scope, was among the best SF stories of the time; Stanley Weinbaum, whose 'A Martian Odyssey' (July 1934), the first intelligent attempt to envision alien lifeforms as genuinely alien, was perhaps the most popular tale to appear in **Wonder Stories** during this period; and John Wyndham, later author of **The Day of the Triffids** and **The Midwich Cuckoos**, who debuted in genre SF with 'Worlds to Barter' (May 1931) and published numerous stories in **Wonder Stories** during this period. Unfortunately, declining sales forced Gernsback to sell **Wonder Stories** in 1936, and while the magazine survived cancellation to re-emerge as **Thrilling Wonder Stories**, it no longer had the cachet it once did, and became eclipsed by **Astounding**.

The second half of the long 1930s were largely the province of John W. Campbell Jr., and **Astounding**. **Astounding** had been around since 1930, but from 1931 to 1933 under editor Harry Bates the magazine had published second- and third-rate material. Under editor F. Orlin Tremaine, from 1933 to 1937, **Astounding** had recovered and become a successful rival to **Wonder Stories**, but nothing more, and for the first 18 months of John W. Campbell Jr.'s reign as editor of

Astounding, starting with its December 1937 issue, the magazine continued to publish quality but not revolutionary work, including stories by Lester Del Rey, L. Ron Hubbard and Clifford D. Simak.

In the summer of 1939, however, Campbell took the next step, giving his editorial philosophy, which emphasized technological and scientific SF, full sway and at the same time bringing in a remarkable group of writers. Isaac Asimov, Robert A. Heinlein, Murray Leinster, Theodore Sturgeon, A.E. Van Vogt and Jack Williamson are among the major names who either debuted in **Astounding** or made it their primary home during the 1939–1941 period. Campbell ushered in what's commonly described as the 'Golden Age of science fiction' with the summer 1939 issue of **Astounding**. The Golden Age lasted through to the end of the 1940s, as long as Campbell's reign as the thought- and taste-leader in the field.

Outside the Continuum

Though **Wonder Stories** and **Astounding** were the dominant SF pulps of this period, they were not the only ones. Outside the Gernsback-Campbell continuum, **Amazing Stories** continued to appear, publishing authors like Nelson S. Bond, David H. Keller, Otis Adelbert Kline, Frederic Arnold Kummer Jr. and Neil R. Jones – none of them major authors of the period, but all prolific in the SF pulps. **Astonishing Stories**, which first appeared in 1940, had a shoestring budget but published such authors as Isaac Asimov, James Blish, Ray Cummings, Damon Knight, Cyril M. Kornbluth and Clifford Simak. **Weird Tales**, though focused primarily on stories of horror and dark fantasy, also published science fiction, including stories by Henry Kuttner, H.P. Lovecraft and Clark Ashton Smith.

Outside of the SF pulps, science fiction thrived in the mainstream pulps during the 1930s. But just as there was a divide between the Gernsback-Campbell continuum of pulps and everything else, so too was there a divide, in the mainstream fiction pulps, between the non-science pulps and the rest of the pulps.

The 'mainstream pulps', used here to represent those pulps that published a variety of genres rather than focusing on one particular genre, had never been hostile toward science fiction. These pulps, which included such long-running magazines as **Argosy** and **Blue Book**, were publishing science fiction long before the pulps displaced the dime novels as the primary purveyor of cheap serialized magazine fiction. So the appearance of science fiction in the mainstream pulps during the second half of the 1930s was not unprecedented. Arthur Leo Zagat, William Gray Beyer and Frederick C. Painton – none of them major science fiction writers, but all capable and competent professionals – were among the writers to publish science fiction in the mainstream pulps during the 1937–41 period.

Outside the science fiction pulps, the more vigorous science fiction appeared among the pulps which specialized in publishing one genre or type of story. Whether a pulp was focused on general thrills, like **Adventure**, or on a particular genre, like **Railroad Man's Magazine** or the hero pulps, that pulp was likely to publish science fiction of the sort that incorporated the particular type or genre of story into it. **Railroad Man's Magazine** published the stories of Charles W. Tyler, about unlucky inventor Hiram Pertwee, whose railroad-oriented

inventions never quite work out the way they are supposed to. **Battle Birds**, an air adventure pulp, became **Dusty Ayres and His Battle Birds** and told Robert Sidney Bowen's near-future story of the invasion of the United States by high-tech-wielding Central Asian invaders. Harold Ward, in **All-Detective Magazine**, published stories about a mad scientist/occultist plotting world domination. All the genre magazines, with the exception of those publishing romance and true-crime, published science fiction.

LEFT AND OPPOSITE: This period saw many science fiction pulps and even some mainstream ones publishing exciting stories about far off worlds and wondrous adventures

OTHER MEDIA

Although magazine science fiction remained the primary driver of the genre, science fiction became commonplace in other media, and in some cases important. SF novels were numerous during the long 1930s; SF movies, though not numerous, broke into the mainstream; SF became a dominant genre in comic strips and comic books; and SF art became an established genre of art.

Novels

Science fiction in novel form was in much the same position during the long 1930s as it had been during the 1926–30 period. There was a substantial amount of novels published, numbering in the hundreds, and some were significant. *Brave New World* (1932), by Aldous Huxley, was perhaps the seminal dystopia of the twentieth century. Olaf Stapledon followed *Last and First Men* with *Odd John* (1935), perhaps the best pre-Superman novel about the übermensch. Later he would publish *Star Maker* (1937), his masterpiece. *It Can't Happen Here* (1935), by Sinclair Lewis, is a prescient look at the threat that native-born fascism poses. *Swastika Night* (1937), by Katherine Burdekin, is a significant alternate history in which Nazi Germany conquers Europe and the Soviet Union, the first such to be published. *What Dreams May Come...* (1941), by J.D. Beresford,

is a contrasting examination of the war-torn present and a utopian future society. But despite these and other works of quality science fiction between hardcovers, science fiction in novel form was still lagging behind. This wasn't an issue of quality so much as an issue of what the majority of science fiction's audience was consuming. To put it another way, while the audience of SF fans and writers was concentrating on the science fiction appearing in the pulps, the general reading audience might read Huxley or Lewis or Burdekin or Beresford and enjoy what they were reading, but they would not consider it the same thing as 'that Flash Gordon stuff'.

Movies

In the movies, science fiction during the 1930s was a popular, if minor, genre; the 124 science fiction films released during the 1931–41 period are only 0.4 per cent of the total film output during that period. However, compared to the 1920s, there was now a surge in the number of science fiction films made, ranging from major productions to B movies. Mainstream movies like *Frankenstein* (1931), *King Kong* (1933), *The Invisible Man* (1933), *Bride of Frankenstein* (1935), *Lost Horizon* (1936) and *Things to Come* (1936) were for the most part successful and well regarded; there were SF serials like *Flash Gordon* (1936), *Buck Rogers in the 25th Century* (1939) and *Flash Gordon Conquers the Universe* (1940) to be seen; and there was a flourishing set of SF-based horror films like *Mad Love* (1935), *The Devil-Doll* (1936) and *Dr Cyclops* (1940).

As in magazine science fiction, however, there was a definite split between mainstream films and the serials, and between the SF-based horror movies and

ABOVE: Movie poster for *The Invisible Man* (1933), directed by James Whale

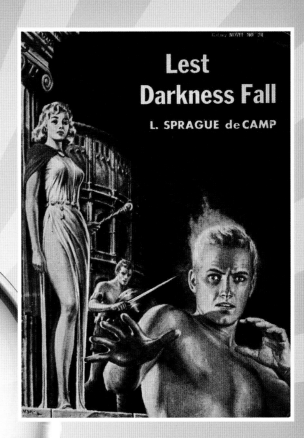

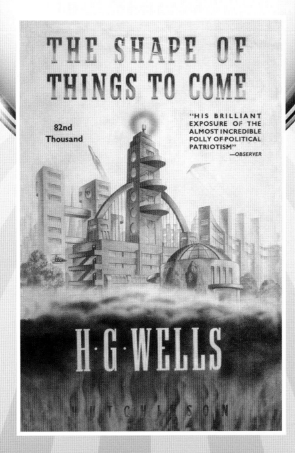

ABOVE: A selection of books from the period; movie poster for *Things to Come* (1936), inspired by H.G. Wells's *The Shape of Things to Come* (1933)

the serials. This divide was not in the quality of the films made but in the central theme of the stories: the potential of science. In mainstream films like **Frankenstein** and **The Invisible Man**, and in the horror movies like **Mad Love** and **Dr Cyclops**, science is a negative thing, something that torments innocents and drives ordinarily intelligent men insane. In these films the only scientists to appear are mad scientists, and the only technology to appear is used for foul purposes. It was only in the serials that science is shown to be man's servant rather than man's master; only in the serials do science and technology create a glorious, colourful and imaginative future.

Stage and Radio Plays

Science fiction was meanwhile appearing in other media, with some success. The SF plays of the 1900s, 1910s and 1920s – plays with titles like 'The Verge' (1921), 'The Unknown Purple' (1922) and 'The Monster' (1925) – gave way to science fiction radio programmes of the 1930s. There were still science fiction plays being written and produced; 'Rossum's Universal Robots' (1920), by Karel Čapek, was a perennial favourite in the 1920s and 1930s, and 'Whispering Walls' (1936), by Wall Spence, had a moment of fame. But generally speaking, during the 1930s, when playwrights wished to dabble in genre, they did so with mysteries rather than with science fiction. Science fiction shifted to the radio, which was in its heyday during this decade, broadcasting shows of every genre and type.

Science fiction on the radio began at least as early as 1929, with the serials **The Cobra King Strikes Back** and **Land of the Living Dead**, but beginning in 1932 science fiction became a regular part of the radio landscape. There were SF serials about individual characters: **The Shadow** (from 1930), **Buck Rogers in the 25th Century** (from 1932), **Flash Gordon** (1935–36) and **Superman** (from 1940). There were science fiction adventure serials, like **Speed Gibson of the International Secret Police** (1937–38) and **Latitude Zero** (1941), greatest of the science fiction programmes of radio's Golden Age. And there were anthology programmes that regularly included science fiction, like **The Witch's Tale** (1931–34), **Lights Out** (from 1934) and **Columbia Workshop** (from 1936). The science fiction on these programmes varied in quality and theme, but they were usually exuberantly science fictional, incorporating the SF tropes, motifs and themes, but telling stories of high adventure and gruesome horror rather than sober portrayals of mad scientists.

Comic Strips and Comic Books

The long 1930s were similarly packed with science fiction comic strips and, towards the end of the decade, comic books. John F. Dille, Philip Francis Nowlan and Dick Calkins' 'Buck Rogers' (from 1929) was the seminal science fiction comic strip, famous enough that within a few years other newspaper syndicates were launching their own SF comic strips. 'Jack Swift' (1930–37), by Hal Colson and Cliff Farrell, and 'Brick Bradford' (from 1933) by William Ritt and Clarence Gray, soon followed with the latter openly science fictional, but it wasn't until 'Flash Gordon' (from 1934) by Don Moore and Alex Raymond that the first exceptional science fiction comic strip appeared. What followed – 'Dash Dixon' (1935–39) by H.T. Elmo and Larry Antoinette, 'Don Dixon' (1935–41) by Carl Pfeufer and Bob Moore, 'Zarnak' (1936–37) by Jack Binder, 'Speed Spaulding' (1939–40) by Edwin Balmer, Marvin Bradley and Philip Wylie, 'Invisible Scarlet O'Neil' (from 1940) by Russell Stamm and 'Vera Ray' (1940–43) by Watt Dell – were all influenced, to a greater or lesser

ABOVE: Janice Logan in *Dr Cyclops* (1940), directed by Ernest B. Schoedsack

degree, by 'Flash Gordon', if only in their approach to science and technology as a source of imaginative wonder.

Although comic books began in 1929, it wasn't until **Action Comics** #1 (June 1938), which featured the debut adventure of Superman, created by Jerry Siegel and Joe Shuster, that the medium of comics began to become truly popular. But science fiction had been integral to comic books from 1935, when **New Fun** #1 – the first comic book from the company that would later become DC Comics – featured 'Don Drake,' a Flash Gordon lift by Ken Fitch and Clemens Gretter. Science fiction strips were a constant part of the pre-Superman comics, which had large assemblages of short comics rather than a single narrative focused on one character.

Action Comics #1 irrevocably changed that medium. So popular was Superman that the impetus in comics quickly swung away from other genres and towards superheroes. (There were four superhero strips published before Superman appeared; after Superman, 35 superhero strips or superhero comic books appeared in 1939 and 158 in 1940.) Science fiction continued to appear, but it lay in the shadow of much more popular genres like crime and adventure. The most successful of the science fiction comics was Fiction House's **Planet Comics** (from 1940), a companion to the Fiction House pulp **Planet Stories**.

Art

While there had often been interior art accompanying science fiction stories, and on occasion that art was memorable, usually it was mediocre at best.

Edgar Rice Burroughs' 'Under the Moons of Mars' (1912), the first major planetary romance, had poor art. 'Under the Moons of Mars' was published as a novel under the title **A Princess of Mars**, which was pleasingly illustrated by Frank E. Schoonover but fell down when it came to illustrating the Martians themselves. There was no tradition of science fictional art, although there had been occasional standouts, such as the illustrations by Warwick Goble for H.G. Wells's **The War of the Worlds** (1897).

Until **Amazing Stories** was launched, with Frank R. Paul as its cover artist, there was no tradition of SF art and no professional SF artists. Paul changed that, painting all of **Amazing**'s covers and much of its interior art while Gernsback was its editor. Paul then went on to paint covers and interior art for other Gernsback magazines (from 1929), other pulps (from 1936) and for comic books (from 1939). Paul, a professional architect by training, applied an architect's eye to his art, portraying detailed cities and technology, and imaginative yet plausible aliens and alien landscapes. Paul was the dominant SF artist of the 1926–41 period; Virgil Finlay (from 1935), Earle K. Bergey (from 1939) and Hannes Bok (from 1939) were more talented artists, especially in their portrayal of humans (one of Paul's weaknesses), but it was Paul who founded SF art as an artistic genre and established the genre's tropes and motifs, and who influenced dozens of lesser-known SF artists.

The End of the Era

The end of 1941, with the attack on Pearl Harbor and the entrance of America into the Second World War, was the end of an era in science fiction as well as in reality.

81

ABOVE: SF movie serials like *Flash Gordon* (1936) were popular in the 1930s

The War had numerous effects on science fiction. Writers of SF were drafted, robbing them of years in which they could have written. Science fiction artists, whether of book and magazine covers or of comic books and comic strips, faced the same problem. The wartime paper drives led to the cancellation of a number of pulps and comic books, and to a decrease in the number of novels published. Wartime restrictions also led to fewer science fictional films being made. What would follow the long 1930s, however, would be a time of transition for science fiction.

82

ABOVE: Charles Middleton as Ming the Merciless and movie serial poster for *Flash Gordon's Trip to Mars* (1938)

ABOVE: Flash Gordon, first appearing in a 1934 comic strip, has inspired various adaptations, such as *Flash Gordon* (1980)

4: A TIME OF TRANSITION

1943

1943 • *The Pocket Book of Science Fiction* •
Simon & Schuster
Critical Book

1943 • *Batman* • Lambert Hillyer
Movie Serial

1944 • *Captain America* • Elmer Clifton, John English
Movie Serial

1945 • Atomic bombs dropped on Hiroshima and Nagasaki
• Japan
World Event

1945 • end of the Second World War • worldwide
World Event

1945 • The Trinity Test, the first nuclear detonation •
Manhattan Project
Science & Technology

1946 • *The Creator* • Clifford Simak
Novel

1946 • Fantasy Press founded • Lloyd Eshbach
Small Publisher

1947

1947 • Fantasy Publishing Company Inc founded •
William L. Crawford
Small Publisher

1947 • Shasta Publishers founded • T.E. Ditky
Small Publisher

1948 • Gnome Press founded • David Kyle and
Martin Greenberg
Small Publisher

1948 • *Ape and Essence* • Aldous Huxley
Novel

1948 • Mahatma Gandhi leads a peaceful transition •
South Africa
World Event

1949 • *Nineteen Eighty-Four* • George Orwell
Novel

1949 • *Earth Abides* • George R. Stewart
Novel

1949 • First issue of The Magazine of Fantasy and Science
Fiction • Anthony Boucher, J. Francis McComas
Pulp Magazine

1949 • First episode of *Captain Video and His Video Rangers*
• James Caddigan, Lawrence Menkin
TV

1950

1950 • First issue of *Galaxy Science Fiction* • H.L. Gold
Pulp Magazine

1950 • *The Martian Chronicles* • Ray Bradbury
Collection

1950 • *I, Robot* • Isaac Asimov
Collection

1950 • First broadcast of *Dimension X* • NBC
Radio

1950 • First broadcast of *2000 Plus* • MBS
Radio

1950 • *Rocketship X-M* • Kurt Neumann
Movie

1950 • *Destination Moon* • Irving Pichel
Movie

1950 • First episode of *Buck Rogers* • Babette Henry
TV

1950 • First episode of *Space Patrol* • Mike Moser
TV

1950 • 'The Helping Hand' • Poul Anderson
Short Story

1950 • *The Dreaming Jewels* • Theodore Sturgeon
Novel

Chronology of selected events in the history of science fiction, from early influences to modern media.

Legend: Philosophy · Science & Technology · Novels · Short Story · World Events · Movies · Magazines · Comics · Play · Pulp Magazines · Radio · Small Publishers · TV · Video Games

1951

1951 • The Festival of Britain • UK
Science & Technology

1951 • 'There Will Come Soft Rains' • Ray Bradbury
Short Story

1951 • *Rogue Queen* • L. Sprague de Camp
Novel

1951 • *The Day the Earth Stood Still* • Robert Wise
Movie

1951 • *The Day of the Triffids* • John Wyndham
Novel

1951 • *Foundation* • Isaac Asimov
Novel

1951 • Japanese release of *Metropolis* • Osamu Tezuka
Comic

1951 • Serialization of *Kimba the White Lion* •
Osamu Tezuka begins serialization
Comic

1951 • First episode of *Tales of Tomorrow* • Mort Abrahamson,
Theodore Sturgeon
TV

1952 • America explodes the first hydrogen bomb • USA
Science & Technology

1952 • First issue of *If* magazine • James L. Quinn
Pulp Magazine

1952 • *The Lovers* • Philip José Farmer
Novel

1953

1953 • *The Demolished Man* • Alfred Bester
Novel

1953 • *Childhood's End* • Arthur C. Clarke
Novel

1953 • *Fahrenheit 451* • Ray Bradbury
Novel

1953 • *The Kraken Wakes* • John Wyndham
Novel

1953 • *Invaders from Mars* • William Cameron Menzies
Movie

1953 • First release of *Astro Boy* • Osamu Tezuka
Comic

1953 • First Hugo Awards given for science fiction & fantasy •
World Science Fiction Society
World Event

1954• *The Fellowship of the Ring* • J.R.R. Tolkien
Novel

1954 • 'Rite of Passage' • Chad Oliver
Short Story

1954 • *Shadows in the Sun* • Chad Oliver
Novel

1954 • *I Am Legend* • Richard Matheson
Novel

1954 • *Godzilla* • Ishirō Honda
Movie

1954 • *Them!* • Gordon Douglas
Movie

1955 • *X Minus One* • NBC
Radio

1955 • *The Quatermass Xperiment* • Val Guest
Movie

1955 • First episode of *Science Fiction Theater* • Ivan Tors,
Frederick W. Ziv and Maurice Ziv
TV

1956

1956 • *Forbidden Planet* • Fred M. Wilcox
Movie

1956 • *Invasion of the Body Snatchers* • Don Siegel
Movie

1957 • Sputnik 1 launched into low Earth orbit • Soviet Union
Science & Technology

1957 • *The Midwich Cuckoos* • John Wyndham
Novel

1957 • *On the Beach* • Nevil Shute
Novel

1957 • First broadcast of *Exploring Tomorrow* • MBS
Radio

1958 • New managing editor of *Amazing Stories* •
Cele Goldsmith
Pulp Magazine

1959 • *Plan 9 From Outer Space* • Ed Wood
Movie

1959 • First episode of *The Twilight Zone* • Rod Serling
TV

1959 • *Starship Troopers* • Robert A. Heinlein
Novel

1959 • *A Canticle for Leibowitz* • Walter M. Miller, Jr.
Novel

THE SECOND WORLD WAR

As it did with so many other things, the Second World War brought a jarring halt to the domination of science fiction by the pulps. The effect of the War on the genre in its various forms led to turmoil, though from that turmoil came high-quality science fiction. Once the War ended, science fiction began to mutate and transform itself from the older style of the 1930s to something much closer to traditional literature, a transformation that would be complete by the end of the 1950s.

The Effects of the War

The American home-front during the Second World War is usually imagined as a relatively placid period, and certainly compared to the British home-front it was. However, there were substantial upsets in the US, from a nationwide surge in crime, to the many labour strikes, to the government-imposed limitations on materials from food to metals. Paper, too, was restricted, and the paper restrictions had a direct influence on science fiction. The United States Government instituted paper restriction in 1942, with increasing limitations

every year to follow. However, the restrictions were not felt in a serious way by publishers until 1943, so that for the first 18 months of the war, publishers were able to freely capitalize on families suddenly flush with spending money thanks to newly available government jobs.

In comics, this meant that by the end of 1943 there were 125 individual comic book titles on sale every month; cumulative sales of those titles topped 25 million, with retail sales for the year 1943 nearing $30 million. In the pulps, this meant although the number of pulp titles decreased every year (as had been the case since 1938), the number of issues of the pulps published declined only very slowly. So the peripheral, worst-selling pulps left the market, but the better-selling pulps continued to produce issues unabated until 1943 and the paper restrictions, when the number of pulps published and issues published both dropped by 12 per cent.

As far as novel publishing was concerned, the War was a time of nearly unabated sales, with the twin demands of the home-front and the military men and women abroad providing publishers with a vast audience, especially for the new, cheap genre paperbacks, which were sold to the military and then given away by the military by the million.

However, this bull market for publishing did not extend to science fiction in all formats. In comics, individual science fiction strips continued to appear throughout the War, as did superhero strips, but as early as 1942 the major comic book publishers had begun diversifying their output and moving away from superheroes and science fiction. Of the 113 titles that debuted in 1942,

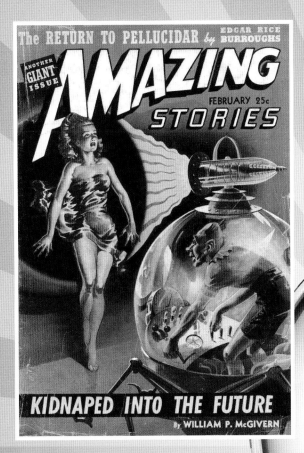

THE RETURN TO PELLUCIDAR by EDGAR RICE BURROUGHS

ANOTHER GIANT ISSUE

Amazing STORIES

FEBRUARY 25c

KIDNAPED INTO THE FUTURE
by WILLIAM P. McGIVERN

VICTORY FROM THE VOID by Wm. P. McGIVERN D. W. O'BRIEN

SEE BACK COVER

Amazing STORIES

MARCH 25c

The METAL MONSTER By E. K. JARVIS

A NOVEL OF THE FUTURE COMPLETE IN THIS ISSUE!

FALL ISSUE

STARTLING STORIES

15c

A THRILLING PUBLICATION

BUY WAR BONDS AND STAMPS FOR VICTORY!

THE TIME TRAIL
An Astounding Complete Novel
By ROSS ROCKLYNNE

THE SPACE DWELLERS
A Hall of Fame Classic
By RAYMOND Z. GALLUN

WORLD OF THE PAPER DOLLS BY DON WILCOX

fantastic ADVENTURES

OCTOBER 25¢

JEWELS OF THE TOAD
By FRANK PATTON

STRANGE ADVENTURES ON OTHER WORLDS—

BRITISH EDITION 9d

PLANET stories

TRADE MARK REG. A.N.C.

Nic Cano was an FFV - but he'd seen too much horror on the new green world
LAST RUN on VENUS
novelet by James McKimmey Jr.

It was 40 years since the last G.C. spacer — plenty can happen in an off-galaxy world in that length of time!

TEMPTRESS of PLANET DELIGHT
a startling novel by B. CURTIS

A NOVEL OF THE FUTURE COMPLETE IN THIS ISSUE!

WINTER ISSUE

STARTLING STORIES

15c

BUY WAR BONDS AND STAMPS FOR VICTORY!

A THRILLING PUBLICATION

THE Giant Atom
An Astounding Complete Novel
By MALCOLM JAMESON

THE LAST WOMAN
A Hall of Fame Classic
By THOMAS S. GARDNER

ABOVE: A variety of pulp magazines from the 1940s and 1950s

76 were non-science fiction and non-superhero. In the pulps, 1941 was the high point for science fiction, with 27 published; by 1945, there were only 10 left, and although the mainstream pulps continued to publish SF, it remained a minority of what they published. Nor did science fiction novels benefit from the military's demand for paperbacks or the home-front's demand for hardcovers. There were 29 science fiction novels published in 1942, 15 in 1943, 17 in 1944 and 20 in 1945 – a minuscule amount compared to the large number of detective and Western novels published during those years.

Astounding was able to publish unabated throughout the War, but *Amazing Stories* only published 10 issues in 1943, five in 1944 and four in 1945, and *Thrilling Wonder Stories*, the successor to *Wonder Stories*, was bimonthly in 1942 and 1943 and quarterly in 1944 and 1945.

Science Fiction in the War

This is not to say that science fiction was dead during the War. *Astounding* continued its run of strong years, with memorable and in some cases all-time classic stories by A.E. Van Vogt, Anthony Boucher, Fritz Leiber, Henry Kuttner, C.L. Moore, Murray Leinster, Jack Williamson, E.E. 'Doc' Smith and Eric Frank Russell. *Amazing* had stories by Edgar Rice Burroughs, Ray Cummings, Nelson S. Bond, Edmond Hamilton and Robert Bloch. The best-selling comics were *Superman* and *Captain Marvel Adventures*, both of which regularly featured science fictional elements in their stories. And certain SF movies – the serials featuring Batman, Captain America and Captain Marvel, the Fleischer cartoons featuring Superman, and the 1941 *Dr Jekyll and Mr Hyde* – were popular. Science fiction was not dead during the War, but neither was it in great health, despite the individually popular authors, stories and films.

LEFT: Spencer Tracy in *Dr Jekyll and Mr Hyde* (1941), directed by Victor Fleming

AFTER THE WAR

After the War, with the return to civilian life of a number of major science fiction writers (including Isaac Asimov, Robert A. Heinlein and Frederik Pohl), science fiction began to expand in popularity to the point that it was one of the (if not *the*) defining genres of the late 1940s and 1950s. As far as science fiction is concerned, the 1946–59 period is more or less a unitary whole. There were significant changes, of course, but like the 'long 1930s' described in Chapter 3, the 'long 1950s' of 1946–59 is a set of years with much in common, but also much to differentiate itself from what followed as far as science fiction is concerned. The intense anti-communist sentiments and activities of the 1950s were on display almost immediately after the War ended; the War was a brief interruption of the American anti-communism that existed before the War and from the early days of the Soviet Union. Similarly, the feeling that America was now the pre-eminent world power, the rise in suburban culture, the interest in going into space, the terrified fascination with (and arms race involving) atomic weapons, the efforts to achieve civil rights for African-Americans – these were all products of the immediate post-War environment in the United States, rather than issues that arose in the 1950s.

Changes During the Long 1950s

Naturally, there were changes taking place during the long 1950s to accompany the continuity of American cultural sentiments. If American cultural trends and obsessions were largely the same from 1946 to 1959, events often altered the way these trends manifested themselves. Anti-communist sentiment was strong in the late 1940s, but became far more intense during and after the Korean War. Suburban culture flourished practically as soon as the G.I.s returned from the War, but the establishment of the Levittowns (the name given to seven large suburban developments created by William Levitt and his company Levitt & Sons) accelerated the process. So, too, did the race to space before and after Sputnik, the civil rights movement before and after **Brown versus the Board of Education of Topeka** (the landmark ruling in 1954 by the Supreme Court that declared state laws establishing separate public schools for black and white students to be unconstitutional) and the obsession with atomic weapons before and after the Soviets acquired the bomb. Even with all this change, the long 1950s were still primarily a decade of sameness rather than of transformation and evolution.

Science Fiction's Continuity

Like the long 1950s of real life, science fiction's long 1950s was marked primarily by continuity rather than by change, although the changes in SF were more pronounced than the changes of the outside world.

ABOVE: A.E. van Vogt's 'Slan' in *Astounding Science Fiction* (October 1940)

THE ASTONISHING ILLUSTRATED HISTORY OF SCIENCE FICTION

The foremost element of continuity during science fiction's long 1950s was the identity of the genre's major authors. The top writers of *Astounding* and *Amazing* listed above – Heinlein, Van Vogt, Smith and so on – were for the most part still producing top-notch work by the time the long 1950s ended, and were still the best-known, best-respected authors in the field. But there were new names among them: Leigh Brackett was producing excellent work during this time, as were Alfred Bester, C.M. Kornbluth, Robert Sheckley and William Tenn. Some of the best-known authors of the 1930s and early 1940s, like Ray Cummings, were publishing less science fiction and had even become obscure – the eventual fate of most authors. But as far as the general fans of SF were concerned, those at the top of the genre in 1946 were essentially the same names that were at the top in 1959.

What being at the top of the genre meant in 1959 was in many ways an accelerated version of what it had meant in 1946. 'Popular' no longer meant 'popular with the limited audience of science fiction fans', but rather 'popular with the readership of science fiction'. Science fiction's readership was much broader and more populous than what had existed in 1946. Science fiction fandom began in the late 1920s, when Hugo Gernsback began publishing letters in *Amazing Stories* with the addresses of fans included, which allowed nearby fans to contact each other and to eventually form reading groups and, in the case of the Science Fiction League, a professionally sponsored science fiction organization. The mystery and Western dime novels of the late nineteenth century had done something similar to this, and in doing so had created nascent fandoms of both genres – fandoms which expanded in the 1910s, with the explosion in popularity of both genres. With the rise of specialty pulps devoted to detective stories and Westerns, these fandoms expanded throughout the 1910s and 1920s. Gernsback enabled science fiction fans to come together in a much more organized fashion than before, which helped with a similar expansion of the SF genre.

During the long 1950s, these fans were not only regular readers of science fiction. They also joined fan clubs, took part in the rising fanzine scene and attended science fiction conventions. Fans were a much smaller group of people (though much more committed to the genre) than science fiction's general readership during this time, not least because a generation had passed since the advent of modern science fiction. A nine-year-old child in 1926, when *Amazing Stories* debuted, was 29 in 1946 and likely had a child or two of his or her own. By 1956 these children would have been reading and watching science fiction. By the end of the long 1950s two full generations of science fiction readers, watchers and fans existed, often with the frame of mind that 'fans are slans', after the superior beings of A.E. van Vogt's *Slan* (1940 as a magazine serialization, 1946 as a novel).

The Business of Science Fiction

This growth in readership had consequences for the business of science fiction publishing. The long 1950s saw an increase in sales for SF novels from the beginning of the expanded decade to the end, both because of the larger audience buying science fiction and because SF was being published by mainstream publishers and appearing in mainstream venues for fiction. The first best-selling science fiction novel was *On the Beach* (1957) by Nevil Shute, but Shute was seen as a popular novelist first rather than a member of the science fiction community. (This, despite his having published six SF novels before 1957.) As has traditionally been the case, science fiction's fandom, though far more committed to the genre and its accessories, was much outnumbered by science fiction's general readership. It wasn't until 1961, with Heinlein's *Stranger in a Strange Land*, that a science fiction novel by a professional science fiction writer reached best-selling status.

CHANGES IN SCIENCE FICTION

Although the increase in sales for science fiction novels and the general sameness among the most popular names undoubtedly lent the long 1950s a feeling of continuity for creators and consumers, there were significant changes taking place, changes that made the long decade more tumultuous, in its way, than the decades before and after it.

Perhaps the most important change was science fiction's transition from primarily an entity of magazines to one equally split between magazines and other media. This change began with the pulps' fall from prominence. The effect of the Second World War on the pulps was deleterious, with the government paper restrictions having a particularly severe effect in 1943, 1944 and 1945. The pulps began to revive after the War ended: 183 titles published in 1946, 194 in 1947, 195 in 1948, 199 in 1949 and 206 in 1950. However, this growth in titles was unfortunately matched by a decrease in the number of issues published from 1946 to 1950; there were more pulps published, year to year, but many of them were publishing on a reduced schedule, or being cancelled and replaced with short-lived titles. After 1950, the number of titles declined precipitously, so that by 1954 there were only 80 pulps published and only 12 in 1960. The science fiction pulps seemed to be immune to the 'fall' part of the other

pulps' rise and fall: five science fiction pulps in 1946, 10 in 1948, 16 in 1950, 15 in 1953, with a decline in issues published seen only in 1953. But a shift in the publishing industry led to a shift in power within science fiction.

The Digest Format

The paper shortages of the War had led magazine publishers to move away from the pulp format (7 x 10 or 6.75 x 9.75) to what became known as the 'digest' format (5.25 x 7.5). The first true digest magazine was **Reader's Digest**, which began publishing in 1922, but as far as genre magazines were concerned, the first digest magazine was **Ellery Queen's Mystery Magazine**, which began in 1941. Smaller and cheaper to produce than pulps – and, important during wartime, using less paper – digests were an attractive alternative to pulps for most genre magazine publishers. As the digest format was increasingly adopted by publishers after the War, when new magazines appeared they were as often digests as they were pulps.

In 1949, the same year that Street & Smith, the major publisher of pulps, cancelled most of them to concentrate on slicks, **The Magazine of Fantasy and Science Fiction** (a digest which quickly became known as **F&SF**) was launched. The following year **Galaxy Science Fiction** appeared. To this point in time **Astounding** (which had gone to the digest format in 1943), edited by John W. Campbell Jr., had reigned supreme in science fiction, both in sales and as a taste-maker, with Campbell's editorial tastes (favouring technological and scientific SF) influencing the entire field. **F&SF** and **Galaxy** changed that and toppled **Astounding** and Campbell from their perch. **F&SF** specialized in literate science fiction, with an

ABOVE : The rocket technology of the War informed the Space Race in the years that followed, and fuelled the imagination of the science fiction writing community.

ABOVE: Authors like H.P. Lovecraft imagined dark tales of ancient and malevolent creatures who threatened the terror of invasion

emphasis on mature and stylish prose, something Campbell had never emphasized (or, arguably, wanted). *Galaxy* became known for its sociological science fiction (one of the 'soft' sciences Campbell disliked) and especially for its satires.

Within a few years – well before the end of the long 1950s – Campbellian science fiction was seen by many fans as an older, less relevant kind of science fiction, one that featured old standbys like Asimov and Heinlein rather than newer, more innovative writers like Robert Sheckley and Philip K. Dick. Magazine science fiction still had life to it, and was still vitally important to the field, but the kind of science fiction that was appearing had changed.

Rivals to Magazine SF

Magazine science fiction, despite its importance to the field, also had rivals during the long 1950s that either had not existed during the long 1930s or had been of significantly less importance and prominence.

Small presses were not new in the 1950s. There had been small presses in the 1920s and early 1930s that published a few science fiction novels, though they were often short-lived. In 1935 William L. Crawford began publishing science fiction and fantasy novels as a small press publisher. His second novel was H.P. Lovecraft's **The Shadow Over Innsmouth** (1936), but his other titles were obscure. In 1939 writers August Derleth and Donald Wandrei founded Arkham House, which was devoted to the works of H.P. Lovecraft and his circle of friends and admirers. After the Second World War ended there was a rapid growth in the number of small presses, including Fantasy Press by Lloyd Eshbach, in 1946, Crawford's Fantasy Publishing Company Inc. in 1947, Shasta Publishers by T.E. Ditky in 1947, and Gnome Press by David Kyle and Martin

Greenberg in 1948. From 1946 to the mid-1950s small press publishers were the primary outlet for science fiction novels. The major publishers were not yet willing to venture into the science fiction field, unconvinced that doing so would lead to good sales. Most (though by no means all) of the novels published by small presses were reprints of novellas and serials that had originally appeared in magazine form, but these were in some cases many years old, and effectively new to the reading audience, thus creating a real alternative to magazine science fiction.

Paperbacks

What killed off the small presses, who published their books in hardcover form, was the rise of the paperback novel. The paperback form achieved prominence in the 1930s in Britain when Penguin Books, which debuted in 1935, published a line of cheap paperbacks in a variety of different genres, including science fiction. Four years later publisher Simon & Schuster brought out the Pocket Books line of novels. Pocket did not usually publish science fiction, with the exception of a 1943 anthology, **The Pocket Book of Science Fiction**. Ace Books (beginning in 1952), Ballantine Books (beginning in 1952) and Bantam Books (founded in 1945 but revamped to publish paperback novels in 1954) did publish science fiction paperbacks. At the same time mainstream publishers like Doubleday and Scribners were venturing into the field, now guaranteed to produce profits. As with the small presses, many of the novels published by these houses were paperback editions of novellas and serials that had previously appeared in the science fiction magazines, but there were a number of significant original novels to appear from these publishers during these years, including Bester's **Demolished Man** (1953), **Fahrenheit 451** (1953) by Ray Bradbury and **Childhood's End** (1953) by Arthur C. Clarke.

SCIENCE FICTION IN OTHER MEDIA

The diminishment of magazine science fiction's influence was hastened by the rising influence of science fiction in other media. The long 1950s saw a downturn in demand for superhero comic books. The post-War environment and changing audience expectations meant that superheroes in comic book form were unpopular (though not on radio or in film). Superhero comics began declining in popularity in the late 1940s, with a wave of cancellations in 1949, 1950 and 1951. However, science fiction comic books became popular at the same time, with titles like DC's *Strange Adventures* (from 1950) and *Mystery in Space* (from 1951), and American Comics Group's *Forbidden Worlds* (from 1951) selling well. EC Comics' family of science fiction comics, *Weird Science* (from 1950) and *Weird Fantasy* (from 1953), is known for works of good quality. Although many of the science fiction titles were adversely affected (usually to the point of cancellation) by the imposition of the Comics Code in 1954, which imposed censorious regulations that most comic book publishers in the United States either would not or could not meet, until that time the comics provided SF consumers with a vigorous alternative to prose science fiction.

ABOVE: Movie poster for *Invaders from Mars* (1953), directed by William Cameron Menzies

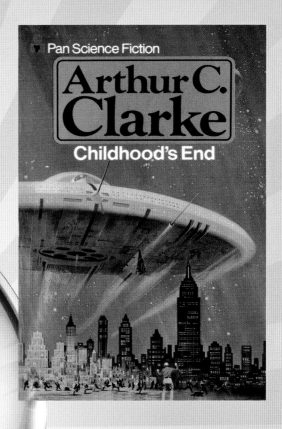

ABOVE: A variety of publications from the 1940s and 1950s; movie poster for *Fahrenheit 451* (1966), based on Ray Bradbury's novel of the same name (1953)

During the long 1950s those consumers disappointed by the disappearance of comic book science fiction from the newsstands could turn their eyes and ears to science fiction on the radio and in the movies. Although the Golden Age of radio science fiction was the 1930s and 1940s, in the 1950s radio listeners had **Superman** (until 1952), **The Shadow** (until 1954), **Dimension X** (1950–51), **2000 Plus** (1950–52), **Space Patrol** (1950–55), **Space Cadet** (1952), **Tales of Tomorrow** (1953), **X Minus One** (1955–58) and **Exploring Tomorrow** (1957–58), among others. Some of these shows used the backlog of stories available from the pulps and slicks, but most of the shows presented original radio plays.

Film and Television

Science fiction in film flourished in the 1950s, compared to the relative desert that had been SF film in the 1940s. There were spaceship films, like **Rocketship X-M** (1950) and **Destination Moon** (1950). There were films about aliens arriving on Earth, like **The Day the Earth Stood Still** (1951). There were message films, like **This Island Earth** (1955). There were pure horror films, like **The Quatermass Xperiment** (1955; in the US, **The Creeping Unknown**). And, of course, there were the many monster movies, the first of which was **The Thing** (1951) but which truly began as a sub-genre in 1954 with **Them!**

Accompanying science fiction at the movies was science fiction on the newly popular medium of television. The first science fiction television series was **Captain Video** (1949–56), which was quickly followed by **Buck Rogers** (1950–51), **Space Patrol** (1950–55), **Tom Corbett: Space Cadet** (1950–55) and a host of others throughout the decade. Most of these were aimed at juveniles

ABOVE: *Destination Moon* (1950), directed by Irving Pichel, explored the dangers of space travel

and had low-quality scripts, productions and performances. There was the occasional television show aimed at adult viewers, like **Tales of Tomorrow** (1951–56) and **Science Fiction Theater** (1955–57).

Evolving Themes

The themes of the science fiction that appeared in all these different media evolved over time. Science fiction in 1959, on the verge of the 1960s, was substantially different from the science fiction of 1946. It is hard to argue that **A Canticle for Leibowitz** (1959, **see** chapter 5 for more) by Walter M. Miller Jr. would have been conceived of in 1946. Its stylistic maturity and contemplativeness would have been unlikely in the immediate post-War environment of science fiction publishing. The novel's religious themes were not, after all, unknown to science fiction in 1946, when Clifford Simak's **The Creator** was published and, controversially for the time, suggested God is an alien. So the following needs to be understood as a discussion of themes and tropes, motifs and concepts which had a surprising longevity throughout the long decade.

The Fall of Campbellian Science Fiction

During the first few years of the long 1950s, Campbellian science fiction held sway. It had an emphasis on recognizable and realistic (for certain values of realism) science and technology; the recurring use of a stereotypical action scientist as a prototypical protagonist overcoming difficulties and enemies with

ABOVE: An alien and his robot companion Gort come to Earth with a message in *The Day the Earth Stood Still* (1951), directed by Robert Wise

a can-do attitude; expansionist and usually imperialist storylines; and most notably an exploration of the influence of new technologies on humans and human societies. Stories with these themes appeared throughout the reign of Campbell at **Astounding** as science fiction's thought leader from 1938 to 1949. Later, the post-War return to productivity of Campbell favourites like Asimov and Heinlein led to new heights that had not always been achieved during the War years.

The appearance of **F&SF** and **Galaxy** in 1949 almost immediately toppled Campbell from his position as taste-maker. This did not mean, of course, that Campbell stopped publishing Campbellian science fiction in the pages of **Astounding**. Campbell remained editor of **Astounding** throughout the 1950s, but his growing interest in pseudoscience, from psionics to Dianetics, and his unwillingness or inability to recognize and respond to new developments in the field, meant that he and **Astounding**, though still popular within science fiction fandom, were at odds with much of science fiction's readership.

New Kinds of Science Fiction

What replaced Campbell and **Astounding** were **F&SF** and **Galaxy**'s approach to science fiction: a new interest in authorial style, in literary qualities, in satirical humour, in sociology, psychology and the 'soft' sciences, and in questioning the sureties of Campbellian science fiction.

One cannot say for certain to what degree this change was influenced by or reflective of movements of the time in the larger culture. Certainly the 1950s,

LEFT: Movie poster for *The Day of the Triffids* (1962), directed by Steve Sekely.   ABOVE: Giant mutated ants are the antagonists in *Them!* (1954), directed by Gordon Douglas

on the surface the era of US power at its height, was also a time when the country was undergoing changes similar to those undergone by science fiction. Works like **The Man in the Gray Flannel Suit** (1955) by Sloan Wilson were questioning men's relationship with work; the rise in sociology and anthropology as serious academic disciplines were questioning cultural truths most Americans believed in; the rise of psychiatry and the public's increasing knowledge of Freud were forcing Americans to question their own personalities in ways previous generations had not. The two Kinsey reports, in 1948 and 1953, were questioning the sexual truths that most Americans held about themselves. **Mad Magazine** (from 1952), **The Realist** (1958) by Paul Krassner and comedy by Lenny Bruce and Mort Sahl were introducing serious satire into the American mainstream. And literary criticism, by Northrop Frye and Edmund Wilson, and the authors of **New Criticism**, was being newly emphasized for American college and university students.

99

So the movements in science fiction mirrored the movements in society at large, with science fiction authors writing stories and novels that particularly exemplified these new movements. **The Lovers** (1952) by Philip José Farmer is a reflection of society's new understanding of sexuality, even if that topic was usually taboo in science fiction magazines and novels. Chad Oliver would regularly make use of formal anthropology in his stories, whether in examining alien cultures as in his short story 'Rite of Passage' (1954), or with aliens examining human civilization as in **Shadows in the Sun** (1954). 'The Helping Hand' (1950) by Poul Anderson, and Philip Wylie's **The Disappearance** (1951), both made heavy use of sociology.

RIGHT: Movie poster for *Forbidden Planet* (1956), directed by Fred M. Wilcox

THE BIG ISSUES

Other recurring themes and tropes in the science fiction of the long 1950s did not neatly correspond to larger current cultural movements, but instead reflected cultural fears and obsessions.

Perhaps the foremost of these was the possibility of nuclear war with the Soviet Union and a corresponding nuclear devastation of America. The news coverage of what the atomic bombs had done in Hiroshima and Nagasaki, and later coverage of the effects of the hydrogen bomb detonation in 1952, led to widespread, even rampant, fear of nuclear war and radioactive fallout. This fear appeared in mainstream fiction, in novels like **Ape and Essence** (1948) by Aldous Huxley and **Red Alert** (1958) by Peter George.

But science fiction had begun to deal with the fear of nuclear war a generation earlier, with **Public Faces** (1932) by Harold Nicolson. After Hiroshima and Nagasaki, the number of short stories and novels about nuclear war increased dramatically; notably fine texts on the subject include 'Thunder and Roses' (1947) by Theodore Sturgeon, 'Not With a Bang' (1949) by Damon Knight, **Shadow on the Hearth** (1950) by Judith Merril, Ray Bradbury's 'There Will Come Soft Rains' (1951), 'Lot' (1953) and 'Lot's Daughter' (1954) by Ward Moore and **Alas, Babylon** (1959) by Pat Frank.

Science fiction film was not immune to the pull of these fears. **Kiss Me, Deadly** (1955) dealt with the fear of the bomb directly. More obliquely, so did the many monster movies of the long decade, which either blamed atomic radiation for the monsters as seen in **Godzilla** (1954) and **Them!** (1954), or symbolically as seen in **Tarantula** (1955) and **The Blob** (1958).

The Red Scare

Attached to the fear of nuclear war and radioactive fallout was the fear of, hatred for and obsession with communists, particularly the Soviet variety. The Red Scare of the late 1940s, reaching its high points with the Alger Hiss affair in the late 1940s and with the McCarthyism of the early 1950s, proved ultimately to be much ado about little, but in the minds of Americans the threat of an international communist conspiracy was very real indeed. Popular culture reflected this, in novels from **Nineteen Eighty-Four** (1949) by George Orwell to **The God That Failed** (1950) by Arthur Koestler, and in non-SF movies like **The Woman on Pier 13** (1949) and **Invasion USA** (1952). Science fiction film also reflected this, in films like **The Whip Hand** (1951), **The Day the Earth Stood Still** (1951), **Invasion of the Body Snatchers** (1956) and **Invaders from Mars** (1953), in which aliens stood in for the communist threat. In science fiction prose the communist menace, and specifically communist aliens, were a product of the pulps of the 1930s and 1940s, and had largely been confined there.

By the time the long 1950s arrived, science fiction writers had for the most part moved beyond portraying communists or aliens as a threat. Some were

ABOVE: Movie poster for *Invasion of the Body Snatchers* (1956), directed by Don Siegel

more interested in portraying them as truly alien – as in 'The Waveries' (1945) by Fredric Brown, and Damon Knight's 'Cabin Boy' (1951) – some depicted them as intelligent and the equal of humanity, though markedly different, as in Arthur C. Clarke's 'Rescue Party' (1946) – while others presented them as essentially human, but wearing different bodies (as in the works of Hal Clement, including 'Mission of Gravity' (1953). The more mundane threat of communism was left far behind.

Disasters

Disasters loomed large in the science fiction of the long 1950s, as they did in the American public's subconscious at that time. It's not that the disasters of the long decade were particularly deadlier than the disasters of the 1920s or 1930s. The 1948 Ashgabat earthquake, the Great Appalachian Storm of 1950, the 1951 Comoro tornado, the 1951 Winter of Terror in Switzerland, these were less severe and less deadly than the 1920 Haiyuan and 1923 Kanto earthquakes, the 1921 Russian famine, the 1928–30 Chinese famine, the 1925 Tri-State Tornado, the Ukraine famine of 1932–33. However, the disasters of the long 1950s were far better reported (with the exception of the Great Chinese Famine of 1958–61), and far sooner, in a mass media that included television and was far more internationally focused than in previous years, and of course took place while the memory of the devastation of the atomic bombing of Hiroshima and Nagasaki were fresh in Americans' minds.

It's fair to say that Americans as a whole were disaster-obsessed in the 1940s and 1950s. Not coincidentally, disasters were a recurring theme in science

ABOVE: Movie poster for *Godzilla* (1954), directed by Ishirō Honda. RIGHT: Atomic radiation was responsible for the eponymous giant lizard in *Godzilla*.

fiction of the long 1950s: **Earth Abides** (1949) by George R. Stewart, in which most of humanity dies because of a viral plague; **The Day of the Triffids** (1951) by John Wyndham, in which humanity is blinded by cosmic rays and then attacked by the mobile plant Triffids; Wyndham's **The Kraken Wakes** (1953), in which an alien invasion of Earth floods the surface world; **I Am Legend** (1954) by Richard Matheson, in which a bacterium has turned humanity into vampires; and **The Death of Grass** (1956) by John Christopher, in which all food plants and grasses are wiped out, with devastating effects on humanity, are among the best.

Religion

Religious issues were also at the forefront of the American consciousness during the long decade. With the population boom (150 million in 1950, 180 million in 1960) and the increase in church attendance (from 57 per cent in 1950 to 63 per cent in 1960), more Americans than ever were religious. But the decade was one in which religious conflicts were numerous: Catholic versus Protestant, mainstream versus underground, liberal versus evangelical, pro-civil rights movement versus anti-civil rights movement. Although these specific conflicts did not for the most part play out in science fiction, religious themes were common in science fiction of the long 1950s, from Ray Bradbury's 'The Man' (1949) to Arthur C. Clarke's 'The Nine Billion Names of God' (1953) to John Wyndham's **The Chrysalids** (1955; published in the US in the same year as **Re-Birth**) to **A Case of Conscience** (1958) by James Blish, culminating in Walter M. Miller Jr.'s **A Canticle for Leibowitz** (1959).

RIGHT: *I Am Legend* (2007) was based on Richard Matheson's novel of the same name (1954)

Art

Science fiction art can be said to have come of age in the 1942–59 period, with pulps, digests and paperbacks all regularly featuring a variety of SF art and artists. Unlike previous periods, during the 1942–59 period artists could make a living as professional SF artists. Frank R. Paul, Virgil Finlay, Earle K. Bergey and Hannes Bok produced well-received art throughout the period, but the most popular and prolific SF artist of the time was Kelly Freas, who began illustrating covers from 1950 onward for a variety of magazines and for several book publishers. His light-hearted portrayals of humans and aliens were a substantial change from the far more serious work of his peers, and SF fans responded positively to them. Other significant artists of the time include Richard M. Powers, who added surrealism to science fiction art, and Chesley Bonestell, whose photorealistic planets and space vehicles were the artistic equivalent of hard SF.

The End of the Long 1950s

The year 1959 was the end of the long 1950s in more ways than temporal. It saw the publication of Heinlein's **Starship Troopers**, the novel that together with **The Genetic General** (1960; better known as **Dorsai!** – as it appeared in magazine and later book versions) by Gordon R. Dickson launched modern military science fiction, which became increasingly popular during and after the Vietnam War. **Starship Troopers** also marks the beginning of Heinlein's move away from the constant innovation he displayed in his science fiction of the 1940s and 1950s – and away from the publication of his science fiction

novels for juveniles – and towards authority worship – a step down from his previous, two-decade-long role as the foremost writer in the field. Heinlein's **Stranger in a Strange Land** (1961) essentially began the 1960s as we think of them, and was influential on the field as a whole.

Cele Goldsmith became managing editor of **Amazing Stories** in 1958, and she transformed it into a magazine which welcomed experimental stories. She brought writers into the field who would be important in the 1960s and 1970s, including Thomas M. Disch, Roger Zelazny and Ursula K. Le Guin. The year 1959 was the last full year that **Astounding** went by its old name; in 1960 it was renamed **Analog**, and although it was still edited by John W. Campbell Jr. and although it won four Hugo Awards in five years, it had lost vitality, and its featured science fiction was increasingly calcified and hostile towards writers who did not fit into the Campbellian scheme, a situation that would not change until Campbell's death. The year 1960 also saw the appearance of **New Maps of Hell** by Kingsley Amis. This was the first critical attempt to explain science fiction to the mainstream, and was influential on critics, readers and writers alike. The difference between the long 1950s and the 1960s is great, and begins not so much with dying traditions in 1958 and 1959 as revolutionary ones beginning in 1960.

103

ABOVE RIGHT: Carole Ann Ford struggles with the plants in *The Day of the Triffids* (1962)

5: REINVENTING THE GENRE

1960

1963

1965

1960 • *Deathworld* • Harry Harrison
Novel
1960 • *New Maps of Hell* • Kingsley Amis
Critical Essays
1960 • *The Time Machine* • George Pal
Movie
1961 • First person in space • Yuri Gagarin
Science & Technology
1961 • *Solaris* • Stanisław Lem
Novel
1961 • *Stranger in a Strange Land* • Robert Heinlein
Novel
1962 • *The Man in the High Castle* • Philip K. Dick
Novel
1962 • *The Drowned World* • J.G. Ballard
Novel
1962 • *A Clockwork Orange* • Anthony Burgess
Novel

1963 • First episode of *Doctor Who* • Sydney Newman,
C.E. Webber and Donald Wilson
TV

1963 • First episode of *The Outer Limits* • Leslie Stevens
TV
1963 • *X: The Man With X Ray Eyes* • Roger Corman
Movie
1964 • New editor of *New Worlds* • Michael Moorcock
Magazine
1964 • 'The Coldest Place' • Larry Niven
Short Story

1965 • 'Dial F for Frankenstein' • Arthur C. Clarke
Short Story
1965 • *Dr Who and the Daleks* • Gordon Flemyng
Movie
1965 • *Dune* • Frank Herbert
Novel
1965 • First episode of *Lost in Space* • Irwin Allen
TV
1965 • *Bill, the Galactic Hero* • Harry Harrison
Novel
1965 • *This Immortal* • Roger Zelazny
Novel
1965 • *The Genocides* • Thomas M. Disch
Novel

Chronology of selected events in the history of science fiction, from early influences to modern media.

1966

1966 • First episode of *Star Trek* • Gene Roddenberry
TV

1966 • *Make Room! Make Room!* • Harry Harrison
Novel

1966 • *Babel-17* • Samuel R. Delany
Novel

1966 • *Fantastic Voyage* • Richard Fleischer
Movie

1966 • *The Solarians* • Norman Spinrad
Novel

1967 • *Dangerous Visions* • Harlan Ellison
Anthology

1968

1968 • *2001: A Space Odyssey* • Stanley Kubrick
Movie

1968 • *Planet of the Apes* • Franklin J. Schaffner
Movie

1968 • Apollo 11 Moon Landing • NASA
Science & Technology

1968 • *Do Androids Dream of Electric Sheep?* • Philip K. Dick
Novel

1968 • *Barbarella* • Roger Vadim
Movie

1969 • *The Left Hand of Darkness* • Ursula K. Le Guin
Novel

1969 • *Slaughterhouse-Five* • Kurt Vonnegut
Novel

1970

1970 • *Tau Zero* • Poul Anderson
Novel

1970 • *Ringworld* • Larry Niven
Novel

1971 • *The Andromeda Strain* • Robert Wise
Movie

1972 • *The Iron Dream* • Norman Spinrad
Novel

1973 • *Rendezvous with Rama* • Arthur C. Clarke
Novel

1974 • *The Dispossessed* • Ursula K. Le Guin
Novel

1975 • *The Female Man* • Joanna Russ
Novel

1975 • *The Forever War* • Joe Haldeman
Novel

1976 • *Man Plus* • Frederik Pohl
Novel

1976 • *The Man Who Fell to Earth* • Nicolas Roeg
Movie

SURFING THE NEW WAVE

'**W**e meet in an hour of change and challenge, in a decade of hope and fear, in an age of both knowledge and ignorance,' said American President John F. Kennedy in a speech at Rice University in 1962. 'The greater our knowledge increases, the greater our ignorance unfolds.' The speech was intended to pitch the space programme to the American public and was a key moment in the Space Race – but it also did a pretty good job of summing up the mood of the era.

These were indeed hopeful and fearful times. The period that saw *Sgt Pepper's Lonely Hearts Club Band*, Woodstock, the launch of Concorde and a TV set appearing in more and more homes also saw the assassination of Kennedy, race riots, the escalation of the United States' involvement in Vietnam, an ever-more chilly Cold War and the subsequent atomic paranoia it provoked.

The Race for Space

Yet humanity did ascend towards the stars. Yuri Gagarin became the first person in space in 1961 and Kennedy's goal of landing on the Moon was achieved in 1969. The future imagined in countless SF novels started to come true, although the mundane realities of spaceflight – the minutiae of calculations, the boxy functionality of the craft themselves, the sheer amount of time spent waiting – fell a little short of the lusty glamour of those Golden Age tales.

Whether as a deliberate reaction to the Space Race or not, SF in the 1960s began to look elsewhere for inspiration. 'The biggest developments of the immediate future will take place, not on the Moon or Mars, but on Earth, and it is inner space, not outer, that needs to be explored,' wrote author J.G. Ballard in the SF journal *New Worlds* in 1962. He called for fewer rocket ships and greater abstract invention.

As the decade progressed, writers would duly oblige. Character evolution, social commentary and countercultural tropes (such as gleeful indulgence in sex, drugs or often both) began to take precedence over the relatively linear lines of the SF that had gone before.

Soft SF

The term 'soft' science fiction was applied (a little retrospectively) to this movement. Author Peter Nicholls is generally held to have coined the phrase in 1975: The Year in Science Fiction' (Nebula Awards Stories 11, 1976) to describe

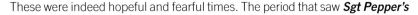

ABOVE: Whilst the 1960s saw America engaging in the Space Race, SF started to focus less on interplanetary adventures

the shift away from the 'hard' SF of physics, chemistry and astrophysics towards 'soft' preoccupations such as sociology, psychology and biology.

SF of the soft persuasion tends to employ technology and world building merely as a staging device for the internal dramas of the characters. Examples might be H.G. Wells's **The War of the Worlds** (1895) or Frank Herbert's **Dune** (1965), in which the precise workings of the Martian war machines or the spice that enables interplanetary navigation are glossed over in favour of how characters react to or use them.

It's probably best not to get too obsessive over the boundaries between hard and soft SF, though, as it remains a subject for debate. Nicholls himself stresses that the term soft SF is 'a not very precise item of SF terminology' (**The Encyclopedia of Science Fiction**, 1979). Instead, it's maybe helpful to think of soft SF as a mood or quality, rather than a definite, codified genre that writers set out to operate within and strayed from at their peril.

THE SOFT PARADE

Ellison, was on a similar mould-breaking mission and collected stories from American SF writers such as Fritz Leiber, Philip K. Dick and Samuel R. Delany.

Open Your Mind

Aldiss later summarized the impact of Moorcock and **New Worlds** in **The Detached Retina** (1995): 'Galactic wars went out; drugs came in; there were fewer encounters with aliens, more in the bedroom. Experimentation in prose styles became one of the orders of the day.'

Whether labelled soft or not, creators of SF in the 1960s (particularly fiction) explored diverse themes that did indeed look within as much as they gazed outwards. Narrative structure and language itself was terraformed by the motions of this 'New Wave' of SF writers as they explored topics as varied as atomic dread, spaceflight, altered states of being and consciousness, the Vietnam War, time, the nature of reality, feminism, faith and the arrival of the messiah (all prevailing cultural preoccupations, as suggested by the 1972 success of David Bowie's *The Rise and Fall of Ziggy Stardust and the Spiders from Mars*, a SF glam rock concept album with many of the same themes at its heart).

His own work certainly reflects this. **Hothouse** (1962) is a mesmerizingly trippy affair set on a no-longer-revolving Earth, where our descendants all live on the branches of a vast tree and intelligence is manifested as a kind of parasitic mushroom, while **Barefoot in the Head** (1969) uses interrupted narrative techniques (poems and songs appear throughout) and slowly fragmenting narration to lead us through the after effects of a war fought with weaponized psychedelic substances.

The New Wave gained its power and momentum from **New Worlds**, a UK science fiction journal edited from 1964 by Michael Moorcock. Under his stewardship the publication became the originating point for much of the literary innovation of the period (until its closure in 1970), featuring work from key writers including J.G. Ballard, Ursula K. Le Guin and Brian Aldiss. It didn't close for long, however, but returned in 1971 in the form of a paperback anthology series initially edited by Moorcock and lasting until 1976. There were also to be other revivals. Across the pond, **Dangerous Visions** (1967), a short story anthology curated by Harlan

Greybeard (1964) however, is painfully, beautifully austere in crafting a vision of a slowly decaying sterile world without children, summoning one of the New Wave's recurring themes: entropy, the gradual decline of order into disorder and the leeching away of energy.

This fascination is made more explicit in **The English Assassin** (1972), part of Michael Moorcock's vast body of work featuring Jerry Cornelius, which is subtitled **A Romance of Entropy** to highlight the theme of dissolution.

ABOVE: SF in the 1960s often explored such themes as altered states of being and consciousness

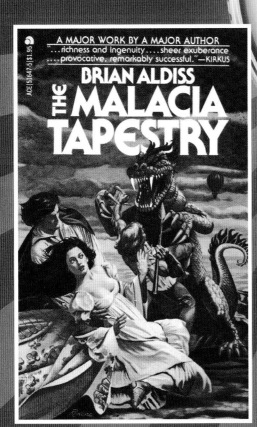

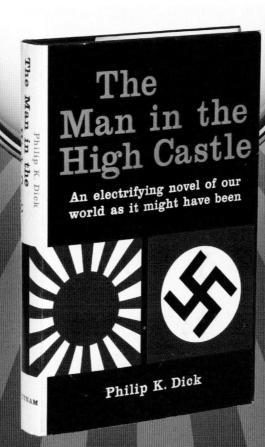

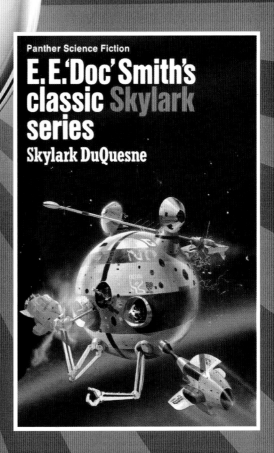

ABOVE: A selection of novels from the 1960s and 1970s

The Messiah Problem

The Cornelius series, which began with **The Final Programme** (1968), goes for the jugular. Jerry Cornelius himself indulges in a constant to and fro of casual sex, returns from the dead as a photo-negative version of himself, commits incest with his mother and sees all of Europe casually destroyed by a hybrid super-being. He embodies the destructive, iconoclastic riffing on the idea of a messiah beloved of some New Wave authors, coming not to keep the world as it is, but to destroy it – sharing the same initials, he is Jesus Christ reimagined as entropic antihero.

Messiah figures abound in 1960s SF literature, perhaps none more strange than the protagonist of John Barth's **Giles Goat-Boy** (1966). In this part bastard-messiah tale, part technophobic nightmare, two super computers make all decisions, anticipating modern obsessions with big data and the knowledge economy by several decades.

Giles, a human raised as a goat, eats straw and believes he is the messiah come to a world now reduced to two university campuses, each ruled by a computer – one in the West, one in the East, again reflecting real-world fretting over Cold War divisions. Long, randy and rambling, the novel's rape scenes and unflinching blasphemy were unsurprisingly shocking to contemporary audiences.

About Time

Faith, but also time and nuclear terror, lies at the heart of a novel that began with the 1960s and whose influence is still felt in modern SF. Walter M. Miller Jr.'s **A Canticle for Leibowitz** (1960) is set in a desert Catholic monastery in the far future, where our civilization has been destroyed by nuclear war and is in the process of rebuilding itself.

The timescale of the novel spans thousands of years, effectively rebooting humanity and running our history again, beginning 600 years after the 'Flame Deluge' (the novel's term for its nuclear apocalypse) and 'Simplification', where all learning and literature is destroyed. Following this, the monks of the Order of Leibowitz attempt to preserve human knowledge in secret.

Gradually humanity makes the same technological advances as before, arriving at the capacity for spaceflight just in time to wipe itself out once more with the use of nuclear weapons. Miller's somewhat pessimistic reading of human nature is that we will always engineer our destruction (there's that notion of entropy again) and that history is set on a repeating loop. That idea, appropriately, would come back around in the also-rebooted **Battlestar Galactica** (2004): all this has happened before, and will happen again.

Stranger in a Strange Land

While **A Canticle for Leibowitz** is built on Catholic doctrine and Catholic orthodoxies, Robert A. Heinlein proposed something rather different in **Stranger in a Strange Land** (1961).

Valentine Michael Smith is a human raised by Martians, who returns to Earth some time after a Third World War has been fought. He has psychic abilities and spends the novel experiencing Earth, its religions, people and pastimes –

ABOVE: *A Canticle for Leibowitz*'s ideas of humans repeating the same mistakes over and over resurfaced as a prominent theme in the *Battlestar Galactica* (2004) reboot

110

in particular hopping from bed to bed in a spirit of free love that would see the book enthusiastically taken up by students – until he founds his own religion, is duly martyred and seems to return in incorporeal form.

The novel shares many of the key themes of the era, offering another take on a messiah figure and our world after a cataclysmic conflict. Its stoner mysticism ('I am God. Thou art God … when a cat stalks a sparrow both of them are God, carrying out God's thoughts') enraptured some and enraged others, but its reach extended beyond the page; the Church of All Worlds, founded in 1968, takes some of its precepts, including (inevitably) polyamory, from the text. Oddly, the novel also seems to be one of the sources of inspiration for the reinvention and patenting of the waterbed.

Dune

Frank Herbert's **Dune** also concerns the coming of a messiah figure to the desert planet of Arrakis (also known as Dune), but weaves in an allegory for the oil industry, feudal struggles, political chicanery, an environmental angle and a blend of galactic mysticism that sees starship pilots taking 'spice', a drug which extends the human life-span and is produced by the giant sandworms lurking beneath Arrakis's deserts, in order to navigate through hyperspace.

Dune's protagonist is Paul Atreides, who vies with Baron Harkonnen for control of Arrakis, whose spice is a key resource of the galactic Empire. Their struggle blends inward-looking soft SF – Paul has psychic abilities and experiences transcendental visions – with aspects of hard SF, namely the deploying of a forbidden nuclear arsenal in order to end the conflict.

The novel and its sequels – including **Dune Messiah** (1969) and **God Emperor of Dune** (1981) – operate on many levels. Arrakis and its ecosystem are very much characters in their own right, setting **Dune** up as an ecological fable on a grand scale; yet there is also Paul's personal journey towards a kind of superhero status, which Herbert saw as a bad thing – charismatic leaders only bring upheaval, as the War 20 years earlier had shown. Further sequels, a film, games, fan fiction and music followed, creating a **Dune** megatext that has seen the imagined world of the novel attain its own shifting life, just like the sands of its all-encompassing deserts.

Interstellar Overdrive

Not every work of SF in the early 1960s was troubled by a God-complex – with Sputnik and Gagarin fresh in the mind, ships were still exploring the stars. Anne McCaffrey's Helva stories, opening with 1961's 'The Ship Who Sang', reimagined the starship as an extension of the body: disabled children are encased in metal shells that wire their brains to the ship itself. Over time female protagonist (and proto-cyborg) Helva learns how to 'be' the starship, all the while developing her own consciousness, in an elegant extended metaphor for both a personal journey through life and humanity's growth towards the stars. McCaffrey pointedly puts a woman in the driving seat, contrasting with the exclusively male roster of astronauts up until that point.

As a counterpoint to the restrained elegance of the Helva series there were rip-snorting adventures to be had in the company of characters such as Harry Harrison's **The Stainless Steel Rat** (1961), intergalactic conman, honourable thief and, notably, atheist. Harrison brought a trademark wit to

III

tales such as **Bill, the Galactic Hero** (1965), parodying space opera tropes of hypermasculinity and also exuberant use of punctuation in crowded-world drama **Make Room! Make Room!** (1966) and alternate Victorian fiction **A Transatlantic Tunnel, Hurrah!** (1972).

Like Clockwork

Straying beyond fun with exclamation marks, the form and function of language was an on-going line of enquiry for SF writers. The influence of Beat generation avatar William Burroughs, who wrote of language itself as a kind of contagion, can be felt throughout the decade, along with the trickledown effect of the Sapir-Whorf hypothesis, a linguistic theory suggesting that our language shapes and affects our worldview. Jack Vance had explored Sapir Whorf in **The Languages of Pao** (1958), and Samuel R. Delany's take on it is **Babel 17** (1966).

These concerns are never more apparent than in Anthony Burgess's futuristic dystopia **A Clockwork Orange** (1962), a feat of linguistic brio in which teenage malcontent Alex narrates his tale of ultraviolence in the invented slang of nadsat. His speech (and tendency to rape, beat and murder) defines him, cloaking him in an 'otherness' that the state tries to erase with oppressive conditioning techniques, transforming the novel into a meditation on free will.

Language and communication also lie at the heart of many of the novels of Stanisław Lem, and in particular the impossibility of meaningful understanding between humanity and alien cultures that share no common ground. In the

LEFT: *Director Steven Soderbergh wanted his version of Solaris (2002) to be close to the spirit of Stanislaw Lem's novel (1961).* ABOVE: Movie poster for *A Clockwork Orange* (1971), directed by Stanley Kubrick.

best-known example, **Solaris** (1961), humans helplessly study a sentient ocean planet, trying in vain to comprehend its mind, while it in turn probes and torments them with unfathomable psychological tricks; the two parties never approach any kind of entente.

Climate Change

A different kind of waterworld troubles Kerans, protagonist of J.G. Ballard's **The Drowned World** (1962). In 2145 the ice caps have melted, leaving London underwater and a carnival of tropical flora and fauna running riot above it.

The Drowned World forms a loose thematic trilogy with **The Burning World** (1964; retitled **The Drought** (1965) and **The Crystal World** (1966); the trio shares ecological musings with **Dune** brought about in part, some critics suggest, by the first images of the Earth from space, published in the same period. It's also concerned with time, which aligns it with Kurt Vonnegut's **Slaughterhouse-Five** (1969), in which Billy Pilgrim experiences time out of order and all at once: there is no single reality or narrative that can be depended upon.

Reality Bites

Exactly what constitutes reality was a near-constant question in the works of Philip K. Dick throughout the 1960s and 1970s. This was partly an existential, metaphysical line of enquiry, but also a direct response to the times he lived in, as he said himself (quoted in David Seed's **Science Fiction:**

ABOVE: J.G. Ballard imagined landscapes riven with economic disaster

ABOVE: The futuristic world imagined by Philip K. Dick in *Do Androids Dream of Electric Sheep?* (1968) would later be captured by the movie *Blade Runner* (1982)

A Very Short Introduction, 2011): 'We live in a society in which spurious realities are manufactured by the media, by governments, by corporations, by religious groups, political groups – and the hardware exists by which to deliver these pseudoworlds right into the heads of the reader, the viewer, the listener.'

Small wonder that Dick's fiction often leaves you wondering where you are. *Do Androids Dream of Electric Sheep?* (1968, later the foundation of Ridley Scott's 1984 film *Blade Runner*) features a world so stuffed with artificiality – in the form of androids, a wildly commercial religion and even fake animals – that it's tricky to know what is and isn't alive, or real. Memory and perception are shown to be just as fallible in 'We Can Remember It For You Wholesale' (1966), in which memory implants are big business. It later inspired two film adaptations: *Total Recall* (1990 and 2012). While the protagonists of the murky nightmare of *Ubik* (1969), and by extension the rest of us, are never sure if they're alive, dead, or some flickering version of both.

High Literature

Dick's unrealities are further enhanced by the mind-altering substances they're often laced with. *The Three Stigmata of Palmer Eldritch* (1965) not only repeats the messianic refrain of the era, but offers a literal trip: taking Chew-Z transports the user to another world. *Ubik*, meanwhile, refers to a multi-purpose can of something that can halt or reverse death (among other things), making it a kind of anti-entropy cosmetic; or is it God revealing himself in a mysterious way? Maddeningly, the point is not to know.

Similarly maddening is *Dhalgren*, Samuel R. Delany's 1975 novel that infuriated Dick himself and remains a challenging prospect for the reader. A complex rendering of the idea of unreliable reality, the novel is notionally set in the crumbling city of Bellona and features a skittish, raving narrative and perpetually shifting perspectives of place and time. The sun rises then sets in the same place. Streets move. The narrator loses all sense of left, right, memory and self. Deliberately unsettling and cyclical (the opening and closing sentences could be read as running into one another, while a notebook found in the novel seems to contain a slightly altered version of the novel itself), it's regarded by some as the zenith of New Wave expression and innovation. For others it's the moment the wheels came off the space wagon.

Alternative Reality

Running parallel to these questions of unreality and perception are the related questions of ideal worlds (or utopias) and alternative histories. What if things had gone differently? Philip K. Dick explores the latter with *The Man in the High Castle* (1962), set in a 1960s where Hitler has won the War and the United States is divided between Germany and Japan.

Division is also central to Ursula K. Le Guin's *The Dispossessed* (1974), which features a prominent wall motif and contrasting planets Urras and Annares that echo the contemporary focus on the division of the Berlin Wall. Elsewhere, Joanna Russ uses a utopian society (among others) to explore feminist thinking and gender barriers in *The Female Man* (1975): in various realities, men are extinct; a woman navigates the world feeling she must pretend to be a 'female man'; the sexes are at war with one another; and the Depression rumbles on.

ABOVE: Rufus Sewell as Obergruppenführer John Smith in *The Man in the High Castle* TV series (2015–), depicting the world of Philip K. Dick's novel (1962), in which Hitler won the Second World War

Gender fluidity (alongside an innate sense of the need for balance and harmony with your surroundings, inspired by Taoism) is also an important part of an earlier Le Guin novel, **The Left Hand of Darkness** (1969), depicting the inhabitants of the ice world of Winter, who have no fixed gender and simply assume one or another depending on their situation.

More Than a Woman

Women's rights and feminism became more loudly discussed as the 1970s progressed, with the publication of books such as Germaine Greer's **The Female Eunuch** (1970). In SF, notions of gender and feminine identity were given an uncompromising working over (albeit with a twinkle in the eye) in the writing of James Tiptree Jr. (real name Alice Sheldon). The one-time CIA operative goes as far as configuring all human space exploration, with its phallic rockets, as a kind of galactic groin-thrust in 'A Momentary Taste of Being' (1975), imagining Earth as 'a planet-testicle pushing a monster penis towards the stars'.

Elsewhere, a man on a space station finds himself sexually obsessed by an alien despite the fact they wouldn't, well, fit together in any way ('And I Awoke to Find Me Here on the Cold Hill's Side', 1972), while 'The Girl Who Was Plugged In' (1973) sees a plain girl, P. Burke, offered a chance to remotely pilot a beautiful elf drone and thus finally be seen as beautiful. It's a comment on male constructs of female beauty as well as more universal recognition of social anxiety, and, as Adam Roberts argues, 'prescient of the 21st-century strategy of mediating social interaction through the online discourse of social media'. Like Burke, we hide our true selves behind a carefully crafted artificial version of 'us' that we're happy with.

Ladies and Gentlemen, We Are Floating in Space

Amid all of this inner questing and tinkering with notions of form, time, entropy and sex, it might be easy to assume that SF literature of the Hard or Golden Age persuasion had simply packed up and left during the 1960s and 1970s. Far from it. Instead, while NASA planned, built and eventually launched its first space station, Skylab, and of course landed men on the Moon, some notable works toyed with the idea of cosmic megastructures.

First, Larry Niven's **Ringworld** (1970) posited the idea of a million-mile-wide ring or band whose circumference is roughly that of Earth's orbit – so large that it surrounds its sun – with its own gravity, day and night, and atmosphere, on which a band of explorers crash land. Arthur C. Clarke's **Rendezvous With Rama** (1973) cast a mysterious alien cylinder into our solar system for humanity to enter and puzzle over.

Meanwhile on Earth, the Vietnam War also cast a long shadow. Joe Haldeman's **The Forever War** (1974), inspired in part by the author's own experiences in Vietnam, sees the time dilation resulting from interstellar travel drag out a conflict with an alien race over centuries – a flinty metaphor for the ceaseless grind of war and its gradual dislocation of combatants from their 'own' time; an experience many returning veterans would share as they came back to a society unsure of what to do with them.

ABOVE: The feminist movement of the 1970s drove the creation of SF TV shows like *The Bionic Woman* (1976–78)

MAGAZINES AND TV SCREENS

There's also an argument to be made for the contribution of Marvel Comics, and Stan Lee in particular, to the field of SF in the period. Iron Man's first appearance in **Tales of Suspense** in 1963 gave the world an injured mortal augmented by technology – certainly an SF trope – who could act as a vehicle for exploring Cold War themes. Likewise the mutated, enhanced X-Men (**The X-Men**, 1963) fought for equality against the backdrop of a real-world society beset with racial prejudices.

Like many of the stories of the period, Haldeman's tale was initially serialized in magazine form. Parallel to the influence and success of *New Worlds*, the big hitters of the Golden Age continued – *Astounding* was renamed *Analog Science Fact* ⌢→ *Science Fiction* to move it away from pulpy sensationalism and reflect the new realities of science fact brought about by space travel. *Dune*'s first appearance was in serial form in *Analog* and the magazine published work from other influential 1960s writers, including Harry Harrison.

Under the editorship of Ben Bova from 1972 to 1978 the magazine continued to evolve, publishing Haldeman's work alongside experimental writers such as Harlan Ellison and Roger Zelazny. **Galaxy** and **If** magazines also had on-going success, the latter publishing Larry Niven's first story, 'The Coldest Place' (about the dark side of Mercury) in 1964. (Unfortunately for Niven, it was established in 1965 that Mercury does not have a permanent dark side.)

SF and the Civil Rights Movement

Indeed, it's pretty difficult not to see an allegory of the African-American civil rights movement of the 1960s playing out in the pages of the X-Men comics. Professor X and arch-villain Magneto effectively represent two sides of the same coin (and therefore to some commentators Martin Luther King Jr. and Malcolm X); both want freedom for their people and to be recognized without hatred, but they have radically different approaches to achieving that goal.

ABOVE: Professor X and Magneto from the *X-Men* (portrayed here by Patrick Stewart and Ian McKellen in the 2000 movie) could be seen as an allegory for the Civil Rights movement

The X-Men themselves are a diverse collective frequently depicted as being on the receiving end of bigotry or racially motivated violence. Their numbers include Magneto and Sabra (Jewish), Dust (Muslim), Nightcrawler (Catholic), Thunderbird (Hindu), Gambit (of Cajun descent), Warpath (Apache Native American) and Storm (born of African-American and Kenyan parents). But of course it is their mutant status that sets them apart, the comics at once championing diversity and decrying intolerance.

Other literary SF works of the era surely echoed with the repercussions of the 1964 Civil Rights Act, the race riots and marches of the decade and the assassination of King and Malcolm X – issues of race and nationality can be seen in the works of Le Guin and Delany to name but two – once again using the medium to look inwards at human nature as seen through the prism of outsiders and strange new worlds. Speaking of which....

Star Trek

A full account of the voyages of the **Starship Enterprise** to strange new worlds could fill (and has filled) entire books, so we must be cruelly brief here.

Broadcast between 1966 and 1969, **Star Trek – The Original Series** was created by Gene Roddenberry and featured the dramatic escapades of the crew of the **USS Enterprise**, a giant starship sent out into the cosmos on a five-year mission of exploration. The show's occasional – all right, frequent – moments of campness, humour and oddness have in some ways come to

ABOVE: The cast of the original *Star Trek* TV series (1966–69): James Doohan, Walter Koenig, DeForest Kelley, Majel Barrett, William Shatner, Nichelle Nichols, Leonard Nimoy and George Takei

define it to the casual viewer, but there's much more going on beneath all that trouble with Tribbles.

Star Trek was pioneering in its use of leading SF writers, including Harlan Ellison, Norman Spinrad and Theodore Sturgeon, to work on its screenplays. While its dramatic core lay in the friendships – what we would now call 'bromances' – between Captain Kirk (William Shatner), Science Officer Spock (Leonard Nimoy) and Dr 'Bones' McCoy (DeForest Kelley), its creative writing team and far-future setting allowed it to explore many contemporary SF themes: racism is tackled in 'Let That Be Your Last Battlefield', while questions about religion and its impact on free will suffuse the melancholic 'Who Mourns for Adonais?'

About Time

The series also strove with varying degrees of success for equality with its diverse, multi-racial crew and balanced treatment of women (it occasionally wobbled on this one), again reflecting contemporary social issues, but it was time that gave the series what many regard as its finest moment.

The Harlan Ellison-scripted 'City on the Edge of Forever' is effectively another 'Nazis won the War' alternate reality tale enabled by a time gateway McGuffin. Stranded in the 1930s, Kirk, Spock and McCoy realize that in order to restore the universe to 'our' version, they must allow pacifist Edith Keeler (Joan Collins), with whom Kirk is in love, to die. The morally complex tale is performed with heart-breaking earnestness by Shatner and won several awards on release.

Time was the central plot device driving another vast, yet less crowded, vessel. **Doctor Who** first aired in 1963, one day after the assassination of President John F. Kennedy. Initially planned as a quasi-educational programme that would inform viewers about historical events through the travels of its titular Time Lord in his TARDIS time machine, the Doctor's adventures soon took a wholly different direction. A cunning 'regeneration' plot device allowed multiple actors to play the Doctor, and as the character evolved, so did the series.

Sofa Time

Early **Doctor Who** featured recurring, almost effortlessly iconic villains – Daleks, Cybermen – pitted against a curiously charismatic protagonist. The Doctor would face adversity with cheer, resourcefulness and a good-natured stereotypical Britishness (and in the case of Tom Baker, the Doctor from 1974 to 1981, a fine scarf). All of which makes it sound jolly. It wasn't.

At its best, 1960s and 1970s **Doctor Who** was as terrifying and unsettling as anything literary SF could conjure. Admittedly their realization on screen requires some suspension of disbelief, but the emotionless, genetically modified fascist tanks that are the Daleks are an unnerving concept. 1971's 'Terror of the Autons' boasts murderous dolls, blank-faced policemen and killer flora – all classic horror tropes – while 'The Brain of Morbius' (1976) features a severed brain falling to the floor. These and many more moments gave rise to the idea of 'watching TV from behind the sofa'.

While tonally very different, both **Star Trek** and **Doctor Who** are important steps in the evolution of SF from stand-alone stories to vast, meta/megatextual enterprises (no

ABOVE: The Starship *Enterprise* from the original *Star Trek* TV series (1966–69)

ABOVE: The first four TV Doctors: William Hartnell, Jon Pertwee & Patrick Troughton, Tom Baker (& Lalla Ward); Peter Cushing faced the Doctor's oldest enemies in *Doctor Who and The Daleks* (1965)

pun intended). Both inspired spin-off novels, radio programmes, comics, cartoons, fan fiction and films – now standard fare for the discerning modern SF property.

Vision On

The two programmes are also way markers on SF's journey from a solely print-based form to what Adam Roberts calls 'a genre dominated by visual media and … what we might call visual spectacularism'. In particular, they highlight the growing importance of television as a storytelling medium – as the 1960s progressed, more homes had sets, and increasingly colour ones.

Other popular shows were quick to take advantage of this wider palette. **Lost in Space** (1965–68) updated the Swiss Family Robinson, while the enjoyably daft **The Time Tunnel** (1966–67) proved that in the case of time-travel themed shows, lightning didn't always strike twice. More startling – and perhaps more in keeping with the vim and vigour of the psychedelic era – were Gerry and Sylvia Anderson's glorious puppets, starring in shows including **Thunderbirds** (1965–66), **Captain Scarlet** (1967–68) and **Joe 90** (1968–69). The last had perhaps the most intriguingly New Wave concept: a youngster can download the skills and attributes of various adults directly into his brain. How very **Matrix**.

Then of course there were the gloomy thrills and surreal chills of **The Twilight Zone** (1959–64) and **The Outer Limits** (1963–65), all adding to the appeal of the little screen in the living room. However, the big screen was about to take SF somewhere else entirely.

SF CINEMA IN THE 1960S & 1970S

We're approaching a monolithic cinema landmark. But there are some other important sights to see first. *The Time Machine* (George Pal, 1960), an adaptation of the H.G. Wells novel, is significant for its visual treatment of moving through time using stop-motion photography: dress styles change in shop windows, sunrises and sunsets race past, and – more gooey – a corpse rots and decays in moments. It also has a point to make about Cold War paranoia, featuring a 1960s nuclear bombardment of London.

121

Apocalyptic terror was served up somewhat contrastingly in **Dr No** and **La Jetée** (Terence Young, Chris Marker respectively, both 1962), the former setting James Bond off on his decades' long romp, accompanied by all the SF trappings of tech and villains with world-killing weapons. The latter, an oblique French affair, raked over the tragic aftermath of nuclear war and the failing attempts of scientists to make things right with time travel.

Meanwhile, **Dr Strangelove** (Stanley Kubrick, 1964) invited us to love the bomb with its coal-black comedy, physical twitchiness (Peter Sellers in the title

ABOVE: The cast of *Lost in Space* (1965–68): Mark Goddard, June Lockhart, Guy Williams, Billy Mumy, Angela Cartwright, Jonathan Harris and Marta Kristen

role excels himself, hand flicking into involuntary Nazi salutes) and satirizing of the authorities with their fingers on the button.

Inside Out

Elsewhere, **The Man With X Ray Eyes** (Roger Corman, 1963) sees only emptiness at the heart of the universe and goes mad, while **Fantastic Voyage** (Richard Fleischer, 1966) sends miniaturized scientists into the human body, rendering organs themselves as fantastical backdrops as it melds hallucinatory visuals with a side order of Cold War jitters. Both literally reflect the more inward-looking preoccupations of New Wave SF.

Barbarella (Roger Vadim, 1968), however, reflected another aspect of the Swinging Sixties: the peace, love and empathy part. At least on the surface. Gaudy, fur-trimmed and lascivious, the film's so-what plot sends Jane Fonda's intergalactic super agent after a doomsday weapon; she carelessly, repeatedly manages to lose most of her clothes along the way. A camp cult hit, **Barbarella** manages the balancing act of slyly sending up the hippy-dippy dream it seems to espouse, while at the same time frankly acknowledging that, as the Vietnam War sank deeper into the mire, what the world actually did need was love, sweet love.

If **Barbarella** was the glamorous, goofy, fun kid at the party in 1968, though, Stanley Kubrick's offering was the absurdly good-looking but serious fellow in earnest conversation in the corner.

2001: A Space Odyssey

Introspective, enigmatic, yet transcendent, **2001: A Space Odyssey** (Stanley Kubrick, 1968) is the high point of 1960s SF cinema. Kubrick's giant leap was to truly understand that the medium could be the message, using music, style and special effects to wordlessly convey the existential and the metaphysical, offering insights that could be grasped intuitively but then never properly explained. It's film as symphony, or Zen riddle – the gateless gate, the wordless word.

The story was developed from Arthur C. Clarke's 'The Sentinel' (1951), becoming both a film and a novel, written in parallel (Clarke later said that the screenplay should be credited to Kubrick and Clarke, the novel to Clarke and Kubrick, hinting at the driving force behind each). There are four acts, or movements: primitive man is exposed to a strange monolith; man ascends to space; the starship **Discovery** explores a new monolith in space; astronaut Bowman travels through a star gate.

The suggestion is that the alien monoliths are responsible for man's evolution, and that we – like the astronauts of the **Discovery** – have merely been passengers on our journey to the stars. The film ends with the cryptic image of Bowman/the Star Child, a vast foetus in orbit around Earth.

Mona Lisa Smile

What does it all mean? The novel is more explicit, but the film was never intended to provide answers. It alludes to a messianic rebirth and many

ABOVE: *Barbarella* (1968), directed by Roger Vadim, was a camp cult hit starring Jane Fonda

other New Wave themes: the influence of the Space Race; the true nature of man; balls-out psychedelia during the minutes-long plummet through the star gate; technophobia and alienation of the self, courtesy of the dwindling sanity of HAL, the **Discovery**'s ever-more-murderous computer. But it offers few conclusions; things are simply there.

The film **2001** is both uniquely a product of its time and quite apart from it. Stately, serious and clinical where **Star Trek** or **Barbarella** were groovy, optimistic and vibrant, it looked (and still looks) like nothing else. That's the key to it, as Kubrick told **Playboy** in 1968. 'How much would we appreciate La Gioconda today if Leonardo had written at the bottom of the canvas: This lady is smiling slightly because she has rotten teeth – or because she's hiding a secret from her lover? It would shut off the viewer's appreciation and shackle him to a reality other than his own. I don't want that to happen to **2001**.'

And Kubrick wasn't done there. Not for one moment, O my brothers and sisters.

SF Cinema 1968–76

While not many other films from the period made the cultural impression that **2001** did, there were still several other important additions to the SF canon. Kubrick's next outing, **A Clockwork Orange** (1971) married a stylistic bravado to the novel's gutsy linguistic tolchocking that has made every successive generation perversely curious to dress up in white boiler suits and bowler hats.

Meanwhile, **Planet of the Apes** (Franklin J. Schaffner, 1968) took Armageddon and ran for the hills with it, positing a deep future where apes rule the world. The final shot has passed into cliché but remains one of the great cinematic rug-pulls. Elsewhere, **Night of the Living Dead** (George A. Romero, 1968) and **The Andromeda Strain** (Robert Wise, 1971), which was based on a 1969 Michael Crichton novel of the same name, looked at extra-terrestrial contamination with dread, posing the question 'It's all very well to go, but what if something comes back?'

Romero's film reverberates with a racial tension that chimed with its age: its black protagonist survives a zombie onslaught but is shot by a posse of white men, an uncomfortable call-back to mob lynchings and the assassinations of Martin Luther King Jr. and Malcolm X. Some contemporary critics also saw, in its violence, an echo of the Vietnam War's horrors. Closing off the period, David Bowie as **The Man Who Fell to Earth** (Nicolas Roeg, 1976), which was based on Walter Trevis's 1963 novel with the same title, used an alien outsider to hold up a mirror to our selfish, sometimes incomprehensible drives and desires. We were still very much looking inwards.

123

ABOVE: *2001: A Space Odyssey* (1968) was the high point of 1960s science fiction cinema. RIGHT: Movie poster for *The Man Who Fell to Earth* (1976), directed by Nicolas Roeg.

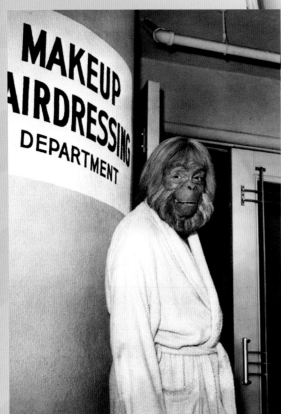

ABOVE: Poster art, stills and behind-the-scenes moments from *Planet of the Apes* (1968), directed by Franklin J. Schaffner

ALTERED IMAGES

As the contrasting styles of the SF cinema of the period show, the 1960s and early 1970s may have been reduced now to lava lamps, flares and bubble lettering, but the truth was much more varied, and not everything was groovy, baby. Artists of the period were no different. Paul Lehr's future fantasies pulsed with technicolour but were always edged in darkness – by contrast, John Harris embraced the vast scale and megastructures of hard SF with his cool, refined lines.

The reality of spaceflight may well have turned out to be less than sexy looking, but it didn't matter: John Berkey and Chris Foss had that angle covered. Berkey's spaceship book covers somehow combine a 1960s *Dr No*-ish aesthetic with a Concorde-in-space vibe that makes them elegant and exciting; Foss used airbrush techniques to create gleaming, functional but thrilling-looking craft (when not doing that, he was the original illustrator of *The Joy of Sex* by Alex Comfort, 1972). Equally soaring but also peering into the subconscious, *Arzach* (1975) by Jean Giraud (Moebius) is a comic without words that blends fantasy and futurism to roam the psyche, just as Ballard had hoped.

Yet despite all of this artistic, literary and cinematic verve, by the mid-1970s it seemed that the promise of Kennedy's speech and the hope and optimism of the era itself was running low. The man himself was dead, the spectre of Vietnam and race riots haunted the United States, and the United Kingdom had endured a period of economic stagnation, unemployment and electricity rationing. Our time on the Moon had ended and it seemed that humanity was truly grounded once more. By 1976 the SF New Wave was faltering. We needed a new hope.

ABOVE: SF artists have always enjoyed a variety of styles, with some preferring bright colours yet dark realities

6: BACK TO THE FUTURE

1977

1977 • *Close Encounters of the Third Kind* • Steven Spielberg
Movie

1977 • *Star Wars: Episode IV – A New Hope* • George Lucas
Movie

1977 • *Gateway* • Frederik Pohl
Novel

1977 • First issue of *2000AD* • Pat Mills, John Wagner, Kelvin Gosnell
Comic

1977 • *Lucifer's Hammer* • Larry Niven and Jerry Pournelle
Novel

1978

1978 • First episode of *Battlestar Galactica* • Glen A. Larson
TV

1978 • *The Hitchhiker's Guide to the Galaxy* • Douglas Adams
Radio

1978 • *Superman* • Richard Donner
Movie

1979 • *Alien* • Ridley Scott
Movie

1979 • *Star Trek: The Motion Picture* • Robert Wise
Movie

1979 • *Mad Max* • George Miller
Movie

1979 • *Kindred* • Octavia E. Butler
Novel

1982

1982 • *Blade Runner* • Ridley Scott
Movie

1982 • *E.T. the Extra-Terrestrial* • Steven Spielberg
Movie

1982 • *Tron* • Steven Lisberger
Movie

1982 • *The Thing* • John Carpenter
Movie

1982 • 'Burning Chrome' • William Gibson
Short Story

1982 • *The Space Eater* • David Langford
Novel

1982 • *Helliconia Spring* • Brian Aldiss
Novel

1982 • *The Crystal Singer* • Anne McCaffrey
Novel

1983 • *WarGames* • John Badham
Movie

1983 • *Frankenstein* • Bernie Wrightson
Comic

1984 • *The Terminator* • James Cameron
Movie

1984 • *Dune* • David Lynch
Movie

1984 • *Neuromancer* • William Gibson
Novel

1984 • First episode of *The Transformers* • Marvel Productions, Sunbow Productions and Toei
TV

1984 • First episode of *Threads* • BBC
TV

Philosophy | **Science & Technology** | **Novels** | **Short Story Story** | **World Events Events** | **Movies** | **Magazines** | **Comics** | **Play** | **Pulp Magazines Magaziunes** | **Radio** | **Small Publishers** | **TV** | **Video Games**

1985

1985 • *Back to the Future* • Robert Zemeckis
Movie
1985 • First episode of *The Twilight Zone* • Rod Serling
TV
1985 • *The Handmaid's Tale* • Margaret Atwood
Novel
1985 • *Ender's Game* • Orson Scott Card
Novel
1985 • *Eon* • Greg Bear
Novel
1986 • Explosion of Space Shuttle Challenger • NASA
Science & Technology
1986 • Chernobyl disaster • Ukraine
World Event
1986 • *Flight of the Navigator* • Randal Kleiser
Movie
1986 • First issue of *Watchmen* • Alan Moore, Dave Gibbons,
John Higgins
Comic

1987

1987 • *Dawn* • Octavia E. Butler
Novel
1987 • First episode of *Star Trek: The Next Generation* •
Gene Roddenberry
TV
1987 • *RoboCop* • Paul Verhoeven
Movie
1987 • *Innerspace* • Joe Dante
Movie
1987 • *Predator* • John McTiernan
Movie
1987 • *Consider Phlebas* • Iain M. Banks
Novel
1988 • *Akira* • Katsuhiro Otomo
Movie
1988 • First episode of *Red Dwarf* •
Rob Grant and Doug Naylor
TV
1988 • First episode of *Mystery Science Theater 3000* •
Joel Hodgson
TV

1989

1989 • The Berlin Wall comes down • Germany
World Event
1989 • *Hyperion* • Dan Simmons
Novel
1989 • First episode of *Quantum Leap* • Donald P. Bellisario
TV
1989 • Invention of the World Wide Web • Tim Berners-Lee
Science & Technology

A CLIMATE OF FEAR

space shuttle launched successfully in 1981, but space shuttle *Challenger* exploded in 1986; in the Soviet Union the Chernobyl nuclear reactor exploded a few months later.

Strange Days

It's possible that the key work of science fiction of the early 1980s had nothing to do with novels, cinema or the genre as a whole. Instead, *Protect and Survive* (1980) was a series of public information broadcasts and leaflets designed to educate the public about surviving a nuclear strike. The 'science' part was sound; the 'fiction', campaigners argued, was that a nuclear strike would be a single event and that nuclear war would do anything but annihilate the human race.

It was with this tone of apocalyptic dread humming in the background that the 1970s ticked over into the 1980s. Nuclear Armageddon seemed not only possible but likely, as the Cold War became ever more tense and newly elected US President Ronald Reagan (1980) promised to consign the 'evil empire' of the Soviet Union to 'the ash heap of history'. Conflict between the UK and Argentina also broke out over sovereignty of the Falkland Islands (1982) in the South Atlantic Ocean.

Into this toxic geopolitical stew were tossed moments of progress and tragedy: the first

Contrasts abounded: corporate power grew against a background of rising unemployment; there was conspicuous wealth and there were miners' strikes. Stock markets boomed, then busted. Music spat out the snarling adrenaline rush of punk, but also the fearless, puckish joy of Michael Jackson's masterpiece, *Thriller* (1982).

Small wonder then that SF of the period was equally contrasting, going for big, broad space operas on one hand, and claustrophobic, Armageddon-flecked techno-nightmares on the other. The Cold War could be felt throughout, as could the cultural back-and-forth over women's rights (or lack of them) and race relations – particularly in the light of South Africa's policies of apartheid. Many novels and films displayed a wariness of governments and the power of corporations. This was the age of political bands like The Clash, satirical puppet show *Spitting Image* and furious stand-up comics such as Bill Hicks.

The one consistent move seemed to be backwards, away from the introspection and narrative juggling of the New Wave and towards the classic tropes of Golden Age SF, unashamedly telling big stories on a grand canvas. And in 1977, the biggest SF story of them all began.

ABOVE: The real world threat of nuclear war influenced a lot of science fiction from this period

SF MOVIES: 1977 AND ONWARDS

and C-3PO) was a lift from Akira Kurosawa's samurai yarn **The Hidden Fortress** (1958), as is their bickering interaction. Lucas has openly acknowledged his debt to Kurosawa's film over the years.

I'm Luke Skywalker, I'm Here to Rescue You

No one could argue for the originality of **A New Hope**'s plot, either – rescuing a princess from a castle (even one in space) was hardly avant-garde story-telling. In fact, Lucas has claimed it was deliberately archetypal, drawing heavily on Joseph Campbell's **The Hero With a Thousand Faces** (1949), a study of comparative mythology that proposed a 'monomyth', or fundamental structure, shared by myths from all cultures over thousands of years.

I t seems only appropriate that a film set 'a long time ago' should have rifled through SF's big box of back issues. To mine the origins of and inspirations for *Star Wars* (George Lucas, 1977, retitled *Star Wars: Episode IV: A New Hope* in 1981) is to delve into the entire history of SF. Lucas plundered pulp comics, early TV serials and films for the raw materials of his game-changing space opera, adding a judicious pinch of Japanese cinema, Arthurian romance and comparative mythology for good measure.

129

In his introduction to the book, Campbell summarizes the monomyth as follows: 'A hero ventures forth from the world of common day into a region of supernatural wonder: fabulous forces are there encountered and a decisive victory is won: the hero comes back from this mysterious adventure with the power to bestow boons on his fellow man.'

Much of the story is built on elements found in the **Flash Gordon** serials of the 1930s. Two heroes dressed as enemy soldiers entering a fortress? Check. A space princess and a giant, hirsute ally? Check. A city in the sky and dogfighting spaceships? You get the idea.

Lucas also used Jungian archetypal figures – characters formed from elements of the collective unconscious, from types of characters that we would all find somehow familiar. Hence the Wise Old Man/Mentor (Obi-Wan Kenobi), or the Hero (Luke Skywalker).

A few more examples of Lucas's magpie-like retro-fitting: **A New Hope** was infused with aspects of pulp comic **Buck Rogers**, and there's more than a little of **Dune** in its desert world of Tattooine. Meanwhile, his narrative approach of telling the story from the point of view of two lowly, servile characters (R2-D2

So, Luke Skywalker (Mark Hamill, the Hero) leaves Tattooine, is schooled in the Force by Obi-Wan Kenobi (Alec Guinness, the Wise Old Man),

ABOVE: The device of telling the story from the point of view of the two robots in *Star Wars* (1977) showed clear influences from *The Hidden Fortress* (1958)

ABOVE: Posters and stills from *Star Wars Episode IV: A New Hope* (1977), *Star Wars Episode V: The Empire Strikes Back* (1980), *Star Wars Episode VI: The Return of the Jedi* (1983)

encounters the Rebel Alliance and Darth Vader (David Prowse/James Earl Jones), destroys the Death Star and returns empowered, ready to fight on against the evil Galactic Empire.

A Cinematic Vision

If all of the above seems a bit dry, it's there to highlight the fact that while the building blocks of **A New Hope** were archetypal, referential, familiar – even dull – the end result was anything but. On screen, the film was miraculous. It looked like nothing else, its 'used future' conceit of a well-worn world actually making it seem more vibrantly alive.

Subsequent films **The Empire Strikes Back** (Irvin Kershner, 1980) and **Return of the Jedi** (Richard Marquand, 1983) further highlighted two magical elements of the series: the alluring mysticism of the Force, and the charismatic performances of its principal actors. Through Luke's training with Jedi Master Yoda the world was gifted endlessly quotable inspiration ('Do, or do not: there is no try'); while the wry asides of Harrison Ford (as Han Solo) or the twinkle-eyed irony of Carrie Fisher (Princess Leia) elevated awkwardly written characters into people to root for and identify with.

Time and again though, it was the visual beats that proved iconic: the **Millennium Falcon**'s spine-tingling cavalry charge from **A New Hope;** the I-am-your-father shock of **Empire** (a secret so closely guarded that Hamill only found out moments before shooting the big reveal scene); the climactic lightsabre duel of **Jedi**. The triumph of **Star Wars** marked a turning point – from 1977 onwards, SF would become more and more a visual form.

Life, But Not As We Know It

Adding to the iconic heft of Lucas's imagined galaxy are the countless outlandish alien creatures that inhabit it. It's another pulp trope – the alien encounter – that was embraced enthusiastically throughout the period as humanity met benign life from the stars, and life that was anything but.

Beginning with the benign, **E.T. – The Extra Terrestrial** (Steven Spielberg, 1982) is unforgettable for its diminutive, Christ-like alien (a motif lying at the heart of so much SF), numinous mood and sheer emotional punch. Lost on Earth, E.T. is sheltered by children, and you never forget the choking terror of dispassionate authority as seen through a child's eyes when E.T. is found and taken away. Likewise, his death, ecstatic resurrection and bicycles-in-flight liberation have lost none of their power over the years. To see E.T. is to experience the transcendent power of compassion, of love as a death-defying force.

Other benign aliens sang a duet with quizzical mankind in Spielberg's other alien movie, **Close Encounters of the Third Kind** (1977); while James Cameron's **The Abyss** (1989) kept its friendly aliens at the bottom of the sea, and is a strange mishmash of deep-pressure tension and suddenly gloopy let's-all-hug melodrama.

131

ABOVE: The iconic flying bicycle scene from *E.T.* (1982), directed by Steven Spielberg

How Do You Like Your Eggs?

There's no hugging to be found in **Alien** (Ridley Scott, 1979), a film that shifted cinematic representations of extra-terrestrial life away from Golden Age conventions of benign indulgence towards something altogether more malevolent. E.T. would make your heart metaphorically burst out of your chest; Scott's xenomorph would do it literally.

The plot is effectively one of a haunted-house movie in space, as the crew of downbeat cargo vessel **Nostromo** (taking cues from Lucas's dog-eared spaceships) are slowly picked off by a scarcely seen alien life-form they unwittingly take on board. The gloomy bowels of the ship are light years away from the cool white of **2001: A Space Odyssey**'s ship **Discovery** and provide plenty of chances for half-lit nightmarish deaths.

Even more arresting is the biomechanical grue of Swiss artist H.R. Giger's alien designs. Technology seems grimly sexual and atavistically predatory; the alien itself is a slavering, teeth-gnashing, monstrously phallic demon. There's no ambiguity here: this is A Bad Guy. Coupled with some truly startling body shocks (in particular the infamous chest-bursting scene, now long passed into cinema lore), **Alien** totally changed the way cinema would approach encounters with the unknown.

Game Over, Man

Alien was also notable because of its hard-as-coffin-nails female action-hero, Ripley (Sigourney Weaver), an unusual screen presence at the time. Instead of

ABOVE: The H.R. Giger Museum Bar in Gruyeres, Switzerland, which is themed along the lines of his biomechanical style as shown in the *Alien* films

playing second-fiddle to a man, or gradually building to a crescendo of terror in contrast to an earlier state of virginal passivity (as with the 'Final Girl' in conventional horror movies), Ripley starts the film tough and ends it tougher. Some feminist readings suggest that **Alien** itself is about womanhood and a stark representation of the female body, as signified by both Ripley (grimy, sweating, blood-spattered and visceral) and the **Nostromo** itself (dark, cavernous, womb-like).

What's worse than one alien? Loads of aliens, of course. **Aliens** (James Cameron, 1986) saw Ripley return to the crash site of the first film, this time with a tooled-up outfit of space marines set on wiping the creatures out. An adrenaline-soaked thunderclap of gun battles and nasty deaths ensues, the aliens again given ferocious life by Giger's set and creature designs. It's a very different film, more crash-bang-wallop than the shadowy terror of the original, but no less successful, and thanks to the shady 'Company' that is secretly trying to bring an alien back to Earth, it has plenty to say about corporate morality in contemporary culture.

The Man Who Fell to Earth

Advances in special effects meant that in 1978 we were promised 'You'll believe a man can fly'; not really a man, of course, but another alien. This time Kryptonian. **Superman** (Richard Donner, 1978) flew into a world that in 1978 probably felt like it needed him: the United States was wearied and wounded from Watergate and the loss of the Vietnam War just a few years earlier, US/ USSR relations were souring, and there was mounting social disquiet on both sides of the Atlantic.

In Christopher Reeve, the Man of Steel found his definitive on-screen expression. His Kal-el is generous, moral, compassionate and with a gentle wrinkle of good humour; when he first appears in costume there's little doubt that he simply **is** Superman. Audiences and critics alike believed and the film soared, along with an even better sequel (**Superman II**, Richard Donner, 1981). Both featured memorable arch villains (Lex Luthor in the first, General Zod the second) and explored notions of a divine being walking the Earth, the Christian God and Christ (in the form of Superman's father and the man himself), the subsequent fall and resurrection, and what it is to be human (or superhuman). Further sequels offered diminishing returns, but the first two were optimistic and glowing with such old-fashioned, Golden Age charm that they remain uplifting today.

133

Fantastic Voyages

While Superman fell to Earth, other films of the period took us on journeys into space, through time and even into the human body itself. **Explorers** (Joe Dante, 1985) is something of a curiosity, as studio pressures meant it was never truly finished and was rushed into cinemas. Yet it has a definite charm (thanks in part to performances from a young Ethan Hawke and River Phoenix) and is surprisingly meta-fictional, presenting both human and alien children going off on sci-fi adventures inspired by watching, yup, sci-fi adventures. There's also a knowing aside that aliens have steered clear of Earth because of our treatment of them in the movies. It's a fair cop.

Equally odd and charming (although now a touch dated), **Flight of the Navigator** (Randal Kleiser, 1986) used the authentically SF trope of time

ABOVE: Christopher Reeve in *Superman* (1978), directed by Richard Donner

dilation – seen in many stories over the last few decades, and still popular in novels of this period such as Dan Simmons' **Hyperion** series, discussed below – to set a young boy eight years adrift of his family courtesy of an alien encounter. Updating **Fantastic Voyage**, meanwhile, **Innerspace** (also Joe Dante, 1987) brought a dose of screwball comedy to the miniaturization drama, while enjoying what updated visual effects could do to build on the original premise.

Who Are You?

Innerspace's hapless hero has something of an existential crisis when he hears voices in his head (actually coming from the miniaturized pod in his bloodstream and its pilot), but his problems pale to nothing compared to the wider identity crisis posed in **Blade Runner** (Ridley Scott, 1982), a version of the Philip K. Dick tale **Do Androids Dream of Electric Sheep?**

Harrison Ford is Deckard, the man charged with hunting down and terminating rogue replicants – synthetic humans looking to override their limited four-year lifespans. Scott conjures a constantly shifting cityscape in his hellish vision of a future Los Angeles, where layer upon layer of accreted culture mashes and bleeds into a mass of painful light, heavy glow and shadow; as Scott said, he was aiming for the overwhelming contrasts of Hong Kong 'on a really bad day'.

There are recurring eye motifs hinting that all is not as it appears, along with an extended riff on wind-up dolls and glimpses of unicorns, all of which leave Deckard – and the rest of us – totally disorientated as to what, and who, is

real. Watching **Blade Runner** is a singular experience, its visual manifestation of Dick's textual identity crisis grimly effective, its cautionary tale of the commodification of consciousness always disquieting.

Rise of the Machines

At the film's climax, replicant Roy Batty (Rutger Hauer) is granted a wistful moment of dying that manages to provoke some feelings of sympathy for a figure that has killed, tortured and menaced without hesitation. Not so **The Terminator** (James Cameron, 1984), a malevolent agent of the apocalypse sent back from a future where mankind's dalliances with AI have cleverly led to us getting mostly atomized in a global nuclear conflict. Where Batty is lithe and cunning, the Terminator is brutally powerful and implacable (Arnold Schwarzenegger is perfect in the title role), a fine incarnation of our electric dreams turning to nightmares and coming after us.

Perhaps not surprisingly, given the tech evolutions (and nuclear convolutions) of the age, other films dealt with similar themes. Paul Verhoeven's **RoboCop** (1987) is a typically Verhoeven-esque splattery body shocker, as 'murdered' police officer Murphy is resurrected as a brusque cyborg, but it's also a savage satire on rampant capitalism, corporate ethics, mass media and government responsibility, as well as a surprisingly touching rumination on what it is to be human.

Tron (Steve Lisberger, 1982) and **WarGames** (John Badham, 1983) also have machines on their mind, one imagining life inside a system (hard-

ABOVE: Movie poster for *Blade Runner* (1982), directed by Ridley Scott

core cyberpunk dressed up as snazzy Disney kids fare), the other the perils of thoughtless hacking – such as starting a global thermonuclear war.

Apocalypse Now

War was on the mind of other films of the period, too, specifically the war in Vietnam. Its treatment in SF gradually evolved from the anguished, guilt-ridden fare of the 1970s in novels such as Joe Haldeman's **The Forever War** (1974) to more redemptive treatments that allowed the United States to come out of the jungle with honour intact.

Predator (John McTiernan, 1987) does just that: in order to fight the technologically superior eponymous alien hunter killing off his elite special

ops team in the South American jungle, Arnold Schwarzenegger must go guerrilla, thereby symbolically re-fighting the war. There's almost humility in his descent from weaponized beefcake to thoroughly mortal survivor, daubing himself in mud and merging with the land he's in, in order to survive. (**Almost** humility; this is still a 1980s actioner, after all, and he does punch an alien in the face.) And before you dismiss the Ewoks of **Return of the Jedi**, it's worth noting that they're guerrilla insurgents battling an arrogant invading army by using booby traps in the jungle, and the good guys are on their side. Just saying.

Where many films of the period understandably pondered the possibility of nuclear war, others imagined a time not long after one. Arrestingly violent and packed with surreal metamorphoses to suggest unstable, shifting identity,

TOP: Arnold Schwarzenegger getting make-up applied for *The Terminator* (1984), directed by James Cameron. ABOVE: Peter Weller in *Robocop* (1987), directed by Paul Verhoeven

diffident biker-teenagers roam post-apocalyptic neo-Tokyo in Japanese anime **Akira** (Katsuhiro Otomo, 1988, based on Otomo's manga). Likewise, the eponymous hero of the **Mad Max** franchise (1979 onwards) wanders a shattered world; its high-octane portrayal of a disintegrating society battling over fuel in killer cars, plus the edgy scorched otherness of the Australian landscape, makes for hauntingly strange viewing.

We Don't Need Roads

Max's customized Pursuit Special is something of a cult movie car, but even it can't hold a candle to the iconic DeLorean of **Back to the Future** (Robert Zemeckis, 1985). This is the moment where Golden Age-inspired 1980s SF cinema truly ate itself, by literally sending itself back to the Golden Age of SF. Editions of pulp magazines (**Fantastic Story** from 1954 in particular) even appear on screen.

Back to the Future is pure escapism, expertly blending its time-travel adventures with a coming-of-age tale told with just the right mix of comic and action beats. It's breezy, sunny, infectiously charming and in Marty McFly (Michael J. Fox) it gave cinema one of its most likeable protagonists, as well as a Merlin/Arthur (or Kenobi/Skywalker) relationship between Marty and Doc.

All of which made **Back to the Future II** (1988) even more startling, with its SF-plus vision of alternative timelines and realities, plus a gleefully meta-fictional moment where Marty travels back to moments seen in the first film. We're still waiting for our hoverboards, but the sequel delivered

THE MAXIMUM FORCE OF THE FUTURE

SAMUEL Z. ARKOFF Presents "MAD MAX"
Music by BRIAN MAY
Written by JAMES McCAUSLAND and GEORGE MILLER
Produced by BYRON KENNEDY Directed by GEORGE MILLER
with MEL GIBSON Color prints by MOVIELAB
RELEASED BY AMERICAN INTERNATIONAL / A FILMWAYS CO.

MAD MAX

ABOVE: Movie poster for *Mad Max* (1979), directed by George Miller

unexpected intrigues and downbeat predictions for a future where a megalomaniacal businessman could wield unprecedented political power. Perish the thought.

Keep on Trekkin'

Throughout the 1970s **Star Trek** was growing in popularity as the original series was re-run. Post **Star Wars**, it was probably an easy decision for Paramount Pictures to green-light **Star Trek: The Motion Picture** (Robert Wise, 1979), one they possibly regretted when presented with the finished film. Suffering from a troubled production, drenched in special effects and wearisomely slow, the film felt out of step with both the original series and the mood of SF cinema in general; even its title felt out of time.

If in doubt, as the genre was learning, look back. **Star Trek** did just that and revived Khan Noonian Singh, exiled by Kirk in the original series and now plotting revenge for 15 years. The resulting movie, **Star Trek II: The Wrath of Khan** (Nicholas Meyer, 1982) captured the spirit of the TV show at its buccaneering, ramshackle best, finding once again the chemistry between the leads and killing Spock in a memorable act of self sacrifice, to the dismay of fans. They needn't have worried: two more films (**The Search for Spock**, 1984 and **The Voyage Home,** 1986) set about bringing him back with an entertaining mix of cosmic melodrama, knockabout comedy, ecological musings and time-travel flimflam. However, by the fifth instalment, **The Final Frontier** (1989) – an incoherent quasi-religious trudge – things were looking tired again. Time for some fresh legs.

ABOVE: Michael J. Fox and Christopher Lloyd as Marty McFly and Dr Emmet 'Doc' Brown in *Back to the Future* (1985), directed by Robert Zemeckis

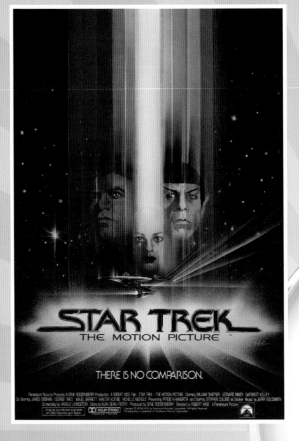 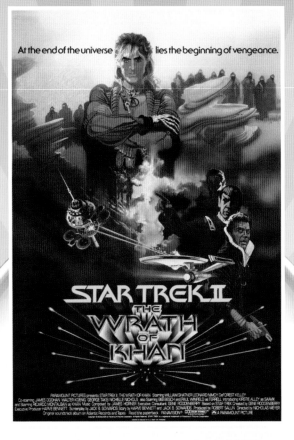 

ABOVE : The first three *Star Trek* movies (1979, 1982, 1984); *Battlestar Galactica* TV series (1978–79); *Back to the Future* (1985); *Tron* (1982)

NEXT GENERATION LITERATURE & TV

Star Trek: The Next Generation (1989, discussed more in the next chapter) gave some indication of the distance travelled since the 1960s both in real terms, via the enhanced special effects and revamped *Enterprise* (although the space-going jumpsuits were less effective)' but also in terms of the SF genre itself. The opening voiceover was updated to 'where no *one*', rather than 'no *man*' has gone before. Counsellor Deanna Troi was on the bridge at the captain's side, the ship's doctor was female and the security officer was Klingon. The ship's captain, Picard, was a diplomat, polymath and somewhat aloof figure – a serious man for less rambunctious times. Serene and gleaming, this harmonious *Enterprise* was the end result of the tumult of the previous decades; but naturally the calm wouldn't last.

Elsewhere on the small screen **Doctor Who** continued, and with **Remembrance of the Daleks** (1988) answered a troubling question: how do Daleks climb the stairs? Under Sylvester McCoy the Doctor became a more ambiguous figure,

somehow more alien – the character would go into TV hibernation soon after. Further out in space, **Battlestar Galactica** (1978) imagined the last humanoid survivors of a deadly war fleeing their Cylon opponents across the universe in search of Earth. The series was heavy with religious portent (thanks in part to creator Glen A. Larson's Mormon faith), which the later reboot would amplify.

Back on Earth, the BBC conjured the sum of all fears with **Threads** (1984), a docudrama about an imagined nuclear strike and ensuing nuclear winter that was so relentlessly bleak (it ends with a ragged survivor delivering a stillborn child among the ruins of society) that it made the future of **The Terminator** look like a pleasant day out with all the nice robots.

Back in Print

Meanwhile, print was enjoying something of a resurgence. The ever-swelling tide of film and TV merchandise included novelizations of many of the hit films of the period (including **Alien**, **Terminator** and of course **Star Wars**), along with original novels set in their universes. **Star Trek** and **Doctor Who** in particular inspired many examples, while the **Star Wars** canon has been expanded massively over the years courtesy of Lucas-approved fiction.

Riding the same tidal wave, much original SF fiction gained in popularity as the genre enjoyed a post-**Star Wars** boost, and market forces being what they are, publishers were happy to oblige. This led to a shift away from the stylings of the New Wave, as Adam Roberts explains in **The Palgrave History of Science Fiction** (2016): 'The majority of SF published during [the period] ... tended

139

ABOVE: *Dredd* (2012), directed by Pete Travis, was inspired by the Judge Dredd comic strip, which first appeared in *2000AD*

to look back to the formats and conventions of golden age SF (to the delight of many fans, for whom such SF represented the acme of the genre).'

The late 1970s saw SF comics gaining popularity, with one title in particular contributing an iconic character (and consistently engaging SF tales) to the genre. Designed to capitalise on the glut of SF movies and with a name intended to far outlive the title's lifespan, **2000AD** launched in 1977 and continues to this day. We have this British publication to thank for introducing uncompromising enforcer Judge 'I am the law' Dredd and the far-future brutalopolis of Megacity One that he patrols, as well as helping to launch the careers of luminaries such as Grant Morrison and Alan Moore.

It's to Moore himself that the key text of the period surely belongs. The witty, breathtakingly nihilistic comic-book series **Watchmen** (1986–87), from writer Moore, artist Dave Gibbons and colourist John Higgins is set in an alternative reality where the US won the Vietnam War and superheroes have been 'out' in society since the 1940s.

Contrasting Creations

Watchmen is a confection of many of the overriding concerns of its era, particularly those around nuclear war and bellicose right-wing ideologies. Moore's 'real' superheroes (read: violent, troubled, sociopathic and sexually impotent when stripped of their capes) stop Armageddon but at great cost, and not through traditional heroics. The only superhuman, Dr Manhattan (able to manipulate life at the atomic level), abandons humanity at the end in

bafflement, as if Superman – or Christ – decided that we're simply not worth the effort.

A few other contrasting novels give a flavour of the late 1970s and 1980s. **Footfall** by Larry Niven and Jerry Pournelle (1985) is a chest-thumping paean to bloodthirsty Republican triumphalism as mankind, though at first defeated, rallies to wipe the floor with a race of thinly veiled communist alien invaders. Somewhat different, beginning in 1987 with **Consider Phlebas**, Iain M. Banks' **Culture** series is a utopian reclamation of the space opera and hymn to left-wing libertarianism, with intergalactic moral intrigues wrapped up in ripping yarns.

Different again, Octavia E. Butler's **Patternist** (1976–84) and **Xenogenesis** (1984–89) series use time travel, speculative alien races and Armageddon to explore themes of self, alienation, community and Otherness. Her best known work, **Kindred** (1979) is an enquiry into gender, race and the legacy of slavery in the US, as an African-American woman protagonist lurches in time from 1976 to the slave plantations of her pre-Civil War ancestors.

Build It Up

Some of the most successful novels of the period focused on building detailed, textured worlds. This is particularly true of Carolyn Janice Cherry – writing as C.J. Cherryh to disguise her gender in a male-dominated field (sigh) – whose colossal novels include **Downbelow Station** (1981) and **Cyteen** (1988) and feature a great deal of politicking, clones, androids and starship standoffs.

ABOVE: *Watchmen*, first appearing in the comic book series (1986–87), and later inspiring the 2009 movie, brought us 'real' heroes

Similarly detailed, the main character in Brian Aldiss's **Helliconia** series (1981–85) is the titular planet itself. The three novels of the series chart Helliconia's development over millennia as humans and aliens co-exist on the planet, which experiences drawn out seasons and challenging environmental shifts on its long orbit around two stars. Aldiss consulted numerous academics to get Helliconia's climate, geology, ecology and so on just right; his reward was a grand stage on which to explore survival in changing environments and how humans might build and rebuild civilizations – relevant questions to society both then and now.

Added piquancy (especially to a modern audience) comes from the gradual revelation that a ship from Earth is orbiting Helliconia, recording events and sending them back to Earth as part scientific study, part interstellar reality TV show.

Tear It Down

Eventually of course humanity on Earth wipes itself out in a nuclear war and the inhabitants of the ship are left to breed and ponder their sudden solitude until, generations later, the last of them dies and the empty ship drifts in orbit. This rather elegiac coda echoes an on-going theme explored by many writers of the period: life on dead or dying worlds.

Gene Wolfe's **The Book of the New Sun** (1980–83) and its sequels begin on a slowly dying Earth (now **Urth**) in the distant future where the sun is cooling. They blend fantasy (society is quasi-medieval) and SF (with starships and time travel) to take us on an oblique quest for God,

encountering false prophets and messiahs along the way through text that divides fans and critics; Wolfe is an acquired taste.

Russell Hoban's extraordinary **Ridley Walker** (1980) can also hold the reader at arms' length at first, courtesy of the arcane speech of its protagonist as he roams a post-apocalypse England, but once we acclimatize (as with Burgess' nadsat in **A Clockwork Orange**) a tale of fall, revelation and rebirth peeps through the layers of language.

Total Wipe-Out

The end of days is a prominent motif in Orson Scott Card's **Ender's Game** (1985), where Earthlings fear destruction at the hands of an alien race (it was ever thus) – though for good reason here as we learn from the book's backstory that aliens have already attacked once – and try to prepare through the gamification of interstellar war. Using virtual reality they train their youth in strategy and combat, until the most gifted, Ender Wiggin, wins the game and totally annihilates the alien threat. Only it turns out that his 'game' was real; his instructions were carried out by actual space fleets, and he has now wiped out an entire alien race. It was their end of days, not ours, and he spends the subsequent novel – **Speaker for the Dead** (1986) – trying to atone.

Sheri Tepper uses a different kind of bait-and-switch tactic to great effect in **Grass** (1989), where the ghastly foxen (basically made of teeth) hunted by aristocratic humans and their alien hippae (amped-up dino-beasts) on the titular planet actually turn out to be the persecuted ones. Protagonist Marjorie Westriding Yrarier slowly unravels the life cycles of the planet and learns to see

141

ABOVE: *Ender's Game* (2013), directed by Gavin Hood, was based on Orson Scott Card's novel (1985)

it anew. In this vein, and for sheer oddness, Alan Dean Foster's **Sentenced to Prism** (1985) gets an honourable mention for its world of silicon-based life, talking blue crystal caterpillars included, which a stranded explorer gradually comes to understand.

Keeping the Faith

Many of these works feature religious themes either explicitly or implicitly, acknowledging the spiritual and theological undertow that has preoccupied SF writers almost from the start. It's a logical line of enquiry: if humanity ascends to the heavens, where is God, and what is God's function?

That question features throughout the interlocked narratives of Dan Simmons' **Hyperion** (1989), told using a **Canterbury Tales**-like structure by a group of pilgrims on their way to the mysterious Time Tombs of Hyperion. One in particular concerns a priest's encounters with an alien race (actually degenerate remnants of an old human colony) whose members have a cross on their bodies, giving him hope for Christ's incarnation on other worlds. In fact, the crosses are parasitical cruciform beings who have infected their hosts and bestow a dreadful kind of immortality.

Faith (and similar plundering of Chaucer) lies at the heart of **The Handmaid's Tale** (Margaret Atwood, 1985), set in a dystopian future where society is run on strictly Biblical principles by a Christian fundamentalist state. This has not led to a compassionate, equal world, and the novel is a furious enquiry into patriarchal power structures and the oppression of women, as Offred

experiences life as little more than breeding stock for her master. The novel reflects a real-world feminist perception that the women's movement had lost ground in the 1980s.

Here's Cyberpunk

A different contemporary social movement, punk, also influenced SF of the period. The cyberpunk genre mirrored its seething sense of social discontent and gloomy iconoclasm, as well as its innate distrust of power structures and contemporary corporate hegemony. Yet it also looked back to the hardboiled noir of authors like Raymond Chandler (**The Big Sleep**, 1939) for both tone and content.

Cyberpunk stories generally take place in the shady underbellies of high-tech societies. That's the thing about all that electric light: it casts shadows. Think of the relentless penumbra through which Deckard moves in Ridley Scott's **Blade Runner**, flitting in darkness between flame and neon. One of the key texts for the genre, **Neuromancer** (William Gibson, 1984), clearly shared common visual influences with the film, with both being inspired by the types of artwork seen in **Heavy Metal** magazine by artists like Moebius.

Neuromancer popularized the term 'cyberspace' (coined by Gibson in another story, 1982's 'Burning Chrome'), gave us the concept of a nebulous 'matrix' and set the template for the genre: one-time super-hacker Case is given a shot at redemption (in this case having lethal toxins cleaned from his blood) if he'll pull one last risky job in cyberspace. A bruising plot of cross and double-cross

ABOVE: Dystopian futures abound in the sci fi stories of this period

ABOVE: Douglas Adams co-wrote the screenplay for *The Hitchhiker's Guide to the Galaxy* (2005), which first started life as a radio broadcast (1978), but he sadly died before production began

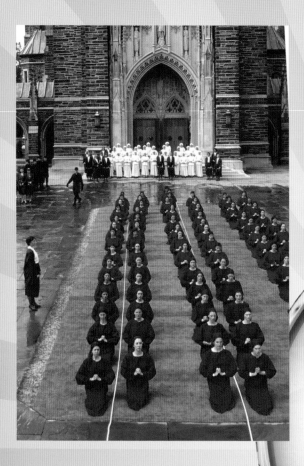

Margaret Atwood

THE HANDMAID'S TALE

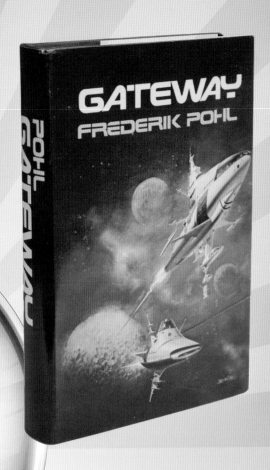

GATEWAY
FREDERIK POHL

POHL
GATEWAY

O
Pan

THE HITCH-HIKERS GUIDE TO THE GALAXY

DOUGLAS ADAMS
Based on the famous Radio series

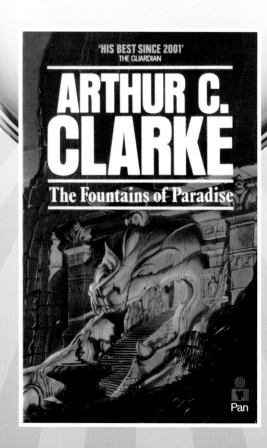

'HIS BEST SINCE 2001'
THE GUARDIAN

ARTHUR C. CLARKE

The Fountains of Paradise

Pan

THE BOOK OF THE YEAR!
WINNER OF THE HUGO, NEBULA AND
PHILIP K. DICK AWARDS!

NEUROMANCER
WILLIAM GIBSON

"KALEIDOSCOPIC, PICARESQUE, FLASHY AND DECADENT...AN
AMAZING VIRTUOSO PERFORMANCE... STATE-OF-THE-ART!"
—WASHINGTON POST

ABOVE: Margaret Atwood's *A Handmaid's Tale* inspired a 1999 movie (seen here), and a 2017 TV series; a selection of novels from the period

later, the case (geddit?) is closed, but the man himself is more or less the same; much like the hardy gumshoes of noir detective tales.

So Long, and Thanks for All the Fish

Cyberpunk gleefully plundered disparate cultural sources – film noir, detective fictions, contemporary Japanese culture, punk rock – to build its patchwork worlds. So too did Douglas Adams's *The Hitchhiker's Guide to the Galaxy*, a dizzying mishmash of SF tropes expertly woven into an offbeat whole that parodies and promotes SF with pan-galactic exuberance.

Existing first as a radio programme, followed by novels, a TV series and a (sadly misfiring) film, *Hitchhiker's* helter-skelter plot encompasses life, the universe and everything. Taking the plots from the books, we start on Earth with *The Hitchhiker's Guide to the Galaxy* (1979) as Arthur Dent is a bit upset to find alien Vogons destroying the planet to make way for an interstellar bypass. We end – for the purposes of this chapter – in 1984 with *So Long, and Thanks For All the Fish*, as Marvin the paranoid android looks with ancient eyes on God's final message to creation. (No spoilers.)

Along the way and through two further novels (*The Restaurant at the End of the Universe*, 1980; *Life, the Universe and Everything*, 1982) Arthur and alien friend Ford Prefect experience snarky computers, artificial worlds, time travel, flight, interstellar war, murderous poetry and a really good cup of tea. And the answer to existence (it's 42). Basically all of science fiction.

ABOVE: Cyberpunk's aesthetic owes much to various cultural sources, from film noir to punk rock.

LUMINOUS BEINGS

SF in the 1980s was much more than simply an era of bombast with one eye on the fallout shelter – there was work of great subtlety and nuance too – but there's no doubt that much of what was done was *big*, in a way that had simply never been seen before.

145

Key artists of the age stepped up to match their own visuals to these stories, such as the great Drew Struzan, whose movie poster art is indelibly linked in cultural memory to films like *Star Wars*, *Blade Runner*, *E.T.* and *Back to the Future*. For many fans (including the one writing this) his work triggers powerful childhood memories of giddy intoxication with the movies he illustrated.

At the same time John Harris, John Berkey, Jean Giraud (Moebius) and Chris Foss continued to define SF's visual aesthetic, while Bernie Wrightson's extravagantly detailed comic art – and in particular his pen-and-ink illustrations for a 1983 edition of *Frankenstein* – have a chaotic, mournful beauty reminiscent of nineteenth-century engravings, and have to be seen to be believed.

Sure, SF creatives in all mediums looked to the past to build their futures. But what they built proved to be fresh, intriguing and, above all else, enduring. The Force will be with us – always.

7: THE INFORMATION AGE

1990

1990 • *Total Recall* • Paul Verhoeven
Movie
1990 • *The Difference Engine* • William Gibson,
Bruce Sterling
Novel
1991 • *Raft* • Stephen Baxter
Novel
1991 • The first website goes online • Tim Berners-Lee
Science & Technology
1992 • *Snow Crash* • Neal Stephenson
Novel
1993 • *Red Mars* • Kim Stanley Robinson
Novel
1993 • First issue of *Wired*, focusing on emerging technologies
• Louis Rossetto
Science & Technology
1993 • First episode of *The X-Files* • Chris Carter
TV
1993 • *Jurassic Park* • Steven Spielberg
Movie
1993 • *Doom* • id Software
Video Game
1993 • *Virtual Light* • William Gibson
Novel
1993 • First episode of *Star Trek: Deep Space Nine* •
Rick Berman, Michael Piller
TV
1994 • *Permutation City* • Greg Egan
Novel
1994 • *Stargate* • Roland Emmerich
Movie

1995

1995 • First episode of *Star Trek: Voyager* • Rick Berman,
Michael Piller, Jeri Taylor
TV
1995 • First episode of *Sliders* • Tracy Tormé, Robert K. Weiss
TV
1995 • *Ghost in the Shell* • Mamoru Oshii
Movie
1995 • *12 Monkeys* • Terry Gilliam
Movie
1995 • *Strange Days* • Kathryn Bigelow
Movie
1996 • The first mammal is cloned • Dolly the Sheep
Science & Technology
1996 • *Independence Day* • Roland Emmerich
Movie
1996 • *The Reality Dysfunction* • Peter F. Hamilton
Novel
1996 • *Voyage* • Stephen Baxter
Novel

1997

1997 • *The Fifth Element* • Luc Besson
Movie
1997 • *Gattaca* • Andrew Niccol
Movie
1997 • First episode of *Stargate SG-1* • Brad Wright,
Jonathan Glassner
TV
1998 • *Half-Life* • Valve
Video Game
1998 • *Dark City* • Alex Proyas
Movie
1998 • *Deep Impact* • Mimi Leder
Movie
1998 • *StarCraft* • Blizzard Entertainment
Video Game
1999 • *Star Wars: Episode I – The Phantom Menace* •
George Lucas
Movie
1999 • *The Matrix* • The Wachowskis
Movie
1999 • First episode of *Futurama* • Matt Groening
TV
1999 • *Sid Meier's Alpha Centauri* • Firaxis Games
Video Game
1999 • *The League of Extraordinary Gentlemen* • Alan Moore,
Kevin O'Neill
Comic

2000

2000 • *Salt* • Adam Roberts
Novel

2000 • *Deus Ex* • Ion Storm
Video Game

2000 • *Revelation Space* • Alastair Reynolds
Novel

2000 • *X-Men* • Bryan Singer
Movie

2001 • *Halo: Combat Evolved* • Bungie
Video Game

2001 • *Planet of the Apes* • Tim Burton
Movie

2001 • First episode of *Star Trek: Enterprise* • Rick Berman, Brannon Braga
TV

2002 • *Minority Report* • Steven Spielberg
Movie

2002 • First episode of *Firefly* • Joss Whedon
TV

2002 • *Spider-Man* • Sam Raimi
Movie

2003 • *Eve Online* • CCP Games
Video Game

2003 • *Oryx and Crake* • Margaret Atwood
Novel

2004

2004 • First episode of *Stargate Atlantis* • Brad Wright, Robert C. Cooper
TV

2004 • First episode of *Battlestar Galactica* reboot • Ronald D. Moore
TV

2004 • *Eternal Sunshine of the Spotless Mind* • Michel Gondry
Movie

2004 • *Forty Signs of Rain* • Kim Stanley Robinson
Novel

2004 • *Hellboy* • Guillermo del Toro
Movie

2005 • *Fantastic Four* • Tim Story
Movie

2005 • *Serenity* • Joss Whedon
Movie

2005 • *Batman Begins* • Christopher Nolan
Movie

2005 • First episode of *Doctor Who* revival • Russell T Davies
TV

2006

2006 • *Superman Returns* • Bryan Singer
Movie

2006 • 'An Inconvenient Truth' • Davis Guggenheim
Documentary

2006 • *Children of Men* • Alfonso Cuarón
Movie

2006 • *Gears of War* • Epic Games
Video Game

2006 • *A Scanner Darkly* • Richard Linklater
Movie

2006 • *The Road* • Cormac McCarthy
Novel

2006 • *Gradisil* • Adam Roberts
Novel

2007 • *BioShock* • 2K Games
Video Game

2007 • *Portal* • Valve
Video Game

2007 • *Mass Effect* • BioWare
Video Game

2008 • *Anathem* • Neal Stephenson
Novel

2008 • *Flood* • Stephen Baxter
Novel

2008 • First episode of *Fringe* • J.J. Abrams, Alex Kurtzman, Roberto Orci
TV

2008 • *WALL-E* • Andrew Stanton
Movie

2008 • *Dead Space* • Visceral Games (formerly EA Redwood Shores)
Video Game

2008 • *The Hunger Games* • Suzanne Collins
Novel

2008 • *Iron Man* • Jon Favreau
Movie

2008 • *The Incredible Hulk* • Louis Leterrier
Movie

A NEW DAWN

What do you do when the long dreamed-of future finally arrives? That's what science fiction had to work out in the 1990s, as the year 2000 stopped being an impossibly distant futuristic mirage and became the near future.

The moment the clocks ticked over from 23:59 on 31 December 1999 to 00.00 on 1 January 2000 felt like it was going to be a momentous one. The new millennium promised a shiny new start, and perhaps even a shiny new world. Things were changing, and the public mood swung between hopeful and fearful as the 1990s progressed.

Social and technological changes (and the social changes caused by technology) were also reflected in fiction. As one millennium melted into another, new hopes and fears captured the public imagination. Science fiction is the genre most interested in following ideas through to their logical conclusions, so science fiction creators snapped up all of those new anxieties and channelled them into their work. The kinds of films, TV shows, books and art made around the turn of the century demonstrate a fascination with technology, with gateways and with transition.

And while the market – or at least marketers – clamoured for known properties, the sequels, remakes and reboots made in the 1990s and beyond all contributed a distinctly millennial perspective on old stories and characters.

The World-Changing Web

Let's cut straight to the chase: the main thing that changed the world (and thus science fiction) in the 1990s was the Internet. The World Wide Web was invented in late 1989 by British computer scientist Tim Berners-Lee, who also created the first web browser in 1990. As it became available to an ever-widening user base, it began to change the way we thought about information, communication and connectedness.

One of the first writers to explore the possibilities of a shared online space in the 1990s was William Gibson. He'd already written extensively about cyberspace throughout the 1980s, most notably in 1984's **Neuromancer**, and he continued to explore similar themes throughout the 1990s. His Bridge trilogy – **Virtual Light** (1993), **Idoru** (1996) and **All Tomorrow's Parties** (1999) – is set in a near-future world where an earthquake has devastated California and created an economic and technological split in society. As always, in these books Gibson is interested in the interfaces between humans and technology, and how information functions as currency.

Gibson's eerie foresight – his ability to tap into emerging trends, to identify and name ideas and phenomena before they become reality – means he's

ABOVE: The advent of the world wide web inspired films like *The Matrix* (1999), directed by The Wachowskis

sometimes seen as more of a prophet than a fiction writer. And his themes are themes that the entire genre would become obsessed with as computers became more and more commonplace and more and more embedded in everyday life, and 'cyberspace' stopped being a fictional construct and became the place we all live our lives.

The early 1990s were littered with Gibson-influenced cyberpunk science fiction movies, from **Hardware** (1990) to **Total Recall** (1990) and beyond. Now, those movies might seem naïve in their construction of how the Internet would change the world, but they weren't wrong about the idea that it **would** change the world – irrevocably so.

The Millennium Bug

The increase in popularity of the Internet – and the rapid development of technology throughout the 1990s in general – opened up some genuinely frightening possibilities. One very real anxiety throughout the decade was the spectre of the so-called 'Millennium Bug': the idea that computers would be unable to cope with the date changing from 1999 to 2000, leading to all sorts of disasters, from crashed banking systems to misfired nukes.

Several movies explicitly traded on that sense of impending doom by setting their stories in the last days of 1999. Kathryn Bigelow's 1995 sci-fi thriller **Strange Days** is one particularly interesting example. In its version of 1999, technology allows a person's experiences and memories to be recorded directly out of their brains and played back for other people to experience.

Strange Days might have been optimistic about how rapidly technology would advance in the next few years (virtual reality still hasn't caught up) but it was also pretty pessimistic about life in general. Its tech didn't make life better – in the film, the SQUID devices are illegal and seem to be mostly used by criminals trading black-market footage of violent crimes – and its version of future Los Angeles is crime-ridden and terrifying, a grim city where the rich travel in armoured limousines to protect themselves from the harsh reality everyone else has to cope with. Tellingly, it ends just as the year 2000 dawns, leaving what would happen next a mystery – almost as if the film didn't quite dare to predict what that might be.

Apocalypse Now-ish

Other movies also caught on to the apocalyptic mood, even if they weren't explicitly set at the turn of the century. Not all of the threat came from technology, either. An awful lot of 1990s science fiction imagined something horrible coming from outer space.

Roland Emmerich's **Independence Day**, released in 1996, depicted that something horrible as a race of invading aliens. In the movie, an enormous mothership arrives in the Earth's orbit, then sends out 36 smaller spaceships, each of which hovers above a major city somewhere on the planet. Though some characters are optimistic about the aliens' intent, hoping that they come in peace, it soon becomes clear they didn't come to party with us – they came to wipe us out.

Independence Day's apocalyptic imagery was bold and impossible to ignore. The scene where the alien ship opens fire on the White House became instantly iconic;

ABOVE: Arnold Schwarzenegger as Douglas Quaid in *Total Recall* (1990), directed by Paul Verhoeven

it may be the most recognizable image from a 1990s blockbuster, never mind 1990s science fiction. It's striking both because the special effects (created using a five-foot-tall recreation of the White House) were so believable and because of what the White House represented. The explosion of the White House, the symbolic home of the most powerful person in the world, felt like an attack on all of humanity, an incredible demonstration of the aliens' power (which just makes humanity's eventual triumph all the more exhilarating).

Crash, Bang, Doom

Two years later, two films put the planet at risk from extra-terrestrial threat again, though minus the aliens: both **Armageddon** and **Deep Impact** dealt with the idea that an asteroid might crash into the Earth. Maybe it's coincidence that both movies were released in 1998, though research was being done throughout the 1990s into the Chicxulub crater in Mexico that pointed to the crater having been caused by an asteroid, which probably led to the extinction of the dinosaurs. So the idea of another asteroid causing the extinction of humanity seems, in retrospect, an obvious path for science fiction to explore on screen.

Disaster novels had long imagined comet- and asteroid-related destruction, of course (one example is 1977's **Lucifer's Hammer**, by Larry Niven and Jerry Pournelle) but depicting large scale catastrophes in print is obviously easier and cheaper than doing it on screen. That might explain why it took until the late 1990s, when computer-generated effects were more advanced – and science fiction movie budgets were bigger! – for these kinds of films to get made.

ABOVE: *Deep Impact* (1998), directed by Mimi Leder, wondered what would happen if an asteroid was headed for Earth

Like **Independence Day**, both films deal with a narrowly averted apocalyptic event, as crews are dispatched to plant explosives to break up the asteroids and the day is saved. Which probably explains why all of these movies were huge box-office successes – because the alternative would be too bleak to contemplate.

Escaping into New Worlds

If life on Earth really **was** in danger of imminent destruction, what would humanity do? Obviously it would depend on the nature of the threat, but one particular strand of science fiction offered an alternative to staying to fight. Instead, we might look for an alternative world. Stories about space exploration were still popular in the 1990s – Kim Stanley Robinson wrote a whole trilogy (**Red Mars** [1993], **Green Mars** [1994] and **Blue Mars** [1996]) about terraforming that planet – but for anyone who wasn't into the idea of jumping on a spaceship, 1990s sci-fi had an alternative. What if you could just step through a door into another world?

That's what happens in Roland Emmerich's 1994 movie **Stargate** (and its later TV spin-offs **Stargate SG-1**, **Stargate Atlantis** and **Stargate Universe**). An archaeological dig unearths a mysterious artefact that turns out to be a portal which, when properly aligned, allows for intergalactic travel via wormhole. Basically, with Stargate technology, all that tedious flying between planets can be cut out entirely, allowing for instantaneous travel between various points in the universe.

Inevitably, it turns out not to be quite as easy as all that, not least because the alien race who created the technology didn't just do it to make interstellar tourism easier for us. But **Stargate** effectively rebranded a sci-fi idea that had been around since the 1940s, giving Einstein-Rosen Bridges the catchier name of 'stargates', and helping to plant the fantasy of jumping through a portal into another world firmly in the public consciousness.

Alternate Earths

Wormholes popped up in various other science fiction stories of the era (including in both of the new 1990s **Star Trek** series), but they didn't always take intrepid explorers to other parts of the universe. In **Sliders** (1995–2000), a wormhole allows travellers to move between dimensions. The show is based around the idea that there are infinite parallel universes that exist alongside our own, each representing a different possible world that could have existed if something had happened differently somewhere along the line.

The show often played these alternative worlds for comic effect: in episode seven ('The Weaker Sex') of the first season, the sliders think they've made it home to Earth Prime when they hear that President Clinton is about to make a televised address, only for it to turn out to be Hillary.

That the sliders ended up unable to find their way home, forever moving between other, mostly terrifying dystopian universes, was a cruel irony that might have ultimately ended up reassuring viewers that they were better off in their own universe, but definitely suggested some degree of dissatisfaction with the way things were going.

151

ABOVE: *Sliders* (1995–2000) followed a group of people 'sliding' between many parallel Earths, trying to find a way back home

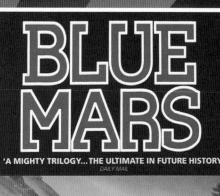

RED MARS

'A staggering book... The best novel on the colonization of Mars that has ever been written'
ARTHUR C. CLARKE

KIM STANLEY ROBINSON

GREEN MARS

'A MIGHTY TRILOGY...THE ULTIMATE IN FUTURE HISTORY'
DAILY MAIL

KIM STANLEY ROBINSON

BLUE MARS

'A MIGHTY TRILOGY...THE ULTIMATE IN FUTURE HISTORY'
DAILY MAIL

KIM STANLEY ROBINSON

STEPHEN BAXTER

RAFT

'GOOD HARD-SCIENCE SF OF A KIND RARELY SEEN NOWADAYS'
JOE HALDEMAN

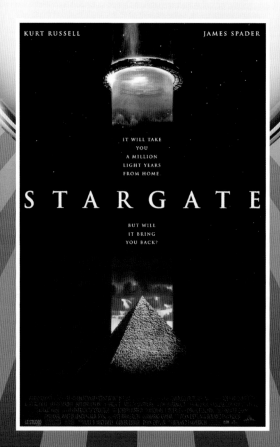

KURT RUSSELL   JAMES SPADER

IT WILL TAKE
YOU
A MILLION
LIGHT YEARS
FROM HOME.

S T A R G A T E

BUT WILL
IT BRING
YOU BACK?

ABOVE: Travelling to new worlds has inspired many SF stories, as seen in Kim Stanley Robinson's *Mars* trilogy (1992–96), Stephen Baxter's *Raft* (1991), *Stargate* (1994) and its spinoff TV programmes

CHANGING TIMES AND ATTITUDES

Dorn as Worf and LeVar Burton as Geordi La Forge) its captain and first officer were still white men. But **Deep Space Nine**, which began airing in 1993, had a black captain (Avery Brooks as Benjamin Sisko) and **Voyager**, which started in 1995, had a female captain (Kate Mulgrew as Kathryn Janeway). Both shows represented obvious leaps forward in onscreen representation, something **Star Trek** had prided itself on since George Takei and Nichelle Nichols were cast in **The Original Series.**

At the beginning of the 1990s, it should have felt like humanity was making massive strides forward. Anti-apartheid campaigner Nelson Mandela was released from prison in early 1990; a few months later, the demolition of the Berlin Wall began, as part of the process of reunifying Germany. And after recessions in both the United Kingdom and the United States at the beginning of the decade, the 1990s were generally a time of prosperity.

Maybe it's notable, though, that neither Sisko nor Janeway ever got to command their ships (or, in Sisko's case, his space station) on the big screen, and in 2001's new series, **Enterprise**, the ship was once again captained by a white guy. Looks like we've still got some work to do on the representation front.

153

Gene Genie

The idea that genetics might define who a person was or could be was often explored in the science fiction of the time. After all, with the Human Genome Project ticking along in the background (it started in 1990, with a rough draft completed by 2000) and Dolly the sheep providing the living proof, in 1996, that living organisms could be successfully cloned from adult specimens, how could genetic tinkering not make it into depictions of an imagined future?

But no era is perfect. The 1990s saw a continuation of various civil-rights movements that wanted to tackle society's lingering sexism, racism and homophobia, and that was also reflected in fiction. As a show that often purported to represent the best of humanity, **Star Trek** might be the best example of how science fiction saw society developing.

Star Trek: The Next Generation started in 1987 and ran until 1994, and while its cast included several women (Gates McFadden as Beverly Crusher, Marina Sirtis as Deanna Troi, Denis Crosby as Tasha Yar) and people of colour (Michael

Andrew Niccol's **Gattaca**, released in 1997, was a deep dive into the potential consequences of being able to 'read' our genetic make-up. In its near future setting, most babies are made to order. Parents can use genetic selection to make sure that their children not only have their desired hair and eye colour,

ABOVE: Ethan Hawke as Vincent Freeman in *Gattaca* (1997), directed by Andrew Niccol

ABOVE: The 1990s and 2000s saw several iterations of *Star Trek* onscreen: *The Next Generation* (1987–94), *Deep Space Nine* (1993–99), *Voyager* (1995–2001) and *Enterprise* (2001–05)

but also aren't genetically predisposed to any congenital diseases; even tendencies to violence, obesity and baldness can be rooted out.

But while breeding out genetic flaws might seem like a good idea, **Gattaca** explored the ways eugenics can go wrong. Its world discriminates against anyone born the old-fashioned way, and anyone unfortunate enough to be at risk of something like heart disease is pushed out to the margins of society, while the genetically superior are handed the best jobs and opportunities. Of course, people are more than just their genes, and **Gattaca**'s complicated hero is an 'In-Valid' who illegally buys the genetic identity of his supposed superior in order to fulfil his dream of going to space. His drive makes him more than his profile says he should be, which is an encouraging sort of message, even if some of the lengths he has to go to in order to maintain his place in the Valid society are pretty extreme.

Disputed Territory

To go back to **Star Trek** for a moment: something else that's noticeable about **Deep Space Nine** and **Voyager**, compared with **The Original Series** and **The Next Generation**, is that there's a contradictory theme of isolation running through them. While the first two iterations of **Star Trek** saw the crew of the **Enterprise** boldly heading off to explore the universe, **Deep Space Nine** was set on a space station in disputed territory in a strategically valuable location coveted by two warring alien races, while **Voyager**'s titular spaceship accidentally ends up stranded in the distant Delta Quadrant. Rather than boldly going where no one had gone before, its mission is to get home.

Both series represent a markedly different attitude towards space exploration than the science fiction of previous decades. It's not that there had never been conflict in **Star Trek** before, but **Deep Space Nine** focused more on interplanetary diplomacy than on new discovery, and **Voyager** put its crew in a position of vulnerability, stranding them far away from home and safety. Both shows also introduced notes of conflict between crewmembers, something **Star Trek** had previously tried to avoid.

Space Diplomacy

Another major 1990s science fiction show to delve into the trickiness of navigating interstellar politics was **Babylon 5** (1994–98). Like Deep Space Nine, the titular Babylon 5 was a space station, a centre for diplomacy that hosted ambassadors from various alien races who had previously been in conflict with one another. Both shows featured double-crossing politicians, unlikely alliances and complicated religious beliefs, and at the time accusations of plagiarism were flung back and forth, with sci-fi fans tending to choose one show and eschew the other. With hindsight, though, both shows had their strengths, and both contributed to a general trend in science fiction of the period: the idea that conflict wasn't always as simple as good versus evil.

It turns out there was a real-world version of these stories happening around the turn of the century. In 1998, the Space Station Intergovernmental Agreement was signed by 15 governments: the United States, Canada, Japan, the Russian Federation, Belgium, Denmark, France, Germany, Italy, the Netherlands, Norway, Spain, Sweden, Switzerland and the United Kingdom.

ABOVE: Rather than being set on a ship exploring space, *Star Trek: Deep Space Nine* was set on a space station, focusing more on interplanetary diplomacy

Assembly of the space station began in the same year, eventually creating a satellite orbiting the Earth that represented a joint effort by former adversaries.

Resistance is Futile

Speaking of former adversaries finally working together, **Star Trek: Voyager** featured a seriously surprising example in the shape of Seven of Nine. Played by Jeri Ryan, Seven was a former Borg drone who was chosen by the Collective to communicate with Captain Janeway in the first episode of season four ('Scorpion'). After a run-in with Species 8472, Seven ends up stranded on **Voyager**. When her connection with the Collective is severed, her body rejects some of her Borg implants, and she ends up staying with the crew, learning how to be human again (she had been assimilated by the Borg as a child when she and her parents had been captured).

The Borg first appeared in **Star Trek: The Next Generation**, in the second season's 16th episode ('Q Who'), and made several appearances in that series before becoming the main antagonists in **Star Trek: First Contact** (1996). A cybernetic species that attempts to assimilate any new culture it encounters, the Borg made for a terrifying spectre of what increasing dependence on technology might look like; it's not hard to read the Borg as a kind of nightmarish warning about Internet addiction.

The Borg are the enemy throughout **Voyager** – but they're not the only enemy, and the addition of Seven to the principal cast started to make them seem a little less scary. Yes, she's there to bring a non-human perspective to the show (much in the same way Spock or Data did in other iterations of **Star Trek**) but she also becomes a kind of halfway house. She's human, but also otherworldly, and while many of her Borg traits are removed – including, crucially, her link to the Borg hivemind – her artificial side turns out to have some advantages. The idea that machines and humans might not be so different after all – that cyborgs might be relatable, even lovable, characters – is one we'll come back to later.

Before we move on from talking about **Star Trek** (at least for the moment) it's worth noting that **Voyager** can lay claim to another first: it was the first **Star Trek** series to use computer-generated imagery for its exterior shots. Previously, whenever you saw a spaceship or space station set against the unending blackness of space, you were seeing a model; after **Voyager**, it was more likely a computer-generated image.

LEFT: *Babylon 5* (1994–98). TOP: The Borg were one of the most feared adversaries on *Star Trek*, even assimilating Captain Picard.,

DIGITAL WORLDS

CGI had been in use since the 1970s, but the 1990s represented a real turning point for onscreen effects. Science fiction, more than any other genre, strives to introduce audiences to new worlds, and so perhaps it's not surprising that science fiction was at the forefront of new cinematic techniques.

When Steven Spielberg set out to make *Jurassic Park* (1993), he initially envisaged using practical effects for the dinosaurs. And most of the effects in the finished film were achieved using either animatronics or stop-motion animation – but some of them were computer generated by Industrial Light And Magic. Steve 'Spaz' Williams was brought in to add CGI motion blur to some shots, but knew there was scope to do more, so he secretly started working on a T-rex walking animation, which he managed to show to *Jurassic Park*'s producers, who were immediately won over.

In the end, there are only five scenes featuring computer-generated dinos in *Jurassic Park*, but that turned out to be enough. Those few dazzling moments, like the scene where a flock of Gallimimus stampedes around (and almost over) actors Sam Neill, Joseph Mazzello and Ariana Richards, revolutionized a whole industry, and sent audiences' expectations rocketing skywards. After all,

once you'd seen real-looking CGI dinosaurs interacting with real environments and actors, surely anything was possible?

Dodge This

The Wachowskis' 1999 cyberpunk thriller *The Matrix* pushed things even further. Visual effects supervisor John Gaeta coined a new phrase for the work he did on *The Matrix* and its two sequels: 'virtual cinematography'. Virtual cinematography involved creating CGI versions of actors and sets that were indistinguishable from the real thing, and then 'filming' them using a virtual camera. It's a complex process, but one that allowed the Wachowskis to include images and scenes in their movies that would either have taken far longer using traditional cinematic techniques, or wouldn't have been possible at all.

The Matrix's most recognizable (and most often copied) effect is what's known as 'bullet time'. That's the effect of slowing down the onscreen action while moving perspective, so that incredibly fast-moving action (like a speeding bullet) can be examined from multiple angles.

It's an effect that fits perfectly into the world of *The Matrix*, where characters who know they're in a computer simulation are able to manipulate the world around them, but has since become a well-worn trope in all kinds of genre movies, often used to demonstrate a character's superhuman reflexes. But though the effect has been emulated many, many times since, that fight scene on the helipad in the first *Matrix* movie is still undeniably effective.

157

ABOVE: Laura Dern, Sam Neill and Joseph Mazzello marvel at a triceratops in *Jurassic Park* (1993), directed by Steven Spielberg

Enter the Matrix

Special effects aside, **The Matrix** might really be the key **fin de siècle** movie. When it was released in 1999, a decade after Berners-Lee first invented the World Wide Web, around a third of homes in the United States had Internet connections; by 2001, it would be more like half. The scene in which Thomas Anderson (Keanu Reeves) wakes up to see his computer screen flashing with a message for him, seemingly acting of its own accord, was one that would have been meaningless to audiences a few years earlier.

But as the Internet became commonplace, the idea of discovering new information (or even uncovering a whole new world) through your computer screen became a familiar one, and that let **The Matrix**'s creepy central premise – that its characters are all unknowingly living in a computer simulation – make a horrible kind of sense.

The Matrix's attitude to technology is a complicated one. As Anderson – aka Neo – investigates the mysterious Matrix more thoroughly, he discovers that his world isn't real; rather, it's a simulation being run by machines which have destroyed the Earth and enslaved humanity. Humans now live out their lives in pods, plugged into a complex simulation designed to be just grim enough that they don't realize something is wrong, while the machines essentially use humans as living batteries. The machines are clearly the baddies.

ABOVE: *The Matrix* (1999) is known for its amazing special effects

Ghost in the Machine

But there's something appealing about the Matrix's virtual reality, too – especially once Neo and co are aware that they're in a simulation, and have learned to bend the world to their whims: mastering technology lets them turn themselves into superheroes. But it's no surprise that some people choose to take the blue pill and forget everything they ever knew about the nature of reality. It's telling, too, that as the movies progress, the story's antagonist, Agent Smith (Hugo Weaving), stops being an intentional feature of the Matrix and becomes a bug, a kind of sentient computer virus. Technology doing what it's supposed to do is one thing, but when it does something it's not supposed to do, that's a whole new problem.

The Matrix blends together anxieties about technology with conspiracy theories about authority figures, and a kind of superhero narrative that gives people with advanced computing skills the ability to download new powers off the Internet and install them into their brains. So perhaps it's no wonder that it was such a massive success, or that it still resonates today. It's a tidy encapsulation of all the hopes and fears that would define the new millennium; being good with computers might have been seen as nerdy or undesirable a decade or so previously, but as computers became so vital to everyday life, being nerdy went mainstream. It even became cool.

Here Comes Everybody

Science fiction itself underwent a kind of image makeover throughout the 1990s and into the new millennium. Formerly the domain of geeks

and misfits, the genre made huge strides towards the mainstream during this period.

An early sign of the genre's increasing popularity was the launch of the Sci-Fi Channel in 1992. Created as part of a joint venture between Paramount Pictures and Universal Studios, the Sci-Fi Channel was inaugurated not with a smashed bottle of champagne but with an onscreen dedication to author Isaac Asimov and *Star Trek* creator Gene Roddenberry, before launching into a screening of *Star Wars*. This was an acknowledgement of the genre's past, but the channel's very existence meant there was an appetite for more – and for new material.

The Internet, too, was proving to be a valuable resource for genre fans. Two different movies lay claim to being the first to have an official website (and of course they're both science fiction): *Star Trek: Generations* and *Stargate*. Both were released in 1994, and which one actually got there first is a mystery lost in the mists of time (neither website survives today) but whichever it was, it seems pretty clear that the distributors were aware of an online fan presence to be tapped.

The Internet would open up all kinds of possibility for fandom; pre-Internet, if you were a fan of something obscure, you might need to send away for copies of photocopied zines or travel miles to meet-ups and conventions, but the Internet made it a lot easier to connect with other fans. Genre fans who might have previously felt isolated were able to sign up for online message boards to share their passions, eventually building communities that could put pressure on networks and creators to make the kind of shows and movies they wanted to see. More on that later, though.

ABOVE: Movie poster for *The Matrix* (1999), directed by The Wachowskis

A SCARY NEW WORLD

If science fiction fans were expecting something massive to happen when the new millennium finally arrived, they were disappointed. No alien spaceships loomed into view, computer systems largely didn't go rogue and turn on their creators, and no portals to other worlds opened up. The end of the world had, apparently, been postponed.

But things didn't quite carry on as normal, either. Because while the beginning of the year 2000 was largely uneventful, the terrorist attack on the World Trade Center on Tuesday, 11 September 2001 did change the world. And rather than the world being united against a common foe in the shape of a scrunchy-faced alien or an errant asteroid, that attack left us all more divided than ever before.

As always, science fiction created in the 2000s reflected the new mood, and audiences flocked to fiction that either offered them some perspective on what was happening, or promised some kind of comfort. It's no coincidence that, post-9/11, superhero movies came back into

ABOVE: David Duchovny and Gillian Anderson as Mulder and Scully in *The X-Files* (1993–2002)

fashion. And while stories about government conspiracies had been commonplace before (*The X-Files*, anyone?) they certainly didn't go away afterwards.

Thanks to the Internet, the world suddenly seemed both bigger and smaller, and information – true or otherwise – could spread more quickly than ever before. Maybe we didn't entirely stop looking for new frontiers, but there was an increased consciousness that the world wasn't as safe as we'd thought, and there were plenty of concerns closer to home to think about.

We Did This to Ourselves

While pre-2000s science fiction tended to imagine planet-level threats coming from outer space, by the mid-2000s, writers and filmmakers were starting to imagine a more man-made threat. As climate change became a reality, dystopian fiction started to imagine a destroyed Earth.

In her MaddAddam trilogy, which began with 2003's *Oryx and Crake*, Margaret Atwood imagines a global pandemic unleashed on the world by a disgruntled scientist working for an evil corporation. The virus is a 'Waterless Flood' that wreaks much the same destruction as the Biblical one.

Meanwhile, in Cormac McCarthy's 2006 novel *The Road*, the actual event that causes the apocalypse isn't explicitly explained, but its effects are thoroughly documented, as an unnamed father and son journey along a dystopian wasteland peopled almost entirely by murderers and rapists.

161

ABOVE: Viggo Mortensen and Kodi Smit-McPhee as a father and son trying to survive a dystopian wasteland in *The Road* (2009), based on Cormac McCarthy's novel (2006)

And in Kim Stanley Robinson's hard sci-fi *Science in the Capital* series, which began with 2004's *Forty Signs of Rain*, man-made climate change has wrought havoc on the planet, eventually leading to the flooding of Washington and the collapse of the Gulf Stream. Scientists are tasked with finding ways to fix the problem, but find themselves hamstrung because the cogs of capitalism just won't stop turning.

The world might not have ended in 2000, but that feeling that it might, at almost any moment, clearly hadn't gone away – and now it came with a side helping of guilt, that our end would be all our own fault.

Holding Out for a Hero

That feeling of looming horror might explain why superhero movies came back into fashion around this time. After all, superhero movies function as a kind of wish fulfilment, on more than one level. Particularly post-2000, superhero movies presented heroes as ordinary people who became extraordinary when circumstances called for it, suggesting anyone could become a hero if necessary, and they also offered a kind of saviour narrative. In an increasingly uncertain and paranoid world, what could be more comforting than the idea that when things got really bad, someone in a cape would swoop in and make everything okay again?

There have been superhero stories for about as long as there have been movies, but they really picked up momentum in the early 2000s. Here's a partial list just to illustrate how many superhero movies were suddenly hitting cinema screens in those first few years after the turn of the century: *X-Men* (2000),

Spider-Man (2002), *X2: X-Men United* (2003), *Hulk* (2003), *The League of Extraordinary Gentlemen* (2003), *Hellboy* (2004), *The Punisher* (2004), *Spider-Man 2* (2004), *Catwoman* (2004), *Elektra* (2005), *Constantine* (2005), *Batman Begins* (2005), *Fantastic Four* (2005), *X-Men: The Last Stand* (2006), *Superman Returns* (2006), *Ghost Rider* (2007), *Fantastic Four: Rise of the Silver Surfer* (2007) and *Spider-Man 3* (2007). Depending on your definition of superhero, there were more besides.

Though that looks like a long list, it doesn't even include the beginning of the Marvel Cinematic Universe as it now stands. We'll come back to that in the next chapter, but the fact that many of those superheroes have since been recast and rebooted (sometimes even more than once) stands testament to just how obsessed with superheroes we've become.

Back to the Future

Speaking of reboots, it's worth noting that none of these superhero stories was original. They're adaptations of comic books, often ones written decades earlier, given a lick of paint and a technological update to make them seem relevant to modern audiences. While much science fiction is concerned with ideas about the future, from the turn of the century onwards there was also a huge trend for looking backward, for dragging old stories into the present.

So the original *Star Wars* movies were re-mastered and re-released before George Lucas got to work on the prequel trilogy (perhaps the less said about that the better). And the programme *Doctor Who* regenerated, first in a 1996

ABOVE: Russell T Davies brought *Doctor Who* back to TV screens in 2005

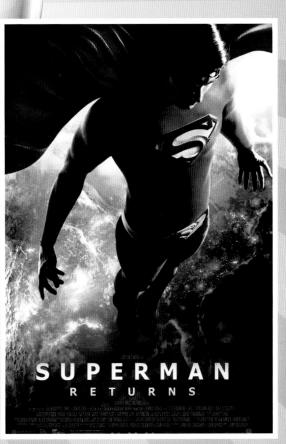

ABOVE: Superhero movies really picked up momentum in the early 2000s

TV movie and then in a full series in 2005. But maybe the most interesting reboot of the period was Ronald D. Moore's *Battlestar Galactica* (2004).

Moore had started his career as a writer and producer on *Star Trek* (with credits on *The Next Generation*, *Deep Space Nine* and *Voyager*) so his space opera credentials were pretty well established by the time he came to develop the mini-series that kicked off the *Battlestar Galactica* remake. But his reboot wouldn't just turn out to be *Star Trek* with the serial numbers filed off. Nope, in this new, post-9/11 world, Moore would create a bleaker, grimmer tale of space exploration, with its own distinct philosophy.

All This Will Happen Again

The new version of *Battlestar Galactica* followed, roughly, the plot of the original Glen A. Larson series from the 1970s, but with some significant changes. The imagery of the initial Cylon attack evoked 9/11, while the *Galactica* was the most suitable ship for humanity to make its escape in because its archaic technology meant it wasn't connected to the network the Cylons exploited. Unlike the perfectly tidy *Enterprise*, *Galactica* was a rust bucket, an old ship that required constant maintenance.

The Cylons, too, had come a long way from the clunky silver robots of the 1970s. Now they came in two flavours: sleek shiny Centurions and humanoid cyborgs who were completely indistinguishable from actual humans. Like the Copies of Greg Egan's 1994 novel *Permutation City*, their consciousnesses could be downloaded into new bodies, and replicated over and over again.

ABOVE: Poster for the *Battlestar Galactica* reboot (2004–09), developed by Ronald D. Moore and David Eick

ABOVE: The cast of the *Battlestar Galactica* reboot (2004–09): Mary McDonnell, Edward James Olmos, James Callis, Jamie Bamber, Katee Sackhoff, Tricia Helfer and Grace Park

These so-called skinjobs were embedded in Colonial society, and that, too, spoke to post-9/11 anxiety: the idea that terrorist threats weren't necessarily coming from abroad, but might be brewing closer to home.

Like **The Matrix**'s Agents, the Cylons weren't just straightforward killing machines. Moore's series saw several Cylons exhibit emotions and even develop relationships with humans. They might be deadly, but they were also complex, well-rounded characters who demanded understanding and even sympathy. In this new millennium, science fiction suggested that future warfare would never be straightforward.

Big Brother's Watching You

The real-world response to the increasing threat of terrorism was to clamp down on personal freedoms, and not just by stopping us packing liquids in our hand luggage. Since 9/11, surveillance laws have changed dramatically, and now that so much of everyday life is lived digitally – either on the Internet or on mobile devices – it's hard not to be paranoid that the Government's watching you. The idea of constant surveillance, of stopping crime before it happens, is the major theme of Steven Spielberg's **Minority Report**, based on the 1956 story by Philip K. Dick.

Released in 2002, **Minority Report** is one of those science fiction movies that's often cited as being spookily prescient. The story of what happens when a team of 'Precogs' can see future murders in time for the police to stop them from happening, it's packed with cool-looking gadgets, including driverless

ABOVE: The cast of *Firefly* (2002–04): Adam Baldwin, Jewel Staite, Alan Tudyk, Gina Torres, Morena Baccarin, Nathan Fillion, Sean Maher, Ron Glass and Summer Glau

cars and the motion-sensing gloves that Captain John Anderton (Tom Cruise) uses to manipulate onscreen images of crimes-to-come that basically predicted the rise of gesture-based computing.

But what **Minority Report** really got right was predicting the way we'd all be tracked while going about our everyday lives. The scene where Anderton's name is called by every interactive advertising billboard he passes feels like a perfect analogue for the way online advertising tracks your browsing history so it can serve you personalized ads across every website you use in the future. And when government agencies can also demand access to individuals' online histories, what are they looking for but thoughtcrime? That's an idea that can obviously be tracked back to George Orwell, but **Minority Report** proves it was a persisting worry.

Doing It for the Fans

As worried as science fiction portrays us being about the rise of the Internet and the dawn of the information age, the genre has massively benefited from online culture. There's never been as much fan-generated art and fiction as there is now, and fans have never before had such a great opportunity to share and develop elaborate theories now that media-specific wikis exist.

And online fandom has also had an impact on the kind of science fiction being made. Back in 2002, Joss Whedon created a steampunk-flavoured space western about the ragtag crew of a decrepit spaceship called **Firefly**. Despite being mistreated by its original network, Fox, which demanded all kinds of changes and then aired several episodes in the wrong order, **Firefly** went on

to develop a devoted fanbase who organized online using the show's official message boards. And when the show was cancelled after a scant 14 episodes, the fans didn't take the decision lying down. A massive fan campaign, which incorporated online petitions, as well as letters and a full-page advert in **Variety** magazine, couldn't quite convince Fox to revive the series, but the show of dedication helped Joss Whedon to convince Universal Pictures to green-light a movie, **Serenity**, that brought the storyline to some sort of closure in 2005.

By the mid-2000s, then, science fiction was in maybe the best shape it ever had been. More mainstream than ever, more credible than ever, it also had access to the most advanced special effects imaginable, and creators had a wealth of inspiration to draw from, as technology transformed the world in perhaps the most significant way since the Industrial Revolution. So where next?

167

ABOVE: Tom Cruise and Samantha Morton as John Anderton and the precog Agatha in *Minority Report* (2002), directed by Steven Spielberg

8: THE FUTURE IS NOW

2009

2009 • *Avatar* • James Cameron
Movie

2009 • *District 9* • Neill Blomkamp
Movie

2009 • *Borderlands* • Gearbox Software
Video Game

2009 • *Star Trek* • J.J. Abrams
Movie

2009 • *2012* • Roland Emmerich
Movie

2009 • *Knowing* • Alex Proyas
Movie

2009 • *The Maze Runner* • James Dashner
Novel

2009 • First episode of *Stargate Universe* • Brad Wright,
Robert C. Cooper
TV

2009 • *Yellow Blue Tibia* • Adam Roberts
Novel

2010

2010 • *Inception* • Christopher Nolan
Movie

2011 • "Wool" • Hugh Howey
Short Story

2011 • *Divergent* • Veronica Roth
Novel

2011 • *The Martian* • Andy Weir
Novel

2011 • *Thor* • Kenneth Branagh
Movie

2011 • *Captain America: The First Avenger* • Joe Johnston
Movie

2011 • *Embassytown* • China Miéville
Novel

2012

2012 • *Avengers Assemble* • Joss Whedon
Movie

2012 • *Prometheus* • Ridley Scott
Movie

2012 • *Looper* • Rian Johnson
Movie

2012 • *The Hunger Games* • Gary Ross
Movie

2012 • First episode of *Arrow* • Greg Berlanti, Marc
Guggenheim, Andrew Kreisberg
TV

2012 • *Blue Remembered Earth* • Alastair Reynolds
Novel

2012 • *The Long Earth* • Terry Pratchett, Stephen Baxter
Novel

Chronology of selected events in the history of science fiction, from early influences to modern media.

Philosophy   Science &   Novels   Short Story   World Events   Movies   Magazines   Comics   Play   Pulp   Radio   Small   TV   Video
              Technology   Magazines   Publishers   Games

2013

2013 • First episode of *Orphan Black* • Graeme Manson
TV
2013 • *Snowpiercer* • Bong Joon-ho
Movie
2013 • *Pacific Rim* • Guillermo del Toro
Movie
2013 • *Gravity* • Alfonso Cuarón
Movie
2013 • *Her* • Spike Jonze
Movie
2013 • *Man of Steel* • Zack Snyder
Movie
2014 • First episode of *The 100* • Jason Rothenberg
TV
2014 • *Interstellar* • Christopher Nolan
Movie
2014 • *Edge of Tomorrow* • Doug Liman
Movie
2014 • *The Girl With All the Gifts* • M.R. Carey
Novel
2014 • *Divergent* • Neil Burger
Movie
2014 • *The Maze Runner* • Wes Ball
Movie
2014 • *Guardians of the Galaxy* • James Gunn
Movie
2014 • *The Abyss Beyond Dreams* • Peter F. Hamilton
Novel
2014 • *Annihilation* • Jeff VanderMeer
Novel

2015

2015 • First episode of *Westworld* • HBO
TV
2015 • *Ex Machina* • Alex Garland
Movie
2015 • First episode of *The Man in the High Castle* •
Frank Spotnitz
TV
2015 • *Mad Max: Fury Road* • George Miller
Movie
2015 • *Star Wars: Episode VII – The Force Awakens* •
J.J. Abrams
Movie
2015 • *The Martian* • Ridley Scott
Movie
2015 • *Chappie* • Neill Blomkamp
Movie
2015 • First episode of *Daredevil* • Drew Goddard
TV
2015 • *Sid Meier's Civilization: Beyond Earth* • Firaxis Games
Video Game
2015 • *The Sandman: Overture* • Neil Gaiman and
J.H. Williams III
Graphic Novel

2016

2016 • First episode of *Stranger Things* • Duffer Brothers
TV
2016 • First episode of *The OA* • Brit Marling and
Zal Batmanglij
TV
2016 • *The Girl With All the Gifts* • Colm McCarthy
Movie
2016 • *Rogue One: A Star Wars Story* • Gareth Edwards
Movie
2016 • *Arrival* • Denis Villeneuve
Movie
2016 • *Batman v Superman: Dawn of Justice* • Zack Snyder
Movie
2016 • *Suicide Squad* • David Ayer
Movie
2017 • *New York 2140* • Kim Stanley Robinson
Novel
2017 • *All Our Wrong Todays* • Elan Mastai
Novel
2017 • *Ghost in the Shell* • Rupert Sanders
Movie
2017 • *Wonder Woman* • Patty Jenkins
Movie
2017 • *Justice League* • Zack Snyder
Movie
2019 • *Star Wars: Episode IX – The Last Jedi* • Colin Trevorrow
Movie
2020 • *Avatar 2* • James Cameron
Movie

HOPE AND DESPAIR

The world we're living in now is, in many ways, the world imagined by the science fiction of the past. Okay, maybe we don't commute to work in flying cars, and we haven't built any space colonies yet. But we can ask Siri or Alexa for a status update and find out what's going on in the world. And we can control our central heating and lighting via the communicators – sorry, smartphones – in our pockets. We can use flying robots to deliver packages or carry out surveillance, we can genetically engineer our crops to be more resistant to environmental pressures, and the whole sum of human knowledge is available to all of us at the touch of a button. We're living in the future, basically.

But if science fiction has taught us anything, it's that dazzling technology comes at a cost. And while we might not be living in a barren dystopian wasteland just yet, we're starting to see some consequences to our actions. The polar ice caps are melting. Unwanted computers and mobile phones are being dumped in illegal waste tips in developing countries. And increased automation is putting people out of jobs all over the world.

The current era began with a couple of key events that signalled both hope and despair for the future. In 2008, Barack Obama became the first black president of the United States, after campaigning on a platform of, well, hope. (Remember Shepard Fairey's campaign poster?) But around the same time, the world faced the worst financial crisis since the 1930s. Were we making progress, or sinking into a mire of hopelessness?

Maybe it's too early to analyse the long-term effects of more recent events, like the election of President Trump or Britain's vote to leave the EU. But then again, imagining the future is what science fiction is for.

The End of the World, Again

We should probably hope science fiction isn't accurately predicting the future, because an awful lot of it seems to be focusing on the end of the world. Though the Millennium Bug failed to materialize, another potentially apocalyptic date loomed during this period: Friday, 21 December 2012.

Though not nearly as credible as the idea that technology would fatally break down at the dawn of the new millennium, the idea that 2012 might mean the end of the world came from an interpretation of the Mesoamerican Long Count calendar, which spanned more than 5,000 years but ended on 21 December 2012. Director Roland Emmerich turned the idea into his 2009 movie *2012*, which saw life on Earth threatened by an errant solar flare, which overheated the planet's core and led to volcanic eruptions, polar shifts and various other natural disasters.

In the same year, Alex Proyas's *Knowing* also imagined a world destroyed by solar flares. The film's Professor Koestler (played by Nicolas Cage) discovers

ABOVE: The movie *2012* (2009), directed by Roland Emmerich, envisioned the end of the world brought about through a solar flare causing a series of natural disasters

a kind of prophecy in a time capsule from the 1950s that predicts various disasters (including, explicitly, the 9/11 terrorist attack) and also predicts that everyone on Earth will die, imminently. The film ends with the world catching fire.

There **was** a big solar flare in early 2009, which scientists were monitoring closely, but it seems more likely that these films were just using an external threat as a stand-in for man-made global warming. Climate change was, and continues to be, a contentious political issue, so using other reasons why the Earth might overheat seems like a smart move; but these films make it pretty clear global warming is going to make some pretty massive problems for all of us, even if it doesn't happen overnight.

Hot or Not

Not all science fiction focused on apocalyptic events. Many writers and filmmakers pictured what would happen afterwards, often with a focus on a world with a very different ecosystem.

Bong Joon-ho's 2013 film **Snowpiercer** is a notable example, because in its vision of the then-near future, humanity attempted to counter the effects of global warming via a disastrous geo-engineering project that ironically catapults the Earth into a new ice age. Rather than the Earth catching fire, it freezes, and so do almost all of its inhabitants. The only survivors are those on board the titular 'Snowpiercer', a massive train that continually circumnavigates the frozen planet, carrying its class-segregated passengers on an endless journey to nowhere.

ABOVE: John Hurt, Octavia Spencer and Chris Evans in *Snowpiercer* (2013), directed by Bong Joon-Ho

A more traditional version of the post-apocalyptic world appears in **Mad Max: Fury Road**, director George Miller's 2015 return to the franchise he created back in 1979. While the original **Mad Max** depicted a society on the brink of collapse, by **Fury Road** the damage has been done, and the world is a nuclear wasteland where only the toughest can survive. Water is society's most valuable commodity, but its supply is controlled by the grotesque Immortan Joe (played by Hugh Keays-Byrne).

And despite the film's triumphant climax, when Joe is killed by his former Imperator Furiosa (played by Charlize Theron) and Max (played by Tom Hardy for this instalment), and his water tanks are opened to his formerly oppressed subjects, it's not really a happy ending. The world's still in terrible shape.

A Time of Monsters

Our mistreatment of the environment is also the cause of a near-apocalypse in Guillermo Del Toro's **Pacific Rim**. Released in 2013, it's set in a near future where terrifying monsters (known as 'kaiju', the Japanese word for movie monsters, literally meaning 'strange beast') are emerging from an inter-dimensional rift deep beneath the Pacific Ocean. Having destroyed

TOP: George Miller returned to direct *Mad Max: Fury Road* (2015), starring Tom Hardy. INSET: Movie poster for *Mad Max: Fury Road*, depicting Charlize Theron as Furiosa

their own world, they're looking to colonize ours – and it turns out this isn't the first time they've tried. Some 65 million years ago, the kaiju tried to move in, but found the environment unwelcoming. Now, though, thanks to the damaged ozone layer and polluted oceans, humans have turned the Earth into a kaiju's dream home.

The apocalypse is averted, narrowly, by an international team of scientists and pilots – whose ability to empathize with one another allows them to cooperatively pilot the gigantic robots needed to battle the enormous kaiju, a metaphor that needs no unpacking – but despite its bombastic robot-versus-monster action, **Pacific Rim** is a film shot through with melancholy. Its world and its characters have lost so much in their battle, and will struggle to rebuild their world even if no further monsters arrive. (Unfortunately for them, the fact that there's a sequel, **Pacific Rim: Uprising**, scheduled for a 2018 release suggests the fight's not over yet.)

What's in the Box?

Another interesting (and environmentally conscious) take on the end of the world that's worth discussing here is M.R. Carey's **The Girl With All the Gifts**. Published as a novel in 2014 and turned into a big-screen adaptation by director Colm McCarthy in 2016, it's set in a post-apocalyptic Britain that's been destroyed by a horrifying disease. This disease turns out to be a fungal infection that turns people into zombie-like creatures known as 'hungries', who'll attack and eat any living thing in their path.

The girl of the title is Melanie (played by Sennia Nanua), a kind of second-generation hungry. Infected in her mother's womb, unlike the newly infected she's capable of logical thought and communication. There's no uplifting message about co-operation and empathy here, though. Melanie ultimately triggers the final act of the apocalypse, unleashing the fungus into the air and transforming all the remaining humans into hungries.

The title of both the book and movie refers to the myth of Pandora, who opened a fateful box and unleashed suffering on the world, finding hope at the bottom. Melanie, too, unleashes suffering, but here the only hope is for the next generation, the evolved children whose bodies have forged a symbiotic relationship with the fungus, and will eventually forge their own world.

Things Can Only Get Worse

Anyone looking for a bleak vision of the future has been spoilt for choice over the past few years. One key franchise was **The Hunger Games**. Suzanne Collins's first novel, **The Hunger Games**, was published in 2008, quickly followed by **Catching Fire** in 2009 and **Mockingjay** in 2010. The first movie, **The Hunger Games**, hit cinemas in 2012, followed by **The Hunger Games: Catching Fire** in 2013, then **The Hunger Games: Mockingjay – Part 1** in 2014 and **The Hunger Games: Mockingjay – Part 2** in 2015.

173

ABOVE: Movie poster for *Pacific Rim* (2013), director: Guillermo del Toro. RIGHT: Poster for the post-apocalyptic *The Girl with All the Gifts* (2016), directed by Colm McCarthy

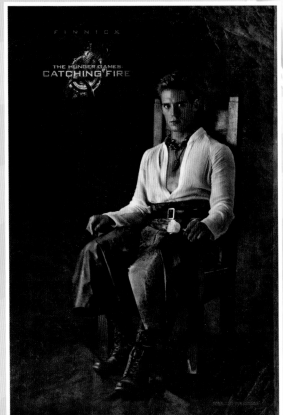

ABOVE: *The Hunger Games* was the start of a trend in popular young adult dystopian novels, and their movie adaptations

The story is set in a future version of America, called Panem, in which children from the various Districts compete with one another in a televised death match to win extra resources from the rich and controlling Capitol. So again, it's down to the children to try to fix the mess they've inherited from their parents. The franchise's heroine, Katniss Everdeen (played by Jennifer Lawrence in the films), is already providing for her family after her father's death and mother's depression when she volunteers to take part in the titular Games to protect her younger sister.

Katniss finds a way to win without playing, by subverting the Games' rules and defying authority, but she's still damaged by her experience. As the books (and films) continue, Katniss begins to suffer from post-traumatic stress disorder. Once again, her victory is a limited one. Her actions spark a revolution that eventually brings down the oppressive government – as well as an alternative but equally grim government – but the scars remain.

The success of **The Hunger Games** saw several other young adult dystopian stories rushed to press and to screen, including the **Divergent** series and **The Maze Runner** series, though none of them had quite the same impact. Still, the overall message got through: the world is damaged, and it's going to be the children who suffer.

The World We Could Have Had

Just as the number of fictional dystopias threatened to become too depressing, science fiction began to come up with stories that highlight the things that

ABOVE: Movie poster for *The Maze Runner* (2014) and the dystopian landscape from *The Maze Runner: Scorch Trials* (2015), both directed by Wes Ball

are currently okay about our world; or at least, okay in comparison to a possible alternative.

The Man in the High Castle (2015–17), a TV adaptation of Philip K. Dick's 1962 novel of the same title, imagines a world in which the Nazis won the Second World War. Set in an alternative version of the 1960s, the show sees America split in two, into the Greater Nazi Reich and the Japanese-governed Pacific States. The characters in the show join up to the resistance after discovering newsreel footage of a world in which the Allied forces triumphed over the Nazis.

In other words, they're living in the darkest timeline, imagining a world that looks rather a lot like our own. It's a compelling setting for a story, and also manages to be oddly reassuring. No matter what might be going wrong in our world, at least Hitler's not in charge, right?

176

Also oddly reassuring is Elan Mastai's 2016 novel *All Our Wrong Todays*. Its protagonist, Tom, comes from a version of the present day in which the invention of a new kind of clean, renewable energy has led to the creation of a kind of utopia. Unfortunately, after a mix-up with a prototype time machine, Tom destroys that world and finds himself stranded in an alternative timeline: ours.

At first, it's obvious that our world is the worse of the two, as Tom finds that even our air is of lower quality than he's used to. But by the end of the novel, there's hope (yup, that again) that we can find ways to fix the damage we've done, and create a better world for everyone.

THE UNITED STATES VERSUS THE UNIVERSE

In case it sounds like all science fiction from the past decade or so was entirely earthbound social commentary, it's worth remembering that in 2009, J.J. Abrams rebooted the cinematic *Star Trek* franchise with, well, *Star Trek*.

The reboot returned to the beginning of *The Original Series*, and followed James Tiberius Kirk (here played by Chris Pine) as he joined Starfleet and rose through the ranks to become Captain of the *Enterprise*.

The film was obviously designed to appeal to a new audience who'd never watched *Star Trek* before, and it focused a lot more on eye-popping action sequences (including one stunning scene where Kirk, Sulu (played by John Cho) and Chief Engineer Olson (Greg Ellis) parachute on to a drilling platform) than on interplanetary diplomacy. Abrams clearly didn't want to alienate Trekkies completely, though; the film includes a cameo by Leonard Nimoy as Spock, which suggests in a suitably geeky way that this film isn't a straight reboot – instead, it's set in a divergent timeline.

ABOVE: Leonard Nimoy and William Shatner as Spock and Kirk from the original *Star Trek* TV series (1966–69)

ABOVE: A movie reboot of the original *Star Trek* series has proved very popular, bringing the original characters to new audiences

ABOVE: Matt Damon as Mark Watney, stranded on Mars in *The Martian* (2015), directed by Ridley Scott

Star Trek was enough of a box-office smash that it's already spawned two sequels, 2013's *Star Trek Into Darkness* and 2016's *Star Trek Beyond*. As if that weren't proof enough of audiences' on-going appetite for space exploration, we've also had two new *Star Wars* movies in recent years: *Star Wars: Episode VII – The Force Awakens* (2015), which saw characters from the original trilogy meet the next generation of Jedi in the form of Daisy Ridley's Rey, and *Rogue One: A Star Wars Story* (2016), a kind of mid-quel that told the story of the Rebels who stole the plans for the Death Star before the events of *Star Wars: Episode IV – A New Hope*. It seems fair to say that audiences are still dreaming of the stars.

The Allure of Competence

Big-name franchises weren't the only place we got to see humanity travelling into space or interacting with extra-terrestrials. The last decade has also seen the rise of carefully researched films about space that almost fetishize intelligence – or, more accurately, competence.

Alfonso Cuarón's 2013 film *Gravity* was an almost unbearably tense depiction of one woman's struggle to survive on a broken-down space shuttle. Dr Ryan Stone (played by Sandra Bullock) is a biomedical engineer whose first trip into space goes horribly wrong after debris hits her spacecraft and sends her crewmate drifting out into the black. Stone has to deal with dozens of other things going wrong around her, all by herself, but despite her evident terror, she manages to find her way back to Earth.

The production was meticulously researched, and watching it on an IMAX screen feels almost too realistic; it's probably the closest any of us will get

to actually being stranded in space ourselves. Stone's triumph plays out like a metaphor for the evolution of life on Earth, making the whole thing feel curiously uplifting after all the trauma.

Similarly, Ridley Scott's 2015 adaptation of Andy Weir's novel *The Martian* (2011) sees an almost preternaturally capable astronaut accidentally left behind on a mission to Mars. With almost no hope of rescue, Mark Watney (played by Matt Damon) has only his own resourcefulness to rely on – and, incredibly, he survives. Watney's good-natured ability to just get on with it, combined with his impressive intellect, makes this another movie in which cleverness and determination conquer overwhelmingly bad odds. Is it surprising that at a time of great upheaval and uncertainty, these are the stories we're drawn to?

Getting the Job Done

There's one more film that fits into this category of so-called competence porn, though this time no one gets lost in space. Denis Villeneuve's *Arrival*, released in 2016, follows linguistics expert Louise Banks (played by Amy Adams) as she's recruited by the military to try to talk to the alien life-forms who've recently landed on Earth. Banks doesn't have access to any universal translator, or anything other than her own brain and a wipe-clean whiteboard, but she nonetheless manages to find a way to speak to the mysterious extra-terrestrials. Slowly but surely, she deciphers their vocabulary, opening her mind to new ways of not only communicating but also thinking.

The film has a complicated, circular structure that mimics the complicated, circular written forms of the alien language. By speaking to the aliens,

179

ABOVE: Amy Adams as linguist Louise Banks making contact with aliens in *Arrival* (2016), directed by Denis Villeneuve

Banks discovers a different way of experiencing time, her perception of her world widening to incorporate a whole new dimension. **Arrival** is an adaptation of a short story, 'Story of Your Life' (1998) by Ted Chiang, which was considered virtually unfilmable until Villeneuve came along. It's a story not just about alien-human relations, but also about co-operation between nations, about determinism and about the difficult choices we face in life. This is seriously cerebral science fiction, and its appeal is in watching how intelligence and compassion win out over fear and suspicion.

Here Come the Girls

Science fiction has made great strides into diversity over the past decade. Just looking at the films already discussed in this chapter, it's clear how much things have moved on, particularly with regard to putting women front and centre in science fiction stories. **Arrival** is about a female linguist; **Gravity** is about a female engineer; **The Girl With All the Gifts** is about a little girl who'll change the world, but also features a female scientist and teacher. Most of the young adult dystopian franchises also revolve around a girl, like **The Hunger Games**'s Katniss or **Divergent**'s Tris. Then

there's **Mad Max: Fury Road**, where Max is less of a badass than Furiosa, and the new **Star Wars** films, which introduce two inspiringly cool female characters in the shape of Rey and Jyn Erso.

There's more work to be done, especially on the racial diversity front. **Pacific Rim** does a pretty great job of including people from all over the world and from all kinds of backgrounds, and the new **Star Wars** films also added some much-needed diversity, with characters played by Diego Luna, Oscar Isaac, John Boyega and Donnie Yen, among others. Even if science fiction still sometimes seems to be better at representing blue and green people than black ones, things seem to be moving in the right direction – after all, **Doctor Who**'s newest companion, Bill Potts (played by Pearl Mackie) is both mixed race and gay.

ABOVE: The many faces of SF: *Rogue One* (2016), *Gravity* (2013) and *Doctor Who*'s 12th doctor

NEW WAYS OF SEEING

The last few years have also seen more advances in filmmaking technology, which have allowed filmmakers to be bolder and more experimental in their work.

James Cameron's eco-conscious adventure ***Avatar***, released in 2009, is the obvious example here. Cameron had been planning the film since at least 1994, but while he initially planned to go into development after finishing ***Titanic***, he ultimately decided that the technology he needed to make the film he dreamed of wasn't ready yet. It took until 2006 for him to be convinced the world was ready. The film was shot in 3D, using the proprietary Fusion Camera System developed by Cameron and his director of photography Vince Pace, but also used motion capture and a special virtual camera system, also developed by Cameron. More of the film is computer-generated than not, in stark contrast to films like ***Jurassic Park***, which were more real than not. More than 900 people worked on the special effects, and Cameron made sure he had complete control over every aspect of the film's visuals.

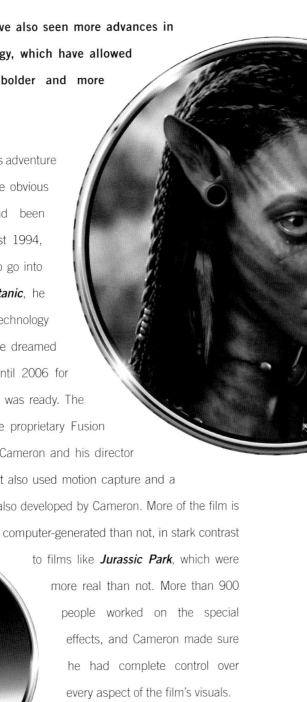

LEFT: Movie poster for *Avatar* (2009), directed by James Cameron. ABOVE: Sam Worthington and Zoe Saldana as Jake Sully and Neytiri in *Avatar*

ABOVE: The *Alien* franchise returned to our screens in 2012 with *Prometheus*, once more directed by Ridley Scott

All that tech didn't come cheap – the film's official budget was $237 million – but it paid off, because **Avatar** became the highest-grossing film of all time. It also reignited audiences' interest in 3D cinema, and demonstrated just what can be achieved when a director with a vision finally gets their hands on the means to make the film they want to make.

Aliens Again

Another project that took a while to come to fruition? Ridley Scott's 2012 movie **Prometheus**, a sort-of-but-not-really prequel to 1979's **Alien**. Scott had actually worked with James Cameron on an idea for another movie set in the **Alien** universe back in the early 2000s, but that movie never quite happened. Instead, there was **Prometheus**; set in the late twenty-first century, it saw archaeologists uncover a map to the stars, then set out to try to make contact with the alien life who had made the original map.

Unfortunately for them, these aliens didn't leave humanity a Stargate to quickly zap them across the universe. Instead, the crew is put into stasis on the titular spaceship, while their android David (played by Michael Fassbender) keeps an eye on their progress.

Scott took full advantage of the advanced visual effects available to him, using around 1,300 digital effects in the film, and shooting in 3D. Much attention was paid to the depth of field in specific shots, as Scott wanted the film to be as immersive as possible. Once, 3D had a reputation for being kind of gimmicky, but films like **Avatar** and **Prometheus** went a long way towards rehabilitating its image, and proving it could be used for things other than making audiences jump at stuff shooting out of the screen at them.

The Laws of Robotics Redux

The tension between the 'real' and the digital doesn't just exist in a film's production; it's also the basis of lots of recent science fiction, as writers and filmmakers struggle to define what 'human' means in an increasingly digital world. And often, that tension turns up in stories about people falling in love with anthropomorphic computers or robots.

In Spike Jonze's 2013 romantic sci-fi **Her**, a man falls in love with the voice of his talking operating system. In Alex Garland's 2014 indie sci-fi thriller **Ex Machina**, a programmer is invited to give an artificially intelligent robot the Turing Test, and falls for her in the process. And in HBO's 2015 reboot of 1973's **Westworld**, an entire amusement park is populated by humanoid androids that guests can choose to fight, rape or even kill.

Each of these stories examines the morality of interaction with non-human intelligence, and questions what it means to be human. Neill Blomkamp's 2015 film **Chappie** offers a slightly different take. **Chappie** doesn't look human, though he's vaguely humanoid; he's a prototype police robot, created to tackle violent crime, but given sentience by

183

ABOVE: Domhnall Gleeson, Alicia Vikander and Oscar Isaac in the psychological thriller *Ex Machina* (2015), directed by Alex Garland

a rogue programmer. When he's stolen by gangsters, his capacity for learning leads him to become a criminal menace despite his pre-programmed morality.

Blomkamp plays some of Chappie's development for laughs, but the film has serious points to make about nature and nurture, too. Its ending, which sees Chappie transferring not just his own consciousness into a new robot body but also the consciousness of his adopted gangster mother into one, too, suggests the lines between real and artificial intelligence might actually be very easy to blur.

Boxset Binges

Providing yet another example of how technology impacts art, as the way we consume media has changed, so too has the media we consume. Just as VHS opened up a new market back in the 1980s, so too has the advent of streaming.

Previously, if you watched a TV show, you probably did it on a weekly basis, tuning in every Tuesday or Thursday to catch the newest episode of your show. You might time-shift your viewing by recording the episode on tape, but mostly, you'd see TV as it was broadcast. But the rise of VHS and DVD (and later Blu-ray) meant that you could catch up on things you'd missed, or binge-watch a whole series in a weekend. The effects of that media change on TV could be seen as far back as the mid-1990s, as shows like **Star Trek: Deep Space Nine** or **Babylon 5** began to move away from the episode-of-the-week format and towards longer story arcs, but those shows were still first broadcast to

the original one-a-week format. Streaming, though, threatened to totally change the way we think about TV shows.

Netflix, which started by sending out DVDs to subscribers, launched its online streaming service in the United States in 2007, and in 2012 in the UK. Rival services, like Amazon Video and TalkTalk TV Store (formerly Blinkbox), launched around the same time, and suddenly, consumers had access to a vast array of TV 'boxsets', which could be watched immediately. Underappreciated shows could be rediscovered, cult shows could increase their fanbases, and viewers could dip in and out of any number of shows without having to commit either to a regular viewing schedule or to an expensive box of physical discs.

Keep Watching

The popularity of these services saw both Netflix and Amazon move from being merely content providers into content creators, and the shows they make aren't designed to be watched one episode a week. They're specifically made for bingeing.

That apparently subtle shift in viewing habits actually meant the way TV episodes were written could be completely rethought. Writers no longer had to structure episodes to make sure viewers would remember to tune in next week; the next episode would probably autoplay before the credits had even finished rolling. And there's no need for recaps, or for catering to new viewers hopping on board halfway through a season; the whole show is always available for fans to catch up on, and there's no risk they'll watch episodes out of order and get confused. TV writers making shows for online

ABOVE: *The OA* (2016) is one of a few science fiction TV shows made specifically for the streaming provider Netflix.

streaming have the freedom to write complex, on-going stories that unfold slowly over the course of several hours, knowing their audience will be able to keep up.

So far, there are only a handful of science fiction shows that have been made for this model (including *Stranger Things*, *The Man in the High Castle*, *Sense 8* and *The OA*) so it's early days yet, but it's clear that the potential exists for sci-fi stories to be more complex and ambitious than ever before.

Masters of the Universe

Speaking of complex stories that expect viewers to keep up, the Marvel Cinematic Universe has evolved since the release of *Iron Man* in 2008, becoming an intricate, interlinked franchise with characters who can lead their own films as well as popping up in supporting roles to help their superhero mates when needed.

Comics have long featured crossovers and team stories, but it took a while for the film adaptations to follow a similar structure. Before building their own franchise, Marvel had been licensing out its properties (Spider-Man, the X-Men, etc.) to other studios, but had made relatively little profit from the practice, so when Kevin Feige became head of Marvel Studios, he tried a different approach. *Iron Man* was followed by *The Incredible Hulk* (2008), then *Iron Man 2* (2010), *Thor* (2011) and *Captain America: The First Avenger* (2011), before all those heroes, plus Black Widow and Hawkeye, were recruited for a gigantic team-up in 2012's *Avengers Assemble*.

Avengers Assemble was a worldwide smash, becoming the third highest-grossing film of all time at the time of its release (it's since been pushed down to fifth place). Marvel Studios got to work on phase two of its cinematic universe, which would involve sequels for the established heroes, plus *Guardians of the Galaxy* (2014) and *Ant-Man* (2015), as well as another massive team-up in *Avengers: Age of Ultron* (2015). After that, phase three, which includes *Doctor Strange* (2016) and *Spider-Man: Homecoming* (2017), kicked off. Marvel had hit on a winning formula, a way of introducing audiences to new characters they might not otherwise have gambled on a cinema ticket to see.

Crossing Over

Marvel's success meant that other film studios also wanted to get in on the shared universe action, so Warner Bros is building a DC Extended Universe through films like *Batman v Superman: Dawn of Justice* (2016) and *Suicide Squad* (2016), with *Wonder Woman* (2017) and the team film *Justice League* (2017) following behind.

Twentieth Century Fox, too, has been experimenting with its comic book properties, and the success of *Deadpool* in 2016 suggests there might be a few more lesser-known comic characters finding their way to the big screen in future, assuming that the studios can find actors as enthusiastic about embodying the characters as Ryan Reynolds was with Deadpool.

Marvel has also been working on small-screen adaptations of some of its characters, launching Netflix Original series based on Daredevil, Jessica Jones, Luke Cake and Iron Fist over the past few years. All of those characters are set to get their own crossover event in the form of *The Defenders*, another Netflix

185

ABOVE: The 1973 movie *Westworld* has been adapted as a TV series (2016–), now with slicker special effects

mini-series scheduled for late 2017. Though there are (and have been) many superhero TV shows over the years, it's notable that it's down to the existence of Netflix that these second-stringers are getting their own shows, and it'll be interesting to see which other characters might move from page to screen if audiences continue to clamour for more superhero stories.

And really, it seems a safe bet that they will. Thanks in part to these mega-budget blockbusters of flying fists and spandex costumes, science fiction has never been as mainstream or as accessible as it is right now, and looking ahead to announced and scheduled films, TV shows and books, it doesn't look like that'll change any time soon – with huge movie series like **Star Wars** and **Avatar** set to continue into the 2020s. There's never been a better time to be a science fiction fan.

ABOVE: World building into the future with thrilling *Avatar* and *Star Wars* franchises

KEY PEOPLE

First Name I Surname I Dates I Role

J.J. Abrams (b. 1966) • Director/Producer/Screenwriter
Douglas Adams (1952–2001) • Author
Brian Aldiss (b. 1925) • Author
Kingsley Amis (1922–95) • Author
Poul Anderson (1926–2001) • Author
Aristotle (384–322 BC) • Philosopher
Isaac Asimov (1920–92) • Author
Joseph Atterley (1775–1861) • Author
Margaret Atwood (b. 1939) • Author
Charles Babbage (1791–1871) • Mechanical engineer
Francis Bacon (1561–1626) • Author
J.G. Ballard (1930–2009) • Author
Iain M. Banks (1954–2013) • Author
Harry Bates (1900–81) • Editor
Antoine Henri Becquerel (1852–1908) • Scientist
Edward Bellamy (1850–98) • Author
J.D. Beresford (1873–1947) • Author
Earle K. Bergey (1901–52) • Artist
John Berkey (1932–2008) • Artist
Tim Berners-Lee (b. 1955) • Scientist
Luc Besson (b. 1959) • Director
Alfred Bester (1913–87) • Author/Screenwriter/Editor
Kathryn Bigelow (b. 1951) • Director
James Blish (1921–75) • Author
Robert Bloch (1917–94) • Author
Neill Blomkamp (b. 1979) • Director
Hannes Bok (1914–64) • Artist
Nelson S. Bond (1908–2006) • Author
Chesley Bonestell (1888–1986) • Artist
Anthony Boucher (1911–68) • Author
Ben Bova (b. 1932) • Editor/Author
Robert Sidney Bowen (1900–77) • Journalist/Editor/Author
Leigh Brackett (1915–79) • Author
Ray Bradbury (1920–2012) • Author
Fredric Brown (1906–72) • Author
Edward Bulwer-Lytton (1803–73) • Author
Katharine Burdekin (1896–1963) • Author
Anthony Burgess (1917–93) • Author
Arthur J. Burks (1898–1974) • Author
Edgar Rice Burroughs (1875–1950) • Author
William Burroughs (1914–97) • Author
Samuel Butler (1835–1902) • Author
Octavia E. Butler (1947–2006) • Author
Dick Calkins (1894–1962) • Author
James Cameron (b. 1954) • Director
L. Sprague de Camp (1907–2000) • Author
John W. Campbell Jr. (1910–71) • Publisher
Karel Čapek (1890–1938) • Playwright
Orson Scott Card (b. 1951) • Author
Chris Carter (b. 1956) • Producer/Director/Screenwriter
Margaret Cavendish (1623–73) • Author/Scientist
George Tomkyns Chesney (1830–95) • Author
John Christopher (1922–2012) • Author
Arthur C. Clarke (1917–2008) • Author
Hal Clement (1922–2003) • Author
Robert William Cole (1869–1937) • Author
Suzanne Collins (b. 1962) • Author
Roy Crane (1901–77) • Author

Michael Crichton (1942–2008) • Author
Alfred D. Cridge (1860–1922) • Author
Alfonso Cuarón (b. 1961) • Director
Ray Cummings (1887–1957) • Author
Harry Dart (1869–1938) • Author
Charles Darwin (1809–82) • Scientist
Russell T. Davies (b. 1963) • Screenwriter/Producer
Cyrano de Bergerac (1619–55) • Author
James De Mille (1833–80) • Author
Samuel R. Delany (b. 1942) • Author
August Derleth (1909–71) • Author
Philip K. Dick (1928–82) • Author
Charles Dickens (1812–70) • Author
Gordon R. Dickson (1923–2001) • Author
Thomas M. Disch (1940–2008) • Author
Anna Bowman Dodd (1858–1929) • Author
Ignatius Donnelly (1831–1901) • Author
Richard Donner (b. 1930) • Director
Arthur Conan Doyle (1859–1930) • Author
Albert Einstein (1879–1955) • Scientist
Edward S. Ellis (1840–1916) • Author
T. Mullett Ellis (1850–1919) • Author
Harlan Ellison (b. 1934) • Author
Roland Emmerich (b. 1955) • Director
George Allan England (1877–1936) • Author
Epicurus (341–270 BC) • Philosopher
Philip José Farmer (1918–2009) • Author
Virgil Finlay (1914–71) • Artist
Camille Flammarion (1842–1925) • Astronomer/Author
E.M. Forster (1879–1970) • Author
Chris Foss (b. 1946) • Artist
Pat Frank (1907–64) • Author
Frank Kelly Freas (1922–2005) • Artist
Alex Garland (b. 1970) • Director
Peter George (1924–66) • Author
Hugo Gernsback (1884–1967) • Publisher
Dave Gibbons (b. 1949) • Artist/Author
William Gibson (b. 1948) • Author
J.U. Giesy (1877–1947) • Author
H.R. Giger (1940–2014) • Artist
Warwick Goble (1862–1943) • Artist
Frank Godwin (1889–1959) • Author
Cele Goldsmith (1933–2002) • Editor
Martin Greenberg (1918–2013) • Publisher
Percy Greg (1836–89) • Author
George Griffith (1857–1906) • Author
Mary Griffith (1772–1846) • Author
Joe Haldeman (b. 1943) • Author
Edmond Hamilton (1904–77) • Author
John Harris (b. 1948) • Artist
Harry Harrison (1925–2012) • Author
Ray Harryhausen (1920–2013) • Animator
Robert A. Heinlein (1907–88) • Author
Frank Herbert (1920–86) • Author
Pierre-Jules Hetzel (1814–86) • Publisher
John Higgins (b. 1949) • Artist
E.T.A. Hoffmann (1776–1822) • Author
Robert J. Hogan (1897–1963) • Author
Ishirō Honda (1911–93) • Director
Charles Hornig (1916–99) • Editor
Robert E. Howard (1906–36) • Author
L. Ron Hubbard (1911–86) • Author
Edwin Hubble (1889–1953) • Astronomer
Aldous Huxley (1894–1963) • Author
Washington Irving (1783–1859) • Author
C.W. Kahles (1878–1931) • Author
David H. Keller (1880–1966) • Author

Donald Keyhoe (1897–1988) • Author
Rudyard Kipling (1865–1936) • Author
Damon Knight (1922–2002) • Author
William H.D. Koerner (1878–1938) • Author
Arthur Koestler (1905–83) • Author/Journalist
Cyril M. Kornbluth (1923–58) • Author
Stanley Kubrick (1928–99) • Director
Henry Kuttner (1915–58) • Author
David Kyle (1919–2016) • Author
Robert Eyres Landor (1781–1869) • Author
Fritz Lang (1890–1976) • Director
Glen A. Larson (1937–2014) • Producer
David Lasser (1902–96) • Editor
Stan Lee (b. 1922) • Author
Ursula K. LeGuin (b. 1929) • Author
Fritz Leiber (1910–92) • Author
Murray Leinster (1896–1975) • Author
Stanisław Lem (1921–2006) • Author
Sinclair Lewis (1885–1951) • Author
Charles Lindbergh (1902–74) • Author
David Lindsay (1876–1945) • Author
Jack London (1876–1916) • Author
H.P. Lovecraft (1890–1937) • Author
George Lucas (b. 1944) • Director
Auguste Lumière (1862–1954) • Filmmaker
Louis Lumière (1864–1948) • Filmmaker
David Lynch (b. 1946) • Director
Fred MacIsaac (1886–1940) • Author
Laurence Manning (1899–1972) • Author
Richard Matheson (1926–2013) • Author
Andre Maurois (1885–1967) • Author
Anne McCaffrey (1926–2011) • Author
Cormac McCarthy (b. 1933) • Author
Johnston McCulley (1883–1958) • Author
Georges Méliès (1861–1938) • Director
Herman Melville (1819–91) • Author
Judith Merril (1923–97) • Author
George Miller (b. 1945) • Director
Walter M. Miller Jr. (1923–96) • Author
Pat Mills (b. 1949) • Author
Edward Page Mitchell (1852–1927) • Author
Moebius [real name: Jean Giraud] (1938–2012) • Artist
Michael Moorcock (b. 1939) • Author
C.L. Moore (1911–87) • Author
Alan Moore (b. 1953) • Author
Ronald D. Moore (b. 1964) • Screenwriter
Thomas More (1478–1535) • Author
William Morris (1834–96) • Author
Samuel Morse (1791–1872) • Scientist
F.W. Murnau (1888–1931) • Director
Andrew Niccol (b. 1964) • Screenwriter/Director
Peter Nicholls (b. 1939) • Author
Harold Nicolson (1886–1968) • Author
Larry Niven (b. 1938) • Author
Christopher Nolan (b. 1970) • Director
Philip Francis Nowlan (1888–1940) • Author
Kevin O'Neill (b. 1953) • Artist
Willis O'Brien (1886–1962) • Animator
E.V. Odle (1890–1942) • Author
Chad Oliver (1928–93) • Author
George Orwell (1903–50) • Author
George Pal (1908–80) • Director
Frank Paul (1884–1963) • Artist
Plato (429–347 BC) • Philosopher
Plutarch (c. 45–120) • Biographer
Edgar Allan Poe (1809–49) • Author
Frederik Pohl (1919–2013) • Author

Gustavus W. Pope (1828–1902) • Author
Richard M. Powers (1921–96) • Artist
Rudolf Erich Raspe (1736–94) • Author
Alex Raymond (1909–56) • Artist
Alastair Reynolds (b. 1966) • Author
J.L. Riddell (1807–65) • Author
Albert Robida (1848–1926) • Artist
Kim Stanley Robinson (b. 1952) • Author
Gene Roddenberry (1921–91) • Producer
Wilhelm Röntgen (1845–1923) • Scientist
J.-H. Rosny (1856–1940) • Author
Joanna Russ (1937–2011) • Author
Eric Frank Russell (1905–78) • Author
Franklin J. Schaffner (1920–89) • Director
Ridley Scott (b. 1937) • Director
Garrett P. Serviss (1851–1929) • Astronomer/Author
Robert Sheckley (1928–2005) • Author
Mary Shelley (1797–1851) • Author
Joe Shuster (1914–92) • Artist
Nevil Shute (1899–1960) • Author
Jerry Siegel (1914–96) • Author
Clifford Simak (1904–88) • Author
Dan Simmons (b. 1948) • Author
E.E. 'Doc' Smith (1890–1965) • Author
Clark Ashton Smith (1893–1961) • Author
Steven Spielberg (b. 1946) • Director
Norman Spinrad (b. 1940) • Author
Olaf Stapledon (1886–1950) • Author
Robert Louis Stevenson (1850–94) • Author
George R. Stewart (1895–1980) • Author
Bram Stoker (1847–1912) • Author
Drew Struzan (b. 1947) • Artist
Theodore Sturgeon (1918–85) • Author
Jonathan Swift (1667–1745) • Author
William Tenn (1920–2010) • Author
J.R.R. Tolkien (1892–1973) • Author
Alexei Tolstoy (1883–1945) • Author
Arthur C. Train (1875–1945) • Author
F. Orlin Tremaine (1899–1956) • Editor
Frank Triem (1905–70) • Author
Charles W. Tyler (1887–1952) • Author
Roger Vadim (1928–2000) • Director
Paul Verhoeven (b. 1938) • Director
Jules Verne (1828–1905) • Author
Auguste Villiers de l'Isle-Adam (1838–89) • Author
A.E. van Vogt (1912–2000) • Author
Kurt Vonnegut (1922–2007) • Author
Lana Wachowski (b. 1965) • Director
Lilly Wachowski (b. 1967) • Director
John Wagner (b. 1949) • Author
Donald Wandrei (1908–87) • Author
Stanley Weinbaum (1902–35) • Author
Andy Weir (b. 1972) • Author
H.G. Wells (1886–1946) • Author
James Whale (b. 1951) • Director
Joss Whedon (b. 1964) • Screenwriter
Jack Williamson (1908–2006) • Author
Robert M. Wilson (1882–1963) • Author
Robert Wise (1914–2005) • Director
Robert W. Wood (1868–1955) • Author
Bernie Wrightson (1948–2017) • Artist
John Wyndham (1903–69) • Author
Roger Zelazny (1937–95) • Author
Robert Zemeckis (b. 1952) • Director

FURTHER READING

Atwood, Margaret, *In Other Worlds: SF and the Human Imagination*, Virago, 2012
Bell, James, *Sci-Fi: Days of Fear and Wonder*, British Film Institute, 2014
Giger, H.R., *H.R. Giger's Film Design*, Titan Books, 2012
James, Edward, *The Cambridge Companion to Science Fiction*, Cambridge University Press, 2003
Jameson, Fredric, *Archaeologies of the Future: The Desire Called Utopia and Other Science Fictions*, Verso Books, 2007
Rinzler, J.W., *The Making of Star Wars: The Definitive Story Behind the Original Film*, Aurum Press Ltd., 2013
Roberts, Adam, *The History of Science Fiction*, Palgrave Macmillan, 2016
Seed, David, *Science Fiction: A Very Short Introduction*, OUP Oxford, 2011

Websites

asimovs.com
This leading sci-fi magazine showcases both prose and poetry from a diverse range of writers.

dailysciencefiction.com
An online magazine that publishes short science fiction stories every day featuring a broad range of topics from time travel to fairytales.

isfdb.org
This online database catalogues extensive information on sci-fi authors, novels, awards, and more.

pulpmags.org
The Pulp Magazines Project is a fantastic resource with biographies, publication information and cover galleries.

scifimoviepage.com
This website offers the latest sci-fi movie and television reviews as well as news from the genre.

scifinow.co.uk
This website will keep you up-to-date on all sci-fi, fantasy, and horror news – from literature to movies to television shows.

sf-encyclopedia.com
An incredible resource: this site aims to provide a comprehensive and scholarly guide to science fiction in all its forms, and the provided entries are free online.

sf-foundation.org
This is a helpful site for those looking to learn more about the genre of science fiction and its benefits.

sffchronicles.com
A fantastic forum for all things sci-fi and fantasy related, whether you seek discussion, advice, or news.

ACKNOWLEDGEMENTS

David Langford (consultant editor & introduction) is a British author, editor and critic, heavily active within the science fiction field. As well as writing fiction, Langford now devotes most of his time to nonfiction and editorial work including magazine columns; his science fiction fanzine and newsletter *Ansible* – for which he has won numerous Hugo Awards; and being one of the four chief editors of the third, online edition of the *Encyclopedia of Science Fiction*.

Pat Mills (foreword) is a comics editor and writer who has played a vital role in British comics since the 1970s. He is perhaps best known for his dystopian comics, such as *Marshal Law* and *Requiem Vampire Knight*, for founding *2000AD* and for playing a crucial role in the creation of Judge Dredd.

Dave Golder (chapters 1 & 2) is a former editor of *SFX magazine* (which he helped to launch), SFX.co.uk and *Comic Heroes* magazine, but he first began writing professionally about science fiction with a regular feature in *Your Sinclair* called 'The Killer Kolumn From Outer Space'. He now works freelance and has written books on *Dystopia* and *Science Fiction Movie Posters* for Flame Tree.

Jess Nevins (chapters 3 & 4) is a librarian at Lone Star College in Tomball, Texas, and is the author of a number of books on nineteenth and twentieth century popular literature, including *The Encyclopedia of Fantastic Victoriana* (2005), *The Evolution of the Costumed Avenger: The 4000-Year History of the Superhero* (2017), and *The Encyclopedia of Pulp Heroes* (2017). He lives in Tomball with his wife Alicia and son Henry.

Russ Thorne (chapters 5 & 6) has published books on *Fantasy Art*, *Cult Horror* and *Superheroes Movie Posters* for Flame Tree and writes regularly for national newspapers including the *Independent*. As a boy, Russ loved reading Fighting Fantasy gamebooks, playing Hero Quest and poring over issues of *White Dwarf*, admiring the cover art in the process. Later he studied English Literature and got to know Homer's heroes and a bit of Beowulf, before beginning a career as a writer and editor.

Sarah Dobbs (chapters 7 & 8) is a freelance writer and digital producer who's contributed to *Total Film*, *SFX*, *SciFiNow*, *Wired*, and *Horrorville*. She was a founding editor on pop culture website Den of Geek, and now co-hosts monthly horror movie podcast Casting The Runes. She owes her love of science fiction to her mum, who got her started on *Star Trek: The Next Generation* and *The X-Files* at an early age.

189

INDEX

We publish a wide range of sf, fantasy, gothic, horror and mystery related books, calendars and journals, all of which can be found on our website, **flametreepublishing.com** where you can also sign up for our newsletter, for updates and special offers.